*f*P

TEA
THAT
BURNS

A FAMILY

MEMOIR OF

CHINATOWN

Bruce Edward Hall

THE FREE PRESS
New York · London · Toronto
Sydney · Singapore

THE FREE PRESS
A Division of Simon & Schuster
1230 Avenue of the Americas
New York, NY 10020

THE FREE PRESS and colophon are trademarks
of Simon & Schuster Inc.

Designed by Pei Loi Koay

Manufactured in the United States of America
10 9 8 7 6 5 4 3 2 1

Library of Congress Cataloging-In-Publication Data

Hall, Bruce Edward.
    Tea that burns : a family memoir of Chinatown / Bruce Edward Hall.
    p.   cm.
    Includes bibliographical references (p.   ).
    ISBN: 0-7432-3659-9
        1. Chinatown (New York, N.Y.)—Bibliography.   2. New York (N.Y.)—
    Biography.   3. Hall, Bruce Edward—Childhood and youth.
    4. Chinatown (New York, N. Y.)—Social life and customs.   5. New York
    (N.Y./)—Social life and customs.   6. Chinese Americans—New York
    (State)—New York—Biography.   I. Title.
    F128.69C47H35   1998
    974.7'1—dc21
    [B]   98-6471
                                                     CIPX

For information regarding special discounts for bulk purchases, please contact Simon &
Schuster Special Sales at 1-800-456-6798 or business@simonandschuster.com

To

Hor Poa

Hock Shop

Herb & Jane Ann

CONTENTS

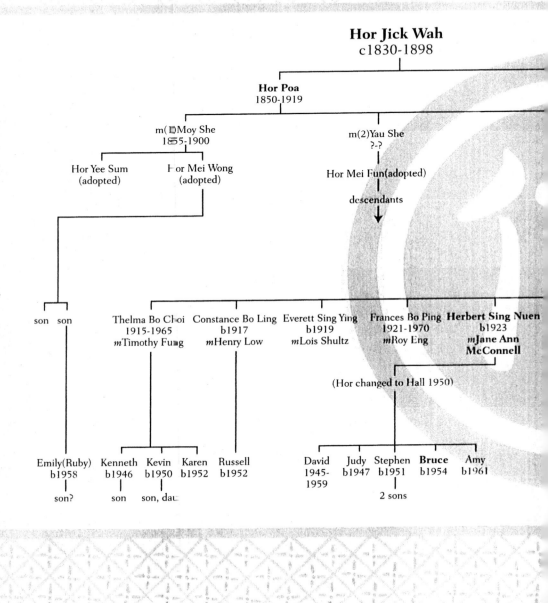

Hor Jick Wah
c1830-1898

Hor Poa
1850-1919

m(1)Moy She
1855-1900

m(2)Yau She
?-?

Hor Yee Sum
(adopted)

Hor Mei Wong
(adopted)

Hor Mei Fun(adopted)

descendants

son   son

Thelma Bo Choi
1915-1965
*m*Timothy Fung

Constance Bo Ling
b1917
*m*Henry Low

Everett Sing Ying
b1919
*m*Lois Shultz

Frances Bo Ping
1921-1970
*m*Roy Eng

Herbert Sing Nuen
b1923
*m***Jane Ann
McConnell**

(Hor changed to Hall 1950)

Emily(Ruby)
b1958

Kenneth
b1946

Kevin
b1950

Karen
b1952

Russell
b1952

David
1945-
1959

Judy
b1947

Stephen
b1951

Bruce
b1954

Amy
b1961

son?

son

son, dau

2 sons

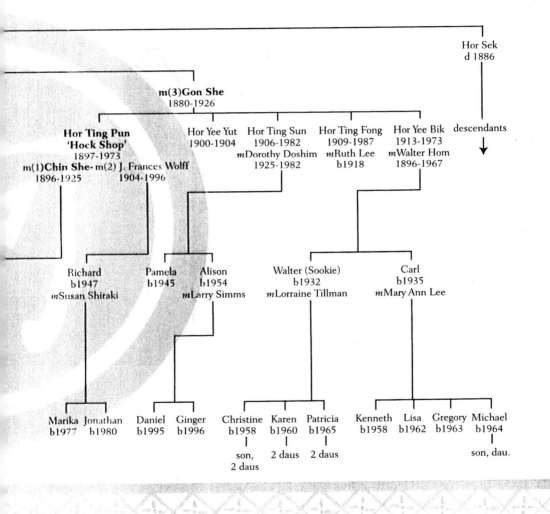

Hor Sek
d 1886

m(3)Gon She
1880-1926

Hor Ting Pun
'Hock Shop'
1897-1973
m(1)**Chin She**- m(2) J. Frances Wolff
1896-1925   1904-1996

Hor Yee Yut
1900-1904

Hor Ting Sun
1906-1982
mDorothy Doshim
1925-1982

Hor Ting Fong
1909-1987
mRuth Lee
b1918

Hor Yee Bik
1913-1973
mWalter Hom
1896-1967

descendants ↓

Richard
b1947
mSusan Shiraki

Pamela
b1945

Alison
b1954
mLarry Simms

Walter (Sookie)
b1932
mLorraine Tillman

Carl
b1935
mMary Ann Lee

Marika
b1977

Jonathan
b1980

Daniel
b1995

Ginger
b1996

Christine
b1958

son,
2 daus

Karen
b1960

2 daus

Patricia
b1965

2 daus

Kenneth
b1958

Lisa
b1962

Gregory
b1963

Michael
b1964

son, dau.

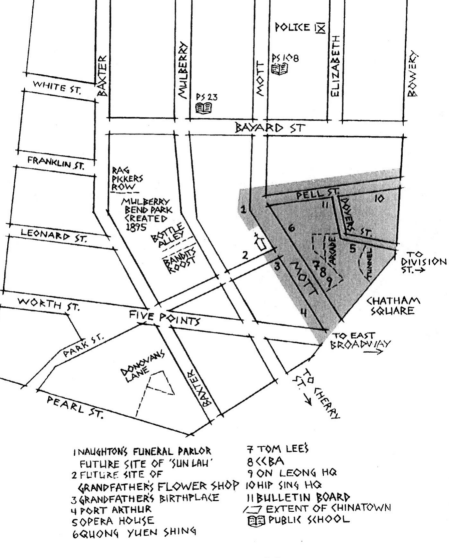

CANAL ST.

POLICE IX

PS 108

BAXTER

MULBERRY

MOTT

ELIZABETH

BOWERY

WHITE ST.

PS 23

BAYARD ST

FRANKLIN ST.

RAG
PICKERS
ROW

MULBERRY
BEND PARK
CREATED
1895

BOTTLE
ALLEY

BANDITS
ROOST

PELL ST.

11

DOYERS

10

LEONARD ST.

1

6

ST.

5

TO
DIVISION
ST. →

2

3

MOTT

7 8
9

ARKE

TUNNEL

WORTH ST.

FIVE POINTS

4

CHATHAM
SQUARE

PARK ST.

DONOVANS
LANE

BAXTER

TO EAST
BROADWAY →

PEARL ST.

ST.

TO CHERRY

1 NAUGHTON'S FUNERAL PARLOR
  FUTURE SITE OF 'SUN LAH'
2 FUTURE SITE OF
  GRANDFATHER'S FLOWER SHOP
3 GRANDFATHER'S BIRTHPLACE
4 PORT ARTHUR
5 OPERA HOUSE
6 QUONG YUEN SHING

7 TOM LEE'S
8 CCBA
9 ON LEONG HQ
10 HIP SING HQ
11 BULLETIN BOARD
     EXTENT OF CHINATOWN
     PUBLIC SCHOOL

CHINATOWN AND FIVE POINTS
c.1897

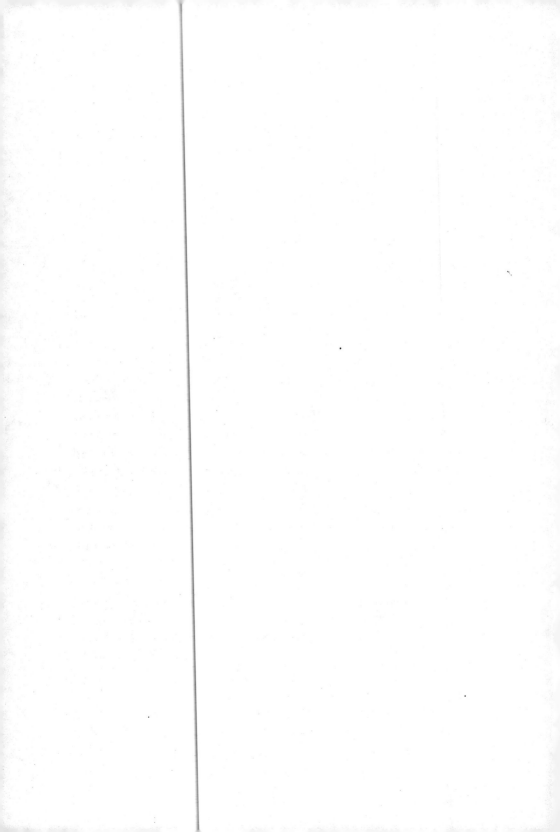

INTRODUCTION

I guess I'm searching for continuity. When I was about eight years old, and living with my family in the fourth house of my short lifetime, I made some remark to my mother about one of our previous homes being where my "roots" were, the place where I had at least made it through two grades of school before my father got promoted and "moved up" yet again. "You don't have any roots!" she exclaimed, laughing, a fact I sadly had to admit was true. I could see roots, however, other people's roots in the old buildings and place names of the Connecticut town that we eventually landed in. I tried to adopt them as mine, but the meld never quite seemed to work for me, a kid with his feet in two hemispheres.

My mother's family hadn't had roots for a long time. Ever since they left Scotland for the Colonies in the seventeenth century their story had been one of Conestoga wagons and homesteading, gold rushes and log cabins. My maternal grandfather lived in a city hundreds of miles away from the small town where my mother grew up, and by the time I knew him, his hobby was buying big, old houses, fixing them up, and selling them for a profit. Every couple of years he seemed to be in a different house, their age and solidity merely an illusion of a family heritage. One time I did see my mother's childhood home, however, when we drove by it on the way to my Great-Aunt Mabel's. There was just enough time to press my nose against the window of the station wagon, before we rounded a corner and it was gone.

We barely even have any artifacts from my mother's family, since my grandfather died without a will and his second wife kept all of his heirlooms for her own children. Oddly, despite the fact that they were married for nearly thirty-five years, she stopped talking to us almost from the moment of his death. The speculation was that the silly old woman was afraid we were going to ask her for something—something of great value, like my mother's childhood dolls, or that spinning wheel my grandfather had promised me, the one that he said had traveled across the country in the covered wagon with his restless ancestors 150 years before. I yearned for that connection to place, even if it was a place on wheels that shifted with the weather and random discoveries of gold a continent away.

Chinatown was the only constant in my life, it seemed, the only spot to which I could always return to familiar surroundings and see the thumbprints of generations that had died before living memory. The crowded, tiny streets, the restaurants we held our semi-annual banquets in, even the ducks hanging in the dusty window of the old grocery store on the corner seemed eternal, although I knew perfectly well that those ducks were freshly killed every day. It was a place with tradition, with customs, with old people who knew my father and would call him by baby names I never heard anywhere else. It was a place that America hadn't homogenized out of existence, and there one could smell the village where the Ancestors had lived for perhaps a thousand years before.

I had a keen sense of what that village was like, even if the Communists wouldn't let you go there to see for yourself. As for my mother's family, the most specific place of origin that anyone could identify was "Scotland and England." Since that could mean anything from Windsor Castle to a sod hut next to some highland peat bog, I had no clear image of a house or a village. I had never heard the voices of those ghosts, nor even knew where to find them.

This is the history of that foreign universe called Chinatown, New York, with my Ancestors providing the string with which to tie together the loose beads of the past. The Chinese side of my family has been in this country longer than the European ancestors of most of my Caucasian friends, and they experienced almost every phase of development of life in Chinatown, from early settlement, to racial apartheid, to Tong Wars, to all-American domesticity. All along the way were generous doses of magic, and poetry, and the exquisite, mystical beauty which was never to be found in the bland, white-bread towns of my youth—which only heightened my hunger for it.

This is a *tactile* history. I want the reader to be able to know what it felt like to live in Chinatown through the years, what it looked like, what it *smelled* like, and I have enlisted the Ancestors to help me in my attempt here and there. But in doing so, they have also refuted some of the modest denials of my Chinese elders, who have always insisted that the Tong Wars weren't so bad, that discrimination wasn't so bad, that our family wasn't so important. They were, it was, and the Ancestors have indicated that they would like a little more respect from their descendants in future.

But I was surprised when these same Ancestors provided some interesting insights as to what makes my immediate family tick, why we always seemed just a shade different from our WASPish neighbors in the suburbia of the 1960s. Despite his Kelly green golf pants and his dry martinis, there is a lot more of Imperial China in my father than he would ever allow. And I guess I have to conclude that there is some of that in me as well.

I have tried not to fictionalize my family's early Chinatown history, although I have had to choose between sometimes conflicting versions of their stories found in old immigration interviews, letters, newspapers, and the municipal records of both New York City and our tiny village of origin in southern China. The home villages were very important to the development of Chinatowns everywhere, since they were where every good Chinese son expected to return one day. Even from an outpost as distant as New York, there was a constant interaction with home to the point that Chinese who had been living on Mott Street for decades were often far more familiar with what was going on at the Imperial Court, some ten thousand miles away, than they were at City Hall, a mere ten blocks away. Chinatowns everywhere were like transplanted Cantonese villages, and like many of his countrymen, my great-grandfather maintained parallel families—three wives, eight children—growing up both in New York and back home. A hundred years ago, the two branches of our clan were so closely intertwined that even now, some strands of their lives still touch ours.

The family left in China earned reputations significant enough to have kept people talking for over a century about fortunes made and fortunes lost, prodigal sons and greedy in-laws—especially greedy in-laws—all basking in the reflected glory of a relation who left for the "Golden Mountain" and made good. The fact that he left in 1873 hasn't dimmed their expectations from their "overseas" family. About ten years ago, after generations of no contact whatsoever, my sister, Amy, was traveling in that part of China and managed to get a message to those very distant relations, living in the crumbling remains of the once-impressive family compound built long ago with American funds. The 96-year-old matriarch was quick to dispatch a two-word reply to Amy's polite introduction: "Bring money." The allure of an overseas relation was just too much for the old lady to resist. My sister chose to stay away.

W ithin these pages I concern myself almost entirely with Manhattan's Chinatown. There are nearby Chinatowns almost as old, those in Brooklyn, Newark, Philadelphia, and Boston. But the juncture of Mott, Pell, and Doyers Streets was the epicenter of that particular universe, and there is more than enough material there for ten books without delving into the satellites.

Also, the reader may notice that I use archaic spellings for the English versions of most Chinese words. My reason for that is simple: I like them. Hong Xiuquan may be the accepted modern way to spell the name of the great nineteenth-century rebel who ravaged the country and almost overthrew the Emperor, but Hong Hsiu-ch'üan is just, well, *prettier*. It is a spelling full of richness, and mystery, and the aroma of sandalwood incense burning before a household shrine. To me, that is what Chinatown is all about. Or at least those are the parts I choose to remember.

1

·

BACKGROUND

There are ghosts in Chinatown. They're all there, lined up, waiting to see me whenever I venture down Mott Street, squeezing past the crowds inspecting the sidewalk vendors' fruit or firecrackers or windup birds that really fly. There are ghosts of men and women, some in exotic clothes, some gambling, bent over little ivory tiles, some eating. No, everyone's eating. Inside a certain shop, there is the ghost of a man in a broad-sleeved jacket, with a long braid, working on an intricate work of art. On a tiny street, a vintage black Cadillac, driven by a little man with a big cigar, careens away from the curb, full of flowers and that day's race receipts. On a narrow sidewalk is the image of a shy young woman in magnificent ceremonial clothes, venturing uncertainly into the sunlight. And then there is the ghost of a little boy with a blue blanket, being carted up a staircase to a mysterious place full of dragons and phoenixes and, once, even a bowl of Chinese Cheerios. These are my personal spirits, shadows of my existence reaching out to me from over 125 years. To me they are dollops of magic—magic that can still be found by those who know where to look.

My father knows where the magic is. Even though he began life there, to him the old neighborhood is still a little mysterious. He is actually third-generation Chinese, born in Chinatown, raised in Brooklyn, and sounding remarkably like Walter Cronkite. His was a classic poor-boy-made-good story—youngest of five children, blessed with exquisite good looks and opportunity, graduating from Columbia at nineteen. As a wartime Army Air Corps cadet in Denver, he married the beautiful Southern blonde he met at a church social, a scandalous move in 1944. Chinatown was far behind him when, as an up-and-coming corporate executive in 1950, he Anglicized his name to Hall from Hor, a name many Chinese-Americans modify for obvious reasons. Pronounced "Haw" and written 乎 it functions in sentences as a question mark. By itself it could mean "What?" although some say it more accurately translates to "Huh?"

Our house *was* the ethnic neighborhood in Madison, Connecticut, and despite the fact that none of us, my father included, spoke Chinese or engaged in any of the martial arts, we were considered somewhat exotic. When meeting us for the first time, my WASPy mother's new acquaintances from bridge at the country club always assumed we kids were Korean War orphans. But Mrs. Hall, ever the Southern Lady, would always smile sweetly and say, "Guess again!"

My friends all had blue-eyed pedigrees. They had middle names like Williston and Carlton followed by a III, a IV, in one instance a IX. In school the teacher pointed to a map of Europe and spoke confidently of where "our people" were from—England, Ireland, Scandinavia, sometimes Italy. I had "people" from those parts as well, but so many generations distant that I no longer felt any direct connection. No, in that world I was always the Chinese kid. The Chinaman. The Chink who spoke real good English. I was never exactly sure where I was from. The closest thing I could come to it was this tiny corner of New York City.

Yet I couldn't entirely fit in here either. I was an outsider with inside connections. An inside/outsider, perhaps, definitely a Connecticut boy, albeit one who could eat with chopsticks. Yet I knew that even Connecticut only went back three hundred years or so, whereas on Mott Street I could almost smell the beginning of time.

I could sense ghosts back then too, but only dimly. The enchantment I felt was stronger for their being just out of sight, heightened by the fact that we would visit only a few times a year. Months of atmosphere and mystery would be crammed into forays lasting only as long as it took to consume a twelve-course banquet, with insufficient time to explore the shadows behind teakwood dragons and mysterious basement doorways.

Over time, I determined to drag those ghosts into the daylight, and find out more about the Chinatown that was tugging on my sleeve. Of course I am talking about "old" Chinatown, those few blocks of Mott Street from Canal south to Chatham Square, and then up Bowery to Doyers and Pell Streets, then west back to Mott—three little thoroughfares to which a whole universe had been transplanted, in miniature.

For my family, that universe is a village of soot-stained mud brick in the waning decades of Imperial China—fifty houses in a jumble of streets so narrow you couldn't lie across them without your head and feet knocking against the opposing walls. Every bit of available space is in use, leaving no room for sidewalks or flower gardens or any kind of personal privacy. There are just the houses, squeezed suffocatingly close, with heavy tile roofs that turn up at the corners into dragon-points that are meant to frighten away evil spirits. As further protection, the village's tiny lanes squirm around in curves and sudden, switchback turns, because, of course, evil spirits can only travel in straight lines and so will come to grief against a wall before crossing some family's threshold. Carved screens or miniature goldfish pools just inside doorways take care of any stray demons that manage to penetrate all other defenses. Household gods and smoldering incense stand guard over the ancestors' tablets in the parlor.

Like all Chinese villages, this one is conceived of as a dragon. The front, where there is a bamboo wall broken by an old wooden gate, is the head. The other end, with the community well, is the tail. There are no street names or numbers. Homes are only identified, for instance, as the second house in the fourth row from the head. Several generations live packed together in each of these dwellings, mostly five rooms running in a line from the "big door" at the front to the "small door" at the rear. The better houses have slightly more elaborate entranceways which might lead into a central courtyard bordered by a largish hall and smaller rooms for various members of the family. Wooden chamber pots sit by the entrances, waiting to be collected so their contents can be sold to local farmers for use as fertilizer—for here, nothing is wasted.

One or two residences, doubling as shops, have no doors or windows facing the street at all, just a big accordion shutter running along the entire front, wide open in the sticky summer heat. But most shopping is done in the market town about three *lis* away. Sundays and Fridays are market days, at which time the men and some of the women of the little village trudge over the fields to the larger town's hundred stalls at which they buy and sell, haggling over clay vessels and iron pots, wooden toys and writing brushes, sticky buns, green vegetables, and slabs of meat, over which a vendor sits silently with a fan to keep the flies from settling too long.

Back home, a few desultory chickens or maybe a pig waiting to be made into a celebratory meal scratch at the hard-packed earth. Otherwise it is quiet, strangely so for a place that is so close and cramped. A visitor during the day will find a village populated by the very old, the very young, and women, many with bound feet, who have been left behind to watch the babies and weary through endless household chores. You might hear the shrill voices of children echoing off the gray-brown walls. A woman with an infant squats by the village well, doing laundry in a basin. Hanging in the air is the *"clack, clack, clack"* which might be the sound of home looms, or of cutthroat mah-jongg games being fought over by the old ladies in their little parlors.

The old men gather in the forecourt of the Ancestors' Hall, where they sit and smoke and complain about their children. They're not really complaining, of course, but bragging is a serious breach of etiquette, so they talk down their sons' various achievements, knowing full well that their friends will read between the lines. Females in their families are never mentioned for any reason.

The old men play mah-jongg too, or maybe *pai gao*, the gambling game played with dominoes, oblivious to the incense smoke rising from the altar behind them. It is faded and well used, but the Ancestors' Altar still provides a little bit of splendor for this essentially utilitarian place. Its lustrous red and green surfaces are heavy with golden dragons lounging among azure clouds and fantasy flowers. There are banners of poetry, venerating the family clan, going back hundreds, even thousands, of years, and someone has burned paper money in the big bronze bowl so the ancestors will have something to spend in heaven.

Ancestors. My ancestors. The family Hor, in the seventh house, fifth row from the head of the village of Hor Lup Chui, in the Toi-shan district of Kuang Tung Province, southern China. Pretty much everyone is named Hor in this village. A bigger community might have two, or even three surnames represented, but Hor Lup Chui has been home to the Hor clan for countless generations, and besides, there are only 438 surnames in the entire nation of China anyway. Still, just because everyone shares a name doesn't mean they are closely related, and individual family trees are scrupulously kept. People of the same surname are not supposed to marry, so boys get wives from one of the other little villages that dot the horizon. Girls are married away, never to return.

Hor Jick Wah was my great-great-grandfather, the oldest Chinese ancestor that I can put a definite name to. I don't really know what he looked like, but I can pretty well guess. He must have had a square face with heavy brows, like my grandfather had, and he was probably skinny like everyone else in China back then. There just wasn't enough food to make anyone fat.

Hor Jick Wah couldn't have been much taller than five feet. After all, his grandson never exceeded five feet three, and even my father, the tallest in the entire family, is only five feet nine. Like every Chinese male in those days, he would have had a shaved forehead and a long queue hanging down his back, a sign of loyalty demanded by the Manchu Emperor in far-away Peking, a mysterious figure who would periodically issue edicts on such subjects as good manners, filial loyalty, and one's moral obligation to pay one's taxes.

Hor Jick Wah may have dressed like many of his country neighbors, with a simple farmer's smock and trousers bound tightly at the ankles with white stockings. But my family has always had some pretensions to gentility, and they would prefer to think that my great-great-grandfather affected the more gentlemanly costume of a short, broad-sleeved jacket over a long scholar's gown. His cloth shoes would have had thick, rounded soles, causing the wearer to rock like a boat in choppy seas.

He was born in Hor Lup Chui during the reign of Emperor Tao Kuang, and family tradition suggests that he was an artisan, probably a woodworker. He built the altars and carved the screens and constructed the intricate window-lattices that regulated demon traffic in and out of people's lives. He also built the coffins in which they took their final journeys. But very likely he hammered out an existence similar to others' in the Toi-shan district during that period—part artisan, part merchant, part farmer of the dry rocky soil that yielded only enough food to sustain the population for four months out of twelve.

He seems to have been a man of modest substance, however, living in a house with a courtyard, and having some education. After all, an artisan was fairly high up on the social scale, higher anyway than people who merely bought and sold things, and certainly his family had enough leisure to allow his son to learn to read and write, no small feat in a complicated language that consists of tens of thousands of unrelated symbols with roots in pictographs created far back in antiquity.

So at the village school opposite the Ancestors' Hall, my great-grandfather joined the other boys in shouting out his calligraphy lessons and refined the art of composing elegant eight-line poetry. Twice a year, troupes of itinerant actors would set up on the threshing floor to perform a days'-long tragedy full of heroes and heroines, demons, dragons, and magic, always magic. Through them, he and his fellows learned the great classics of drama, and even illiterate farmers delighted in quoting the time-honored verse by heart.

Of course if Great-Great-Grandfather had been really motivated, he could have educated his son to be a scholar, who would then be qualified to take the grueling Civil Service exams held annually a day's ride away in Canton, the entry to a lucrative career in the Imperial bureaucracy. Young men studied obsessively for years to pass these exams, memorizing hundreds of pages of Confucian doctrine, word for word, for candidates were ruthlessly tested on their knowledge of the great philosopher and the classics of Chinese literature. However, only a tiny fraction of the applicants went on to the next level, and had my ancestor successfully passed the exams, my history might be radically different today.

It was in the 29th year of the Emperor's reign, the Year of the Monkey, a.k.a. 1850, that my Great-Grandfather Hor Poa was born. Chinese counted time according to the number of years that the current emperor had been on the throne, and Tao Kuang was sixth in the line of long-reigning monarchs of the Ch'ing or Manchu Dynasty, which had, until recently, been a period of peace and prosperity for the great Chinese Empire.

But soon after Hor Poa's birth, young Prince Hsien Fêng ascended as Emperor of *Chung Guo*, or the Middle Kingdom, an event that would have been celebrated with feasting and firecrackers all across the nation. The people of Hor Lup Chui may have considered this dawn of a new reign a good omen for the baby Hor Poa's future. But the omens were not so good for China and Toi-shan.

In those days, the country was wracked with chaos and starvation and social upheaval. By 1850, the population had soared to an estimated 410 million from about 150 million in the previous century. The first Opium War had ended only eight years before in 1842, with Great Britain humiliating China into opening her markets to foreign trade and ceding them the island of Hong Kong into the bargain. The British bought up Chinese tea and silk, and built a city on their luxuriant stolen isle. They also made billions by flooding the country with opium produced in British India. China quickly became a nation of addicts, thus making Victoria the world's first international drug Queenpin. The Emperor imposed disastrous taxes on his subjects to pay the costs of losing a war.

Furthermore, just as Hsien Fêng ascended the Peacock Throne in 1851, the Tai-ping or "Great Peace" Rebellion was getting underway in southern China. A messianic maniac named Hong Hsiu-ch'üan fought to set himself up as a rival god-emperor. It would be fourteen long, hungry years before Hong and his movement were finally exterminated by the Chinese army, but the anarchy he generated continued to take its toll.

All across the southern provinces of Kuang Tung and Fukien there was massive unemployment. Armies of bandits from "Secret Societies"—terrorist groups ostensibly formed to restore the Ming Dynasty, out of power for some two hundred years—ravaged the countryside. Travelers were compelled to move about in large groups, and then only at night, with armed guards and lanterns covered by deep shades lest their light attract hungry bands of brigands. Village fought against village in bloody inter-clan feuds. Sometimes warring villagers would steal out under cover of darkness to dig up hillocks and move giant boulders in an attempt to destroy their rival village's *feng shui*, the spiritual balance determined by the physical arrangement of the landscape. It was just one more way to bring ruin upon their enemies' lives.

Meanwhile in 1856, the fifth year of Hsien Fêng's reign, and the sixth year of Hor Poa's life, the Opium Wars started up again, adding even more devastation to the mix. European invaders ultimately chased

Hsien Fêng and h s court from the vast splendor of Peking's Forbidden City to a crumbling palace in the hills, where the hapless monarch died in 1861. He was twenty-nine years old.

Hsien Fêng's successor was Tung Chih, a six-year-old boy controlled by his scheming mother, a former minor concubine of the late Emperor, who for the rest of the century would stop at nothing, including royal murder, to hold onto her newfound power. The reeling Chinese Empire was steadily being gnawed away by hunger, war, and drug addiction, afflictions which killed an estimated twenty million people. Some say it was more like sixty million. The swirl of misery created a chasm which foreigners rushed to fill.

The people of Hor Lup Chui knew there had been Foreign Barbarians, also known as White Devils, visiting the nearby city of Canton for centuries. But ever since the Emperor had been forced to create "treaty ports" for foreign trade, it seemed that White Devils were everywhere—huge, ugly, pasty-faced men, with big bellies and hair sprouting from all over their bodies. Occasionally, there would be strange straw-haired women, walking brazenly in the street, wearing bizarre gowns that flared out from their waists like giant bells. They all came from barbarian lands far across the sea, in big wooden ships crowned with heaps of white sails or tall smoke-belching chimneys.

All through Hor Poa's growing years these White Devils, also known as Big Noses, told stories of gold—mountains of gold in a country called California, where one could go and become rich by just plucking the stuff off the ground. Chinese middlemen in their employ traveled around the villages, spreading the tales of this land of riches. The Big Noses had ships, they said, that could take a person to their country. The middlemen just needed money—a lot of money—and you could sail away to wealth, guaranteed. Or, if need be, a loan could be arranged. The middlemen would pay the passage in exchange for a little work until the money was repaid. It was easy, they said. You will be rich.

In other parts of the country, people were skeptical of these stories. Every Chinese knew that all other places on earth were beneath the notice of those who lived in the Middle Kingdom. Besides, life was too hard, the burden of tradition too great to allow them to be curious about unknown lands across the sea. But here in Toi-shan, where living had been particularly difficult for so long, people were looking for ways out of their misery. The stories the White Devils told sounded good to hungry men and women. The lure of gold began to ease the disapproval from the spirits of a hundred generations of ancestors and overcome any fear of the unknown.

It had been in the 27th year of Emperor Tao Kuang, a.k.a. 1848, that two men and one woman first went aboard one of the alien ships and disappeared into the mists. Months went by. But eventually, little packets of nuggets and gold dust started to arrive for their families. The following year, nearly eight hundred men and two women followed their compatriots. The year after that, more than three thousand men and five women—and finally by 1852, 27,000 Toi-shan residents were seeking treasure beyond the sea.

Many bought passage and sailed off on their own to try their luck. But some shipowners, under contract to western masters, had their middlemen—or k'o-t'ou, who were often returned emigrants themselves—recruiting shiploads of young men for laboring jobs in an assortment of distant places. The Chinese only knew that they were going off into the unknown to make money. But while some jobs were in the California gold fields, many more were on sweltering tropical plantations surrounded by the malarial rain forests of Cuba, or South America, or Malaysia, where the workers, referred to by the Big Noses as "coolies," died like flies.

Then, by the middle 1860s, the White Devils had stopped talking about gold and were actively recruiting men to go to California and work on something called a Rail Road. No one in the village knew exactly what a Rail Road was, but it apparently provided good, steady work, and could make a man rich. Some of the contracts offered by the k'o-t'ou to these mostly illiterate laborers promised payment of their passage in exchange for a certain number of years of labor for the sponsoring company. This "credit-ticket" system was nothing more than indentured servitude. Many called it slavery.

Early on, the Imperial Court was suspicious of Chinese mixing with foreigners. Emperor Hsien Fêng didn't want any of his subjects going abroad to work for these uncouth Barbarians who had forced opium upon his nation and more or less hijacked Hong Kong into the bargain. Thus, starting in 1855, the émigrés had to contend with an

Imperial decree branding them traitors to the Manchu Dynasty, and mandating death by beheading for anyone trying to leave the Middle Kingdom. Ambitious bureaucrats were promised merit points for every ten illegal emigrants they captured. The heads of one hundred emigrants meant a promotion in rank.

However, the siren call of gold, plus the great "face" or prestige of having a relative working in California, taught families how to elude the authorities. They could sell a water buffalo or pawn some jewelry to come up with the exorbitant fare demanded by the *k'o-t'ou.* Some used money-lenders to raise the cash, and many traveled under the credit-ticket system.

But however the money was obtained, there was still the leader of the local garrison to bribe, and maybe a payment to the regional magistrate or government official. It was then a fairly simple matter to take a junk down the Pearl River to one of the big ships standing in Hong Kong harbor and start the long, long voyage to another world. Most thought their sojourn would be a temporary one. For many, their exile is not yet over.

It was an arduous journey, especially for country boys—for they were very nearly all young men expecting to return to their women—who had never been out of sight of land before. Three months of being tossed about on the Pacific Ocean ensued, crammed into holds that had carried cargo on the outgoing journey—but then, the passengers were little more than cargo themselves. Everyone was sick on the first days out, made all the worse by the fact that they usually were forced to stay below decks, just like on the African slave traders that had stopped plying the Atlantic only a few decades before. Food, such as it was, consisted of whatever fare could be carried aboard by the passengers themselves and kept for ninety days in the era before refrigeration. Many even had to supply their own water, which they carried in distinctive cylindrical wooden casks. Some captains supplied hardtack and dried peas, which could be boiled down into a gruel, with maybe a piece of saltpork on occasion. Perhaps a load of rice would have been taken aboard before sailing. Of course, rats could fry up to make a special treat.

But nothing could stop the contagious diseases which sometimes ravaged the ships, the close quarters only accelerating the spread of infection. In the 1850s and 1860s, dozens of these vessels met with disaster caused by overcrowding, such as the *Lady Montague*, where 300 of the 450 passengers sickened and died. There were 338 out of 380 who perished on the *Providenza* before she passed Japan. On the *Dolores Ugarte*, desperate Chinese locked below decks started a fire as a ploy to get the crew to open the hatches. Over 600 were burned to death in their floating prison.

Troublemakers were beaten with rods by the Caucasian crews or locked in bamboo cages. Many were chained with iron shackles or even hanged by captains fearing mutiny. Some merely gave up and committed suicide. Yet even so, they sailed. As one Chinese survivor would later write, "To be starved and to be buried in the sea are the same."

For those lucky enough to avoid death from starvation or disease, the devastating seasickness eventually wore off, and the men grew accustomed to sitting with the others in the semi-darkness of their quarters. They had long since sought out those with the same surname or others from the same region. It wasn't family, exactly, but they had grown up in a society where people weren't so much individuals as part of a group and it was essential for them to merge with others. So they passed the time, smoking and gambling, gambling, gambling with their little *pai gao* dominoes, or perhaps they played *fan tan*, where they bet on the number of beans shaken from a cup. "Strings of cash"—Chinese copper coins with holes in the middle, carried on loops of string—began to clutter the winners' pockets.

A stop for revictualing in the Kingdom of the Sandwich Islands, also known as Hawaii, brought a little relief to the passenger-freight below decks in the form of fresh water and maybe some dried fruit or vegetables. They were not allowed to go ashore, of course, but that didn't matter, as all they were interested in was their final destination.

The arrival in San Francisco, some ninety-five days after leaving home. The bewildered boys would stumble down the gangplank, two by two, wobbly from their weeks of inactivity and the constant movement of the ship. Customs officials would fall upon their baggage, consisting of wooden boxes, wicker baskets, and rolls of cloth tied with cord. The essentials for a civilized existence in a barbarian world were spilled upon the ground. Chopsticks, porcelain teapots, bamboo steamers, and iron woks; family portraits, scrolls of calligraphy, ivory mah-jongg tiles, and skeins of silk; smoking tobacco, delicate pipes, dried lizards, and live snakes for use as medicine were pawed through by white men looking for boxes and bags of one item and one item only—opium. It wasn't that these Government officials were there to seize contraband. They had to make sure that they collected the very substantial duty which was charged, for opium was not then illegal in this country, nor would it be for decades to come.

Teams of Chinese representing the Six Companies—the Chinese-run benevolent associations that controlled every aspect of Chinese life in San Francisco—met these new immigrants as they reassembled their belongings. Groups of boys would recognize a summons in their own local dialect, and separate from the group to follow the speaker, who would pile them into carts for the trip to "Chinese Street," which the whites called by the name of Jackson. Narrow alleys running off to the sides were crammed with cheap wooden houses and shacks in which hundreds of Chinese men slept on hard wooden bunks. The crowding and sanitation were not much better than in the hulls of the immigrant ships, but the newcomers were largely indifferent to their surroundings as long as they could make money. Their newfound friends from their home district would soon help them slide into jobs in this rapidly expanding frontier town.

The earlier arrivals mostly worked for white prospectors, digging and panning out hastily-staked claims. They were allowed to keep half of whatever gold they found, which sometimes amounted to what seemed like a fortune to these cash-poor peasants. Claims abandoned by their original white prospectors were hastily taken over by Chinese, who hungrily squeezed gold dust out of the discarded tailings.

After 1864, shiploads of Chinese men were imported to work on the Transcontinental Railroad. Called "Crocker's Pets" after Chester Crocker, the railroad mogul who first conceived of this method of amassing cheap labor, ten thousand Chinese were toiling away at any given time. They worked long, backbreaking hours without complaint, their small, lithe bodies perfect for creeping into rocky crevasses to plant dynamite for blowing away obstacles. Often they were dangled down sheer cliffs in order to reach otherwise inaccessible places. The expression "Chinaman's chance" referred to the likelihood of their being killed in a fall or a badly-timed explosion. For all this they were given board and $30 per month in gold.

It was largely due to Chinese labor that the Transcontinental Railroad was finished in an amazing five years, but not a single Chinese face appears in the famous photograph of the ceremony surrounding the driving of the final spike in 1869. It is estimated that between five hundred and a thousand Chinese laborers were killed in those five years. Many believe the numbers were far higher.

Even so, the Chinese were appreciated by their white bosses for their energetic hard work, although some of their habits truly astounded them. At the insistence of their white co-workers, Chinese prospectors and railroad workers alike lived in separate camps; there their own cooks could prepare a semblance of the food they knew at home. American eyes were exposed to the mysteries of chopsticks and stir-frying for the first time. White men were further amazed to see Chinese carefully wash themselves every day—*every day*—coiling their long, braided queues on the tops of their heads to keep them out of the way. And then there was the strange Chinese habit of drinking nothing but tea—sans milk or sugar, no less—with the cooks keeping vats of water constantly on the boil so as to provide a constant supply. No one could figure out why the Chinese seemed never to get sick, while the Big Noses, also known as Round Eyes, who drank cold water directly from streams, were often doubled over with dysentery.

After 1869 the gold mines were getting depleted and the Transcontinental Railroad had been finished. Although thousands of Chinese were kept working on another branch of the railroad, thousands of others suddenly found themselves without work. Long practice in scrambling for subsistence in Toi-shan had taught them nothing if not resourcefulness, however, and the men just joined the swelling ranks of those who worked in various businesses catering to the ballooning Chinese expatriate community.

All sorts of skills were needed, like those of the Chinese immigrants in 1870, among whom were found six herbal doctors, seventy-one carpenters, fourteen stone-cutters, three bakers, seven barbers, and twenty-seven tailors to construct the loose-fitting blouses and trousers for the thousands of their countrymen who had preceded them. Scribes wrote letters for their illiterate compatriots. Troupes of actors entertained with classical Chinese opera. And then there were the importers who provided all that tea and other essentials from home.

Some Chinese were opening restaurants. Of course the cooking was just basic bachelor fare—a dim imitation of what they were used to eating in Toi-shan. Yet it was this plain country, Cantonese food which became the staple of the restaurants that were springing up in cities and towns where the railroad had dumped its men. Whole new dishes were invented to appeal to Round Eye palates. For instance, there is a legend of a group of drunken white miners breaking into a Chinese restaurant after hours and demanding food. The proprietor just scraped together table scraps and garbage and called it "chop suey," which means either "leftovers" or something vastly more rude.

Still others founded laundries, a desperately needed service for the sweaty white men who disdained clothes-washing as an effeminate task fit only for women. But with not very many white women to take care of all those men, some of these newly rich, western pioneers actually sent their laundry all the way to Hong Kong to be washed and pressed, rather than besmirch their manhood by doing it themselves. The Chinese stepped into the breach, and all over the West Chinese men sweated over great tubs of steaming water, boiling and pressing white people's clothes.

Others found work in the rapidly expanding cigar-making factories, where Chinese were favored over "Bohemians" for their dexterity and hard work. Tobacco would be shipped to San Francisco direct from Cuba, with over a million finished cigars per month sent East for $18 to $50 per thousand. The Chinese cigar-maker would earn four to twelve dollars for producing the same amount.

Some Southern plantation owners whose black slaves had run off after Emancipation turned to cheap Chinese labor to work in their fields and live in the old slave quarters. In the Northwest, loggers valued the strong, agile men who could scamper up a tree as well as wield an axe. These qualities made them even more valuable in the silver mines of the Rockies, where they could reach into the narrowest fissure.

Chinese found work as servants, as shoemakers, and in all manner of factories. Many operated their own truck farms, supplying two-thirds of all the vegetables eaten in California by 1872. And all the while, these good Chinese sons hoarded their money and sent a substantial amount to their honored wives and parents back home—for first and foremost, a Chinese son's duty is to his parents. After all, a hundred American dollars could make a family rich in Toi-shan. It could provide for a bride price, or a bigger house, or more farmland, or just food— sumptuous food, like squab, and crabs, and duck, hot and juicy, for everyone to become sleek and fat, the envy of their neighbors.

Besides, none of these men expected to stay in California for long, and they dreamed of the day when they would be able to return to their villages and bask in the honor reaped from their Barbarian-acquired riches. The upshot was that in the 1850s and 1860s so much money was sent back that Toi-shan became the most prosperous region in China. The United States became known as *Mei Guo*, "Superlative Country," while the sons in California were referred to as *Gum Shan Hok*, or "guests of the Golden Mountain."

After 1866, even the Emperor's Government—that is to say, the Emperor's mother—realized the benefits of so much hard cash being sent into Chinese coffers, and in 1868, the thirteen-year-old Sovereign affixed his seal to the Burlingame Treaty, which provided for free emigration between the U.S. and China, and further confirmed the rights of Chinese to use American schools and pursue naturalization. Those were not rights that most Californians thought should be granted, but then Anson Burlingame was a great fan of the Chinese.

Meanwhile, in the little village of Hor Lup Chui, my great-grandfather, Hor Poa, was playing with his friends in the surrounding hills, hunting, fishing, or just plain exploring with one of the village's many pet dogs. Of course the children never went out at night, because that's when demons from the surrounding graveyards roamed, looking for young inductees to the netherworld. But through daylight and darkness, there was always one thing present—the distant smell of gold in his nostrils.

He waited longer than many of the other young men of his region to make the big trip. Perhaps things were good enough at home so that there was no urgency. Perhaps they were so bad that he couldn't afford a ticket. At any rate, in the twelfth year of Emperor Tung Chih, a.k.a. 1873, twenty-three-year-old Hor Poa took the junk down to

Hong Kong and there boarded the *Oceanic* with some 725 of his countrymen for passage to San Francisco. His fare: $45.25. The *Oceanic* was one of a new fleet of steamships built specifically for the Pacific passenger trade since 1869. No longer locked below decks in dank holds designed for cargo, immigrants could now sleep in berths and cross the Pacific in about a month. Food, albeit strange Barbarian food, was provided by the line. Richer passengers could even enjoy the comfort of private cabins.

He did well. Family tradition says that Hor Poa worked on the new southern spur of the Central Pacific Railroad, but not as a common laborer, God forbid. We have always been solemnly informed that our Chinese-American Patriarch worked in the somewhat more genteel position of cook to the workmen. Still, whatever he did, Hor Poa sent a steady stream of money home to old Hor Jick Wah, waiting expectantly in his little village. And after fewer than six years, Hor Poa had fulfilled the dream of every immigrant Chinese man in California—he had saved enough money to return home in style.

It was in January of 1879 that Great-Grandfather set sail for Hong Kong on the *Gaelic*. Maybe he even splurged and went cabin class, with a stateroom of his own, along with dour-faced missionaries and other returning big-shot small-town boys. Regardless, he would have arrived in triumph at Hor Lup Chui village just in time for the New Year, 4577, the Year of the Rabbit, and the fifth year of the Emperor Kuang Hsü.

Back in 1875, just as he grew old enough to assert himself, nineteen-year-old Emperor Tung Chih had "ascended the dragon"—in other words he had died. Some say he had contracted a venereal disease from prostitutes after his mother denied him access to his wife, whom he had married over her fervent objections. However more people believe that he was murdered, perhaps by means of a poisoned towel handed to him by his own mother, Tz'u Hsi. His beautiful teenaged Empress followed him a few days later, forced to take an overdose of opium so the Court could officially announce to the world that Her Imperial Majesty, prostrate with grief, had committed suicide. Tung Chih was replaced with another boy-child, a cousin, while his mother, the ruthless ex-concubine, now styled Dowager Empress, continued her absolute regency.

None of this was on Hor Poa's mind, however, as he was showered with admiration by his family and dispensed the presents expected of a dutiful son. A bag of gold, a clock, some other Western mechanical treasures—as such were the things that were held in high esteem—only heightened the aura of romance around the returning sojourner as he looked forward to a long-delayed milestone in his life—marriage. Of course it would be to the girl his parents had chosen. This was Wife Number One. Eventually there would be a Wife Number Two, and my great-grandmother would be Wife Number Three—but now I am getting ahead of the story.

About Wife Number One I know little except that she was of the Moy family, and she had natural feet. Apparently her parents were not aristocratic or pretentious enough to bind their infant daughters' feet into "Golden Lilies"—painful, tiny knots of bone and flesh that would nearly cripple them for life. Starting in early childhood, but occasionally beginning as old as ten or eleven, girls' feet were tightly bound with silk bandages, forcing the big toe upwards and back and the others down. The arch eventually folded in on itself, resulting in a deformed appendage some three inches long. To retain the desired shape, the bandages would have to be regularly reapplied for the rest of the woman's life. Walking, insofar as it was possible, was done on the heels in aching, minuscule steps. Tiny feet were one of a Chinese lady's greatest claims to beauty and gentility, but Hor Poa's parents decided that he didn't need a mere ornament at home. Or rather, *they* didn't need one. Their son's wife, like all sons' wives, would be there only to work hard for them, while she found time to bear sons between household chores.

The Moy family was from Chung On village, 15 *li* across the fields from Hor Lup Chui. Their daughter's betrothal to Hor Poa had probably been arranged when both were still children, or possibly while he had been in California. A go-between—an elderly female relative or a marriage broker—would have arranged the union, trundling back and forth, extolling the virtues of the two parties, checking genealogical lines to make sure they weren't related. She also would have negotiated a "bride price" from the groom's family, for Hor Jick Wah was essentially buying a wife for his son, who now had the added luster of being a Guest of the Golden Mountain. Of course the two young people had no say in the matter.

By the time of Hor Poa's return to China, both bride and groom were a little old for marriage—he was twenty-nine, she twenty-four. One reason for the delay was that Hor Poa had been away seeking his fortune. But then also, Miss Moy had been born in this, the Year of the Rabbit, and the Elders would have known that a wedding at this time would be desirable because this was to have been an especially propitious year for her to bear sons.

Anyhow, on the actual day of the wedding, a date reckoned in the West as June 1, 1879, this daughter of Moy would have traveled from her father's house to the groom's in a closed sedan chair carried by two bearers. One or two female attendants, most likely elderly relatives, would have walked alongside. A cart with her trousseau would follow, stuffed with linens, and embroideries, and select pieces of bridal furniture. At the gates of the village, little boys would have met her procession with a hail of firecrackers, the elders whaling away on shrill little gongs. Her emergence from the chair would have marked the first time she and Hor Poa had ever seen each other, but there was no time to get acquainted. For Miss Moy and her attendants immediately retired to a bedroom where she was changed from her ceremonial traveling robes into a new gown, the second of the four she would wear to mark each part of the ceremony. All of her wedding clothes were a dazzling red, the color of prosperity and good fortune.

The actual marriage ceremony would have consisted mainly of the intonation of "a few lucky words" by Hor Jick Wah and the exchange of the red generational papers detailing each party's lineage going back three generations. That was all. Hor Poa could now be formally be known by his marriage name, Hor Lup Chut, while the Moy daughter could add the Chinese suffix *She,* for Mrs. or Madame, to her maiden name, thus becoming Moy She. Her own given name, bestowed upon her by her parents, would never again be used, and would remain unknown to almost everyone, including her children. It would not be long until it would be forgotten forever.

The formal worship of Hor Poa's ancestors would come next, a short ritual in front of the ancestral tablets in the parlor with incense and offerings—he first, and she imitating him. In this way she left her own father's family forever, and joined her new husband's line. Now all her obligations would be to Hor Poa, Hor Jick Wah, and the long trail of

Hor family predecessors. If she was a traditional Chinese mother-in-law, my great-great grandmother, whose name is lost to my generation, would have made Moy She's life a misery. At least until she provided a grand-son—or two—or three.

But that was still in the future as, following the ancestor worship in the parlor, there would have been a day-long celebration of feasting and drinking in the village banquet hall—with the women separated from the men, of course, for a good wife never ate with her husband. And that night, the entire wedding party, spouting astonishingly rude jokes made all the more lewd by the liberal imbibing of rice wine, would have escorted the couple to their wedding bed, a great canopied fantasy of teakwood dragons and lucky birds flying among flowers and vines. It was time for Hor Poa to fulfill his obligation to his ancestors and give them that son they had been clamoring for, so they could brag about him in heaven. Three days later, Hor Jick Wah would send a gift of ten-der young pigs to the Moy parents in Chung On village, a traditional confirmation that their daughter was, in fact, a virgin. Not to do so would have been a mortal breach of etiquette.

But despite the auspicious omens provided by the Year of the Rab-bit, as well as entreaties to dead generations, it seems that Moy She did not conceive. So, not able to wait any longer, Hor Poa agreed to the adoption of a girl-child, very likely from some impoverished widow trying to raise money for her husband's funeral; such an arrangement was very common and simple. This girl, named Yee Sum, or "Good Heart," was provided basically so that his lonely wife would have someone to wait on her. A son would have provided greater face, but there would be time for that later. Adopted daughter waited on adopted mother who waited on parents-in-law in Hor Jick Wah's house in the fifth row from the head of the village. But the father was long gone. For four months earlier, Hor Poa had returned to the Golden Mountain. It would be years before he saw any of them again.

In California, there had been a measure of hostility towards the Chinese almost from the beginning. With the number of immigrants increasing from three to something over 25,000 between 1848 and 1852, the white population of San Francisco feared imminent obliteration by the seeming hordes arriving every day. Granted, at first the educated opinion was that they were good for the country—"Sober, diligent, laborious, orderly people—economical in their habits, and in all respects a desirable population," wrote one observer. Yet as early as 1849, there was mob violence against Chinese gold miners, and by the mid 1850s individual communities started banning Chinese miners altogether. In response to the growing anti-Chinese rallies held in San Francisco and elsewhere, exorbitant taxes were levied on the remaining mine workers, as well as on Chinese laundries, restaurants, and every other kind of Chinese enterprise. An attempt was made to deny the Chinese business licenses of any kind. In 1870, San Francisco prohibited the hiring of Chinese for municipal works. In 1879, an amendment to the California state constitution prohibited any corporation from hiring Chinese at all. Laws were enacted specifically to harass them: prohibiting the use of poles to carry burdens in the street; prohibiting firecrackers and ceremonial gongs; mandating the cutting of queues; and preventing bodies from being shipped to China for burial. The latter two were both cruel dilemmas. For most Chinese men intended someday to return to their native country, where they could be beheaded for *not* wearing a queue, the symbol of loyalty to the Emperor. And all of them believed that if they weren't buried in their home soil, their souls would wander, lost and aimless, forever.

Flouting the 1868 Burlingame Treaty, which promised the Chinese civil rights equal to any other foreign residents, local laws were passed to prevent Chinese from owning real estate, attending white schools, or even fishing, whether commercially or for pleasure. There was even a California law enacted threatening jail for people who slept in a space of less than 800 cubic feet—an obvious attack on the notoriously crowded Chinese neighborhoods. This measure backfired, however, when it was realized not only that tens of thousands of Chinese would have to be incarcerated, but also that the space allotted to them in jail was considerably less than that prescribed by law.

Chinese immigrants were baselessly accused of spreading leprosy and bubonic plague. Between 1854 and 1872, they were forbidden to testify against whites in Californian courts. Since they could not legally protect themselves, this left them open to all sorts of abuse from their Caucasian neighbors. And since Asians did not technically fall into the categories of "white persons, Africans, or those of African descent" specified by the Fourteenth Amendment to the Constitution, Chinese people were denied naturalization. Since they couldn't become citizens, they couldn't vote. Since they couldn't vote, politicians ignored them.

Yet all these were the least of the indignities suffered by Chinese in the American West. The very few Chinese women present were commonly assumed to be prostitutes and liable for deportation, as on the occasion in September of 1874 when some two dozen women were brutally forced onto the China-bound steamer *Japan*, their "screams and wails" filling the quayside air. Whenever they ventured into white neighborhoods, Chinese men could expect streams of abuse from white children, who would pelt them with stones and pull their queues. Chinese mining camps were regularly attacked by whites wielding clubs, rocks, and shotguns. There were wholesale massacres: Twenty-two killed in Los Angeles in 1871, thirty-one miners in one 1887 raid, a "so-called massacre" of "only five or six" laborers by a gang of white thugs in 1877. Despite the fact that the perpetrators were usually well known, courts could not be found that would even indict them. Communities of Chinese were routed out of towns all over the West. In Seattle and Tacoma their homes were looted and burned by angry white mobs. The Knights of St. Crispin, a rapidly growing anti-Chinese labor group, declared in their founding statement that "one effect of a thorough organization here would be to deter the Chinese from coming, as they would think it unsafe." Led by the St. Crispins, California exerted greater and greater pressure to force Washington to ban Chinese immigration altogether.

The Six Companies pleaded for tolerance in appeals to San Francisco's white population: "We hoped you would, by knowing us, learn to like us, and be willing to protect us from some evils we now suffer . . ." But by 1876, the popular opinion concerning the Chinese was expressed in this typical commentary in a California newspaper ". . . he is a slave, reduced to the lowest forms of beggarly economy, and is no fit competitor for an American freeman . . . his sister is a prostitute from instinct, religion, education, and interest, and degrading to all around her . . . they defy the law, keep up the manners and customs of China, and utterly disregard all the laws of health, decency, and morality . . ."

Once again, desperate Chinese started looking for a way out. Then, early in 1880, a fare war erupted between the Central Pacific

Railroad and the Pacific Mail Steamship Company. The railroad wanted to eliminate competition on transcontinental travel once and for all, and started offering tickets for the unheard-of low price of $35. Frugally-minded Chinese jumped at the opportunity and started to buy.

Their destination: New York City.

2

.

NEW YORK

The arrival of some 150 Chinese men in New York City during the week of March 4, 1880 was a big event in the nation's largest metropolis. Big enough, anyway, to draw newspaper reporters and curious spectators down to the Chambers Street pier where the travelers were to land after taking the ferry from the Jersey City terminal. Unfortunately for them, few Chinese were actually spotted, but that didn't stop the intrepid reporters from digging up a story anyhow. "The car in which they rode came into Jersey City a model of cleanliness, as compared with those occupied by white emigrants . . . ," wrote one breathless observer before heading downtown to see if he could expand on his story. Still, even though these few "Celestials," as they were called, caused such a stir, they weren't totally new. After all, there had been Chinese living in and around New York for years.

It had been in 1796 when a Dutch merchant who had been trading in China settled in Philadelphia with five Chinese servants. Pung Hua Wing Chang was the supposed name of a Chinese valet working for John Jacob Astor in New York in 1808. Ten years later the first of five Chinese boys arrived to study at the foreign mission school in Cornwall, Connecticut. And in 1825, a Chinese sailor who had taken the name "William Brown" arrived in New York City, where he married an Irish woman named Rebecca and had a son, whom they named after his father. The trickle had begun.

Still, it would be a long time before there was a Chinese "community" to speak of. After William Brown, Senior, there had been the occasional Chinese visitor to New York—sailors, ship's stewards, or maybe a merchant once in a while—arriving on one of the American trading ships bringing spices and silk from Canton. Then in the late 1840s there was another handful of Chinese students sent over by their aristocratic families, as well as a few more domestic servants living at fashionable addresses uptown on Lafayette Street or on Union Square with employers such as the Delano family—grandparents of that famous Delano who would one day occupy the White House—who brought a Chinese manservant and nursemaid back from their sojourn in Canton, where they had grown rich in the opium trade.

P. T. Barnum took over the successful Chinese Museum on Broadway between Spring and Prince Streets in 1850. The "Extensive View of the Central Flowery Nation" not only featured "Ten Thousand Things on China and the Chinese," but one "Miss Pwan-ye-Koo . . . the first Chinese *lady* that has yet visited Christendom." Here Mr. Barnum was being disingenuous, to put it politely, because he himself had sponsored appearances of another "Chinese Lady," Afong Moi, who had first turned up in New York in 1834, went on the stage with the diminutive General Tom Thumb in 1845, and was still being "exhibited" as late as 1847.

Still, she seems to have been largely forgotten with the debut of Barnum's latest "discovery," the seventeen-year-old Pwan-ye-Koo, who boasted bound feet reportedly only two and a half inches long. She was being trotted around the world by the great circus impresario along with a retinue billed as her maid, her "Professor of Music," his two small children, and an interpreter. But it was the girl and her tiny feet that were the main attraction.

New York City schoolchildren learned about China from the Chinese Museum, like twelve-year-old Andrew Archibald, who wrote, "The china People is very Industrious. they have very small feet. they are bound in iron shoes when they are young and when they are Men and Women their feet stays so and also they whear wooden soles to their shoes and their feet is very tight with their shoes and they have very long hare. it is so long that it would make a whip. and they also eat cats and mice and pupies." [The spelling is Andrew's.]

As for the adults' reaction to the Chinese Lady, a reporter for the *New York Herald* sighed, "We had no idea that a woman of that country could be so good-looking . . ." Unfortunately for him, Pwan-ye-Koo soon left for London.

Mott Street was then still firmly in Irish hands. Yet the tide was beginning to turn that would bring Chinese to make a life in that neglected neighborhood way down on the Lower East Side—a neighborhood that would someday be transformed into a hazy replica of a Kuang Tung village half a world away.

New York City, during the first year of Emperor Hsien Fêng, a.k.a. 1851. Back in China, the Tai-ping Rebellion is picking up steam. Great-Grandfather Hor Poa is just learning to walk and his parents may already be looking for a suitable bride for him. But here, mass immigration from Europe has recently caused the population to surge past 500,000, more than double what it was twenty years ago. Construction is spreading north at a breakneck pace, and sumptuous mansions of the rich are being built on Fifth Avenue, up to and even beyond the new Madison Square, located between 23rd and 26th Streets. A grand new public park has been proposed that will cover more than eight hundred acres of scrubland (as well as obliterate at least one Free Black village) in an area unimaginably far uptown. Its supporters are firm in their belief that this new "Central" Park will someday be engulfed by development. Mayor Ambrose C. Kingsland, a Whig politician and dry-goods salesman, has given his official endorsement to this plan. He also presides over a City Council popularly known as "The Forty Thieves" for their rampant greed and corruption.

Meanwhile, below Canal Street, between Broadway and the East River, the Five Points neighborhood is the worst slum in town. Some say it is the worst slum in the world. On its southwestern corner is an area that will eventually be known as Foley Square, but it was until 1808 the location of the Collect Pond, a small lake referred to as "a very sink and common sewer" because of the refuse from the manufactories located on its shores. The city had drained and covered over this body of water by 1811, but the soil remained marshy, and the buildings of the new neighborhood built to the east of it soon started to sink and crack. The smell from marsh gases and decay, mixed with the stink from horse manure and back-yard privies, drove away its more well-heeled residents. All that could be found to replace them were the most desperate of the poor.

At the center of Five Points is "Paradise Square," a block east of the old Collect Pond, formed by the intersections of five tiny streets— ultimately known as Baxter, Worth, Park, Water, and Mulberry. There stands a decrepit brick building known as the Old Brewery, famous enough as an emblem of the slum so that tourists and visiting V.I.P.'s are taken there to gape at the degradation. In the 1790s, the place had actually been used to brew the then-famous Coulter beer, but since the 1830s it has been broken up into a warren of dark squalid little rooms, housing an unbelievable 1,200 desolate people on its five crooked floors. Supposedly, in this one building alone there is one murder per week.

It is not just the Old Brewery however, but all the buildings here that are "dens of death . . . houses into which the sunlight never enters . . . that are dark, damp, and dismal throughout all the days of the year and for which it is no exaggeration to say that the money paid to the owners as rent is literally the 'price of blood.'"

Unventilated soil pipes open onto many floors or empty into basements which remain perpetual swamps of raw sewage. A typical house is described as "damp and rotten and dark, walls and banisters sticky with constant moisture." Buildings have been squeezed into many of the tenements' back yards, reducing any open space behind them to airless, lightless courts, hung thick with laundry and ringing with the cries of the children playing there in the gloom. The outdoor privies reek with the odor from "night soil . . . within a *foot and a half* of the seats." Water is obtained from public pumps or fountains, around which it is the custom to leave the carcasses of dead animals for easy collection and disposal.

On Bayard Street between Mott and Elizabeth is one "big flat" tenement with room for 100 families. Others live in the little alleys which run behind the streets, giving access to the cellars made "horribly foul" by the accumulation of sewer gases and fecal matter oozing up through the floor. Back-yard shanties go for one dollar per month.

Some people just rent part of a grimy bunk—three to a mattress, 15 cents each, for eight-hour stretches. Others sleep in the streets along with the pigs, which roam wild, serving as the neighborhood's sanitation department. Children run barefoot. Human waste and garbage are thrown out the windows, which are often dark at night for want of money to buy lamp oil.

Mulberry, the principal street of the neighborhood, has been nicknamed "Death's Thoroughfare." Indeed, the whole neighborhood is putrid with disease. Smallpox, yellow fever, and cholera are frequent visitors. One house will have twenty cases of typhoid in a single year. By the 1860s, it is certain that 17.5 percent of the neighborhood's population will die in the course of each year. The annual infant mortality rate will eventually be reckoned as one in five.

People's bodies are covered with little bite marks from fleas, lice, and bedbugs. In 1852, a public bathhouse will be erected on Mott Street just north of Canal at the astronomical cost of $42,000. It is the only place for blocks and blocks where a person can get a real bath, with soap and hot water. It will close by 1860 for lack of patronage.

The people of the Five Points are fruit dealers and cobblers, day laborers and peddlers, collectors of junk, rags, and bone. Some residents are black, descendants of a group of ten freed slaves who settled near Chatham Square in 1645. Some are from "Russian Poland," others from little German grand duchies and kingdoms such as Brunswick, Saxony, and Württemberg. Far more are Irish. There are enough Irish, in fact, to make Five Points the largest Irish community outside of Dublin. At any rate, the neighborhood is supposedly the most densely populated spot in North America.

Although there are people who manage to provide themselves with a few small luxuries, more typical might be the family found by one charitable worker. The father is an unemployed painter. Their dinner, laid out on an old crate, consists of stale bread and bones. A basket of coal can only be bought with the sale of the household's last chair. When asked if the children might not be better off in an institution, the mother says that they'll "all hang together" as long as they can, and "if necessary . . . starve together."

It is no surprise, then, that in Five Points there is rampant gambling and prostitution, begging too, anything that can bring in a few

Tea That Burns

cents. It is notorious as the place where one can indulge in any conceivable vice, that is if one can tolerate the filth. The scant earnings of the inhabitants are quickly spent on meager bits of food, on fuel, on cheap rum or homemade gin that might kill you, or maybe only make you blind.

Gangs with names like the Dead Rabbits, the Shirt-Tails, and the Plug Uglies—so-called because of the oversized plug hats they wear virtually resting on their ears—battle with each other and keep the population cowed through terror and extortion. Their special domains carry names like "Bandits' Roost," "Thieves' Alley," and "Kerosene Row." The police only venture into Five Points in pairs—if at all.

Toward the edges of this neighborhood Mott Street runs parallel to Mulberry, one block to the east, and James and Pearl Streets snake along the southern rim on their way across Cherry to the docks of the East River. These are streets where no respectable New Yorker would walk, let alone live. These are also the streets where the first Chinese in the City are able to make their homes.

Once the haunt of Colonial-era aristocracy, Cherry Street runs parallel to the waterfront, crossing Pearl about a block inland. George Washington had lived here in a handsome three-story brick house during his first term as President, but by the late 1840s Cherry Street had grown seedy and disreputable. Its once-stately mansions had been broken up into cheap boardinghouse rooms and flophouses.

It is Cherry and nearby James Street that have for the past few years been the location of the boardinghouses favored by the dozen or so transient Chinese sailors who can be found in New York. At least two, at 61 Cherry and 78 James, are actually operated by Chinese. Living among the echoes of past grandeur in their lofty rooms stacked high with wooden bunks, the Asian lodgers stay pretty much to themselves, even further isolated by divisions of dialect. The Cantonese live in one boardinghouse, those from Shanghai in another.

The men just sit and gamble over their cards and *fan tan* cups. Or they shut out their solitary lives in New York entirely, reclining in opium-induced stupors in their rough wooden bunks. Catering to their more basic needs is one Ah Sue, who in 1847 opened a tobacco and candy store in an old house at 62 Cherry. It was apparently the first Chinese-owned business in New York. He too has a "boarding house" upstairs, with his and others' tenants coming from a variety of unexpected sources.

The Chinese junk *Key-Ying,* with two giant eyes painted on either side of her prow, had caused a sensation when she sailed into New York harbor in 1847. She was fitted up as a floating Chinese exhibit for curious Yankees, and thousands paid the 25-cent admission to visit her teakwood decks during her summer-long stay. Her main cabin, painted Imperial yellow and adorned with fantastic pictures of birds and monkeys, was fitted up as an exhibition room, lined with cases filled with exotic wonders from the Middle Kingdom. Furthermore, her twenty-member European crew was supplemented with thirty to forty Chinese men who, while in New York, occupied themselves visiting Barnum's Chinese Lady and gamely experimenting with such Barbarian toys as cigars and forks.

Unfortunately, most of these men had been duped into making the long voyage from their homeland by the white owners of the vessel, having been contracted only to sail to Java, not halfway around the world. *Key-Ying's* European captain, Charles A. Kellett, used violence to keep his crew in line, eventually refusing to pay them their promised eight-dollar-per-month salary. But at the end of August, twenty-six of the Chinese men were "rescued" by an American couple and a Mr. Lin King Chew, a "Chinese gentleman of education, and of distinction and property in his own country [and] a devoted Christian." While these twenty-six were eventually sent home, it seems that a few others stayed on. It was a major addition to New York's embryonic Chinese community.

In 1853, the Tong Hook Tong Dramatic Company stops in New York to perform one of their classic opera tragedies. These are elaborate affairs that can take many days, if not months, to complete, with an all-male cast decked out in fantastical make-up and spectacular costumes of heavy embroidered silk. To Chinese spectators, Tong Hook Tong's theatrical conventions are comfortingly familiar. They know that the different colors of the tiny flags stuck into a general's robes denote various allegiances and the size of armies. Two generals fighting is an apocalyptic battle. Willowy maidens are portrayed by female impersonators singing in a traditional falsetto, while the orchestra saws away at melodies and rhythms created in the Middle Kingdom many centuries before.

Of course, with only fifty to seventy-five Chinese in the city, most of Tong Hook Tong's audience is white, but the troupe are confident of repeating their recent success in San Francisco with an engagement at the Niblo Theater at Broadway and Prince Street. It is a wish that will remain disastrously unfulfilled, however, for as soon as they arrive from California on the *Cortes* in May, their New York sponsors declare bankruptcy and renege on their commitment to pay the company's expenses. The dumbfounded actors are left stranded without resources, while the captain of the *Cortes* puts a lien on their sumptuous costume collection as collateral for their unpaid passage. It is only the first blow.

Hopeful that they can earn the money to pay him, they go ahead with their Niblo's engagement anyway, but attendance is disappointing. Some White Devils find the opera performance interesting, but most consider it almost ludicrously unintelligible; the Chinese music is especially confounding to them. Disappointment is turned to catastrophe when Tong Hook Tong's American booking agent absconds with what profits there are. The second blow.

Increasingly desperate attempts are made at mounting further performances, with the company trying to adapt to white tastes. The plays are drastically reduced in length. Some of the sensational acrobatics are lifted out of the operas and performed on various vaudeville stages in the City. But attendance is still discouraging. The Tong Hook Tong troupe faces real disaster.

New Yorkers are not without compassion, however, and efforts are spearheaded to help the stranded Chinese. The manager of the Castle Garden Theatre, scene of the soprano Jenny Lind's recent triumph, offers his premises for a benefit performance. Newspapers run advertisements free of charge. There are donations of money and services, but it is too little, too late, and the actors' fortunes sink even lower. "What shall become of us now?" the company manager writes through an interpreter. "We did not come to this country as beggars. Honest ourselves, we were deceived by putting too much confidence in those persons who brought us into the miserable situation we are in now; therefore we really think we do not deserve our unfortunate fate." But the final blow is yet to come.

The company's creditors will wait no longer, and the valuable costumes, without which the actors cannot perform, are seized and auctioned. Appeals are made to charities and in the newspapers for financial assistance, at first to send the company back to China, then just to keep them housed and fed, but by now there is only a tepid public response. The owner of the Shakespeare Hotel extends their credit as long as possible, but ultimately the forty-one members of the Tong Hook Tong Dramatic Company, which includes managers Li Koon and Min Chu, interpreter Leong Mun Gao, and two cooks, are evicted and left to wander the streets, dazed and penniless.

The splendor of the Chinese opera is far behind them as some are sent to Blackwell's Island, New York City's penal colony for homeless paupers, where they are put to work making cigarettes. While there, at least one attempts suicide. Others are to be found selling what remains of their personal possessions on street corners. There is no record of any of them returning home in the years that follow. It is in this manner that New York's Chinese community tops 100 in number.

Maybe the disenfranchised actors find a place among the cigar-makers. At 391 Pearl Street there is a gate leading into a covered gangway, only wide enough to allow one person to pass at a time. The gangway skirts the side of a brick tenement, ending in a small, dim yard. At the back is a row of outdoor privies. Along the side is an old, dilapidated wooden structure. A doorway in this building conceals a flight of rickety, uneven stairs leading down to a large basement room, low-ceiling'd and thick with tobacco smoke. The feeble light from the door—for there are no windows—needs to be supplemented by a tallow candle. There is a work-table in the center of the room, covered with a woven mat and surrounded by a mixed assortment of wooden chairs. The walls are a shiny dark brown—not from paint, but from long exposure to the greasy fumes from cooking and heating fires.

Nineteen-year-old Ah Kam has set himself up in this basement room in 1851. He has tried to make it a little more homey by adorning the walls with a few oddments of decoration—a scroll or two of poetry, some cheap pictures, a simple household shrine to the kitchen god with a bowl for food offerings and constantly burning sticks of incense. He supports himself as a cigar salesman, rolling and finishing the product right there in the cellar and hawking them on the street. White New

Yorkers know Ah Kam as Mr. Akkomb or even Mr. Akkbo. Apparently the Big Noses don't realize that the honorific *Ah* is not part of his name, but means something vaguely akin to "Comrade."

Ah Kam's rent is steep—$13 per month, much more than a white man would have to pay. So, ever vigilant for ways to make money, he has made his room into a kind of boardinghouse for other Chinese cigar peddlers—fourteen of them in fact—who pay $3 a week for the privilege of sleeping there. Bunk beds line two sides of the room, as in the hold of a ship, with the men sleeping two and three to a bunk. But food is also included in the rent, with Ah Kam doing the cooking, mostly plain rice with a few vegetables to go with it. A nice hot bowl of tea is provided before bedtime. Twice a month they have boiled chicken as a special treat.

Before their arrival in New York, some of these men had been employed as "coolies," or semi-slave laborers, in the tropics. Theirs had been a much harder story than those of the miners and railroad workers in California. For victims of the "coolie trade" often were tricked into signing up with a Chinese labor-broker, or even kidnapped outright from their homes in China. At treaty ports like Amoy and Shanghai they were imprisoned in long warehouse-like barracks—just like the African slaves of an earlier generation—before being stuffed into the holds of clipper ships and hauled off to Latin America, where they sweated away hacking plantations out of the jungle or doing other hard labor. Many of the men living with Ah Kam, for instance, had been digging guano on islands off the coast of Peru. At their first opportunity they fled, joining the crews of trading ships as cooks or stewards and jumping ship in New York.

In Ah Kam's basement room, they take up the cigar business, buying cheap remnants from local tobacco dealers and, singing the monotonous chant of a working song like black slaves in a cotton field, they join their landlord in rolling the stinkers at his center table. Each man produces perhaps 150 to 180 per night, selling their cigars in the streets in all weather for three cents apiece. They suffer the indignities of having their queues pulled by boys or adult thugs, and young punks cockily take cigars at will, without paying. It's grim, hard work, but the money's good. Some cigar-sellers can earn up to $20 or even $25 per week, which is two or even three times more than the average American factory worker.

Of course they save every penny possible and, like good Chinese sons, send a portion home to their parents.

They also look out for each other. When any of them becomes too ill to work, the others pool their money and pay his expenses. In the first five years, four die in that room. The rest pay for their funerals and send their bodies back to China, where their souls can finally be at rest.

Ah Kam's "boardinghouse" averages over $100 per month profit for him, which, added to his earnings from selling cigars, nets him a tidy little sum. It may be that he is able to give up the hard life of peddling on the streets, and he may, in fact, be the legendary "Ah Ken" who supposedly, in 1858, opens a little smoke shop on Park Row. At the same time this same Ah Ken is said to rent a small house on lower Mott Street, the first Chinese to do so. Of course he hires out bunks to the slowly increasing trickle of Chinese immigrants to New York. Is this the moment when Chinatown is born?

Cigar-selling seems to be the main occupation of New York's Chinese, although some also sell "that peculiar preparation known as Chinese candy." Like the cigar men, they station themselves on the street corners, with little portable wooden tables or boxes covered with crumbly bits of brownish rock candy, which they sell for a penny apiece. And throughout the 1850s there are a few Chinese traveling uptown to work in the fancy tea shops found there. Some are clerks, but some are just hired for atmosphere, their broad-sleeved jackets, cork-soled shoes, and long, trailing queues adding to the exotic decor. They sit forlornly on the sidewalks in front of these stores, wearing sign boards that advertise the wares within while they suffer the open-mouthed stares of Barbarian passersby.

There is one who is busily learning English. It is his often-expressed hope to marry a white girl and become an American citizen. He tries very hard to fit in, and is "quite dandyish in his appearance, wearing a shawl, and all that" over his American ready-made suit. He may even have adopted an American name, Charles Miller, and is already well on his way on the road to prosperity.

He seems to be living at 78 James Street, also the home since 1855 of Ah Bao, the most popular of the tea-shop clerks. He works at 50 Spring Street, speaks English with a flair, and is perceived by whites as a leader of the little Chinese community. Somewhere along the way, Ah

Bao has picked up the vaguely Western first name of Quimbo, and thus is known to the Big Noses as "Mr. Quimbo Appo." He had been born Chu Fi Bao, in "the interior of China" in the fourth year of Emperor Tao Kuang, a.k.a. 1825. Finding himself in Shanghai during that city's bombardment by the British during the first Opium War, he was compelled to flee after some unspecified criminal activity. There followed a decade or so of wandering which took him from China, to California, to Boston on the *Vandalia,* on which he worked as a cook, to New Haven, and finally to the James Street boardinghouse. It had been while sojourning in New Haven in 1853 that he had acquired a wife, "a very intelligent Englishwoman" (Catherine Fitzgerald, who was actually Irish), and had two children. The elder died, but the second, born on the fourth of July, 1854, was christened George Washington in honor of the day, and moved with his parents to New York.

Quimbo Appo is not unique in his choice of spouse. Several of New York's Chinese men have married Irish girls. It is interesting that these earliest Chinese settlers marry not the German, not the Polish, not the African women found all around them in the Five Points slum, but almost exclusively the Irish. Of course, Chinese women would be more acceptable, but Chinese women are totally lacking on the East Coast, and the menfolk are lonely.

As for them, why would good Irish Catholic girls consent to unite with these strange and exotic "Mongolians"? Perhaps it is because it is a way out of the grinding poverty that their new American lives have provided them. Perhaps it is because Irish girls of the period are at the absolute bottom of New York's white society and can't find anyone else. One thing is certain—it is a sign of desperation on both sides that one would agree to consort with the other. After all, this is still Five Points, where conventional morality is stretched to fit around any circumstance that hunger and poverty can provide.

So the Chinese boys and the Irish girls marry—at least both parties claim to be married—and as a result the first generation of Chinese children in New York is actually Eurasian. The Irish women's more well-heeled, "respectable" uptown neighbors use these unions as evidence of their natural depravity. During the Draft Riots of 1863, Irish mobs in the Fourth Ward attack any Chinese man "suspected of liaisons with white women."

Still, George Washington Appo is a beautiful child, with dark, delicate features touched with the slightest hint of exotica by dint of his Chinese blood. Lively and precocious, his future seems promising. After all, his father, working at a successful tea business and speaking English, has earned the admiration of white New Yorkers, who view him as a quaint and charming curiosity. The gregarious Chinese makes a habit of visiting the police to inform them of illegal activities among his countrymen. Of course, that's not as much of a betrayal as it might seem, as he is from Shanghai and most of them are from Canton and speak another dialect. To Quimbo Appo, these Southerners are almost as foreign as the White Devils with whom he is trying so hard to assimilate.

However, despite his friendliness with the Metropolitan Police, Quimbo's history with the law is a troubled one. It was so not only in Shanghai but also in California, where he killed two Mexicans, albeit in self-defense or so he claimed. It is in 1856 that he gets into a late-night argument with his wife, Catherine Fitzgerald. He had found her drunk after she returned from celebrating the birthday of their landlady, Mary Fletcher, at their new lodgings in 47 Oliver Street, and starts shouting at her and then beating her. Mary Fletcher and eight of her Irish women friends rush to Catherine's defense, ganging up on the man they call the "China Nigger," striking him repeatedly with their fists, a flatiron, whatever comes to hand. Brandishing a knife, Quimbo stabs out blindly and strikes Mrs. Fletcher, whether intentionally or not is unknown. She tumbles backward down the stairs and dies.

As the women run shrieking for help, a neighborhood Irish mob tries to lynch the hapless Chinese man. He is rescued by the police, but it doesn't really matter. Quimbo Appo soon becomes the first Chinese in New York State to be sentenced to death.

Unlike what he could expect in California at this time, however, in New York there is public sympathy for Quimbo. Christian missionary workers loudly complain about the inadequacy of his defense, and the man is granted a new trial in 1859, where he is convicted of a lesser charge and sentenced to ten years. But even though there is a much-vaunted conversion to Christianity, and Quimbo is pardoned early in 1863, the die has been cast.

In 1869 he marries an Irish woman known as "Cork Maggie"—not, reportedly, because of her city of origin, but because of the composition of her false leg. It seems that Maggie has something of Robin Hood in her personality, because she steals Quimbo's money and gives it away. They fight. He stabs her. Maggie survives, but Quimbo goes to prison for another year.

Later there is more violence, more killing, until Quimbo Appo is finally branded a demonic monster by the New York press and put away for good. Bald, toothless, and covered with Roman Catholic tattoos, the little man ends up in an institution for the criminally insane, raving and delusional. For the rest of his long, unhappy life, he is convinced that he is the Emperor of America. His palaces and legions of retainers forever await him, just out of reach, on the other side of his prison walls.

As for Catherine Fitzgerald, in 1859 she leaves for a new life in California with their three-year-old daughter, but after a three-month voyage, her ship is wrecked on rocks mere yards from its destination. Mother and child are drowned. Meanwhile, as his world completely disintegrates between Sing Sing and the California coast, beautiful little George Washington Appo is left to live by his wits among the pickpockets and prostitutes of the festering Five Points ghetto. With new teachers like "Nigger" Hannon and "Dick the Tinker" Flannigan, George Washington soon learns to follow in his father's footsteps.

Others in that first generation of Eurasian children are more fortunate, however. In 1862, a sailor named Lou Hoy Sing, 42, jumps ship and moves into one of the Cherry Street boarding houses. He follows the example of his countrymen and marries an Irish girl, by whom he is to have two sons. One of these will become a truckman like his father, and the other a New York City police officer, the first Asian on the force. The son has brought great face to his people and his family name.

It isn't Chinatown yet in 1870, but it is a start. The census states that there are 63,254 Chinese in the United States. The population of New York City is nearing one million, and in the Fourth and Sixth Wards there are 16,925 white people, 129 black people, one Indian, and ten insane persons (no race listed) in the streets on both sides of Chatham Square where almost all the Chinese in the City live. Their number in this neighborhood is listed as 58. It is a count which is undoubtedly low.

Even if the legendary Ah Ken lived on Mott Street in 1858, he doesn't now. No Chinese seem to be recorded as living on Mott in 1870, but since addresses aren't exactly specified in the Census records it's difficult to tell for sure. At any rate, on nearby streets one can see the mix in this not-yet-so-Chinese community. Some live alone, like 25-year-old "John" Ah Bock, a cigar maker. He is the single Chinese in a boardinghouse with eight Irish, Italian, and "Russian Polish" families, forty-one people in all. Elsewhere, Ah Ling and Ah Kim, both cigar-makers, share a room. So do confectioners Ah Wang and Sing Doon.

Meanwhile, Ah Kam, who has married an Irish woman named Kitty and now lives with her somewhere south of Chatham Square, has several boarders; Ah Fat, Ah Wah, and Ah Fung. All four of these men have adopted the Christian name "John," but then white people have, for some time, been referring to all Chinese men generically as "John Chinaman." Irish-born Anna, married to Ah Fung, also lives there. The women can read and write, but the men cannot, at least not in English.

Even so, Ah Kam's life has gone rather unusually well since the days when he ran his little basement establishment on Pearl Street some fifteen years before. He had served as a steward on a Union gunboat during the Civil War, and was twice wounded, perhaps the only Chinese to be able to make that claim. Now that he is married, he has settled down to a domestic existence, selling cigars and running his little boardinghouse. There seems to be nothing but promise in his future.

A couple of doors down the street are fifteen Chinese living together, including one who calls himself George Smith, a sign of either an early attempt at assimilation or some White Devil who couldn't pronounce his real name. George Smith, probably a cigar peddler, is either very careful with his money or hasn't moved up very far in the world in the last decade and a half. He has quite possibly lived crowded into this same bunk-lined room since the middle 1850s.

Fifty-year-old candy-seller "John" Ah Man is married to, or at least lives with, a thirty-year-old Irish woman named Ellen, one of at least nine neighborhood Chinese thus paired. Thirty-six-year-old seaman William T. Ah Kee is married to twenty-year-old Margaret, sharing their rooms with "John" Ah Lok.

Ship's steward James Wing, forty-eight, and his wife, Bridget,

Tea That Burns

thirty-eight, have four children: Charles, fourteen; Catherine, nine; Martha, four; and Thomas, two. These children, like all of the fourteen Chinese-Irish children surveyed, are officially reckoned as Chinese, even though they were born in the United States.

James Wing, along with his brother John, had become a naturalized American citizen by 1867 when both were living at 65 Cherry Street. They are two of about ten Chinese in the entire country to have received citizenship despite widespread attempts to deny Chinese that right. James is also reportedly in possession of $800 worth of personal property. In an era where the average American worker might make $300 per year, he is well on his way to achieving the American dream.

For most, however, the dream is more elusive. There is a Chinese man who seems to have landed in New York via Cuba, who calls himself Antonio Como. Every evening he walks the five blocks from his boarding house at 10 Baxter Street to the sidewalk in front of Central Hall at 33 Bowery, where he sets up his portable cigar stand. Central Hall is a cheap theater exhibiting sideshow attractions and on this particular June 15, the "flaming posters" in front of the place advertise "a monstrosity in the shape of a negro girl with two heads"—a spectacle that proves irresistible to the low-life Bowery crowd.

The crush becomes oppressive, and as Como and his cigar stand are penned in by a jostling swarm of adolescents, he testily tries to warn them off. But these are streetwise youths who won't stand to be reprimanded by a mere "Chinaman," and soon Como is being taunted and baited. Nasty epithets are hurled. Perhaps someone grabs at Como's queue or tries to steal a cigar. Goaded into a blind rage, whatever the exact provocation, the Chinese man lashes out with a penknife and stabs twelve-year-old James Moore in the side. The boy sinks to the pavement with a wound that will prove fatal. Como, realizing what he has done, hurriedly packs his wares and tries to walk rapidly away under cover of the ensuing confusion. A fleet-footed police officer catches him at the corner.

This incident only serves to inflame the emotions of a group of New Yorkers who are organizing an anti-Chinese rally to be held in Tompkins Square Park in two weeks' time. It seems that a few days before the death of James Moore, some seventy-five Chinese between the ages of 14 and 22 had been imported from California to replace

striking shoe-factory workers in North Adams, Massachusetts, 150 miles
to the north of New York City. "Their little, oblique almond eyes take in
a great deal of what is going on around them . . .," remarked one white
observer. "With their utter ignorance both of the craft and of our language, it is a matter of surprise how speedily and thoroughly they have
mastered the technicalities of the business, and what they are shown
once, they rarely forget or need to be shown a second time." The factory
owner rates them a great success.

The striking Caucasian workers, represented by the Grand Lodge of
the Knights of St. Crispin, are not so impressed, however, and rally to
protest "this new attempt to crush the Crispin Order by introducing for
that purpose a class of servile laborers from Asia who cannot become permanent citizens of this country . . ." They are referring to a court ruling
that because of the Fourteenth Amendment to the Constitution, Chinese
cannot be legally naturalized, even though some New York judges have
ignored the precedent. Also, they somehow assert that the St. Crispin
organization "knows no distinction of race or color . . ." Despite that claim,
it seems that a group of Chinese walking in a North Adams street very
early in their tenure had "a bucketful of dirty water . . . thrown on them.
[They] took it very meekly and manifested no resentment."

It is a relatively small group of New Yorkers who perceive the
imported shoemakers as the vanguard of a great yellow invasion bearing down on them from California. The rally in Tompkins Square Park
on June 30 is held to support the Crispins in particular and oppose
Chinese immigration in general. Three oratorical platforms are
erected, two for English speakers and one for German. Although there
are many women and children present—apparently to enjoy the
refreshments and the warm, night air—the working male population
targeted by the rally is so noticeably absent that the start of the
speeches is delayed for half an hour.

Finally, a long roster of resolutions is laboriously read out, and
Mayor A. Oakey Hall is introduced. He compares Chinese to blacks as
"another kind of tawny slave labor," and huffs that "men who [are]
debased in morals [are] being brought here to compete with free
white[s]." The response from the small crowd is anemic.

In September, sixty-eight Chinese workers will arrive under cover
of darkness to work at a giant steam laundry in Belleville, New Jersey,

just outside of Newark. Before the year is out, On Yung, the brother of one of those workers, will open New York City's first Chinese hand laundry, at the corner of Catherine Street and East Broadway. Its success will start a trickle, which will soon develop into a flood, of Chinese laundries opening all over New York and Brooklyn.

It is also about this time that a lone New Yorker, one Miss Sarah Goodrich, starts a school on White Street specifically for the Chinese population. This genteel Presbyterian lady had been a volunteer at the Chinese Mission started at the Five Points House of Industry in 1868 by Reverend Thomas Railsback, but now, with the blessing of her church, she strives to teach English—and Christianity—to an inoffensive people that she sees being victimized and cruelly treated all around her. It is a small seed of charity that within a decade will grow into a movement that will do as much good as the Crispins can do harm.

Meanwhile, Mayor Hall will be twice indicted for corruption in his involvement with the Tweed Ring.

It is the 11th year of Emperor Tung Chih, a.k.a. 1873. Great-Grandfather Hor Poa first arrives on the West Coast, the *New York Times* predicts that Chinese immigration will soon explode outward from California, and the "Chinese Quarter" in New York is taking definite shape.

Many Chinese still live in the Cherry Street boardinghouses. Ko Lo Chee, who has been running the late Ah Sue's old place at Number 62 since 1867, has enhanced his local reputation (and pocketbook) by appointing himself the defender of Chinese sailors and stewards on any and every merchant ship tying up at the docks nearby, fearlessly marching on board to seek out his countrymen and check on their conditions. One ship's cook had been so badly abused and underpaid that Mr. Ko indignantly took legal action against the captain, eventually forcing the man to pay his servant $2,000 in damages. Of this, Ko Lo Ciao supposedly retained $1,200 in "fees."

Meanwhile, Ko has been trying to lure new Chinese immigrants to New York. At first he meets only massive indifference, but with the completion of the Transcontinental Railroad and the subsequent increase in unemployment, some Chinese have begun thinking of greener pastures.

For the last four years Ko's entreaties have been met with increasing, though still modest, success.

One of the newest arrivals, at Number 66 Cherry, is a Chinese doctor, lately from New Orleans, seeking to set up a practice among the new immigrants here. He is a small man, about forty, wearing the broad-sleeved jacket, baggy trousers, and cork-soled shoes of his countrymen, although he differs from others in the neighborhood in that he keeps his queue wound in a coil on top of his head. In a small third-floor room at the back of the house, he sees his patients, dispensing a vast array of herbs, roots, and ground animal parts in an attempt to achieve balance between the body's heat and moisture. Bewildered white visitors attempt to define the doctor's additional practice of acupuncture as a way to release pent-up gases within the body through little holes made by the needles. However, what really appals them is the presence of several white teenaged girls, who "brazenly looked the visitors in the face," sitting in a line among the Chinese men. Apparently, the white girls weren't exhibiting the required amount of shame at their discovery in such dissolute company.

The real news, however is what is happening on Mott Street, which virtually overnight has become the center of Chinese life in New York City. Wah Kee has just opened a store at Number 34. It is the first Chinese store on Mott, having previously been located on Park, and before that, way down on Oliver near Cherry. Situated in what had once been the front and back parlors of a townhouse, Wah Kee sells silks and jades, rice bowls and cookware, clothing, herbs, ceremonial paper money to burn for the ancestors—just about everything a Chinese can need. Favored customers are honored by a pot of tea and polite conversation as they peruse his wares, and purchases are figured up on a baffling import from the Orient—an abacus. Starting with an investment of $40, Wah Kee has built up an extremely lucrative business, making him one of the richest Chinese men in the Eastern United States. His store becomes the central meeting place for the Chinese community in New York City, which, according to the New York State census of 1875, numbers a grand total of 172.

At Number 13 Mott there is a new Chinese "boardinghouse." It is not a house, really, just the basement of one, which the Chinese proprietor has divided into six little chambers with cheap wooden partitions.

The front room is for entertaining. It has an old beat-up sofa, some rickety cane-bottomed chairs, and the ubiquitous scrolls of poetry hung on the walls. The rear room is the kitchen, with a coal stove, a long wooden table with a couple of benches, and a glass-fronted cabinet with broken glass, containing an assortment of mismatched china and crockery. In between are four lightless cubicles, with ten beds crammed in any which way. One of these spaces is apparently devoted to opium smoking, the requisite equipment standing at the ready. Meanwhile, the landlord—whose name as rendered by the New York press, comes out as "Aslug"—does all the cooking, providing beef, chicken, and rabbit when available. Water is always on the boil for rice and tea. Room and board costs $4 per week here. But for $3 per week, one can just come and eat, for as yet there are no Chinese restaurants in the Chinese Quarter.

However there are two benevolent societies, either Village or Family Associations, in operation now, one at 34 Mott Street, one at 12 Baxter Street. There have been community- or clan-based organizations for the welfare of the people for centuries back in China, a country where the Government is principally concerned with collecting taxes and cutting off the heads of those who don't pay them. The famous Six Companies scrupulously look after Chinese interests in San Francisco. Likewise, here in New York, these Associations shepherd the Chinese community, or at least those from those villages or families that give them the right to belong. For between 25 and 50 cents per week, they can gather at one of the clubhouses for a game of mah-jongg or a meal, energetically stir-fried in a giant pan on a wood stove in the corner. Many of the men are employed as stewards and cooks on overnight riverboats and coastal steamers. When in New York, they sleep two to each of the myriad of beds crammed into one of the Associations' dormitories. New arrivals looking for work will come here to be placed wherever there is an opening. The indigent are fed. The needy are provided loans to start a new business or pay for a funeral at Brooklyn's Green-Wood Cemetery, although earlier dead were buried in a Chinese plot in the New York Bay Cemetery in the Greenville section of Jersey City.

But wherever they are interred, after a few years' time the bodies will be dug up, the flesh burned off, and the bones cleaned and polished for easy shipment back to China, for these men would never have come so far without making sure that at least their souls would be at peace in their native land and they have paid a fee to their Association to cover any such eventuality. For a departed "good boy" who cannot afford a Green-Wood funeral, a candle and incense are burned for three months in front of his picture, right there in the common room, flanked by mourning poetry written on red paper. "Chinese friends in big, strange land . . . make him a little memory here," explains an old man to a curious visitor.

The "Poolon Kun Cue" Society at 34 Mott Street is the larger of the two associations. It is a two-and-a-half-story house, the basement being divided into two rooms where all business and social activity is conducted. On the first floor is Wah Kee's store, with the remaining space upstairs used as dormitory and a workshop where men sit and methodically roll cigars, an activity occasionally broken by a rest with an opium pipe. Up here they are also frequently visited by young white girls from the surrounding Five Points neighborhood. Opium helps the girls forget their dismal lives, while the lonely Chinese men find their companionship welcome.

Number 12 Baxter is also home to a Chinese temple. It is in the back parlor of the former residence. Thirty men can be accommodated on the six benches that face the altar, which takes up the rear wall. It is just a large table, really, upon which a kerosene lamp is kept continually burning, along with sticks of incense which fill the room with their musty fragrance. There are bowls of food offerings—fruit, nuts, rice—in case the deity gets hungry. Two red silk lanterns flank the altar, and above it on the wall is a huge, fantastically-colored picture of someone who may be Buddha or may be one of the pantheon of Taoist gods. But all the walls, decorated as they are with scrolls of poetry, are dark with soot from the burnt offerings and grease from the bacon, which the attendant is incongruously cooking on a stove in the corner. Is that part of Buddhist ritual, a Big Nose wants to know? "Chinese secret—No tell," comes the inscrutable reply.

To celebrate the coming of the Year of the Dog, a grand banquet is held here, costing a whopping $75. But first, honor must be paid to the Ancestors, the worshippers circling the room and kowtowing three times before the altar. Making sure all bases are covered, the nearby Chinese Mission School at the Five Points House of Industry teaches the rudiments of Christianity and the English language. Mr. A. H. Kembell and Miss Sarah Goodrich from the Fourth Avenue Presbyterian Church conduct classes every Sunday evening and during every day except Saturday, while Miss Goodrich's White Street School is still going strong. Kembell and Miss Goodrich like to believe that they are converting the heathen. "[The] pupils quickly learn to conform themselves to the usages there instilled," they say. That may be so, but the Chinese also find the Bible classes helpful in learning English.

The northeastern United States is continuing to draw the attention of Chinese scattered around the country. In Beaver Falls, Pennsylvania, white workers are in despair, as Chinese are paid $25 per month for jobs that the whites had been paid $80 to perform. Meanwhile, the several hundred workers imported to work in the Belleville, New Jersey laundry are thriving. As they cavorted together at a festival just after Christmas, one startled white observer said that "the kicking up of their capacious trowsers [sic] during the dance caused [them] to resemble a room full of insane women." Many of these workers are still drifting away to start their own metropolitan-area laundries, like the ones up on Third Avenue or on Park Row, which have just begun to appear.

There are more well-heeled visitors as well. Delegations of Chinese businessmen take the train to New York from California to scope out commercial opportunities. Thirty Chinese "ladies and gentlemen . . . of much fairer complexion" than that of the laboring classes, arrive in the East to be educated with Imperial scholarships.

And in Providence, Rhode Island, a Chinese diplomat on some undefined mission arrives for an extended stay. Charmed by the presence of this obvious aristocrat in their midst, society hostesses strive to outdo each other in entertaining their exotic guest, made all the more dazzling by the company of his exquisite wife and sister. When the wife bears a son—"the exact image of the typical infant portrayed on Chinese fans"—the society ladies go wild and shower the happy couple with presents. Tea and firecrackers are welcome. A basket of sparrows' nests is puzzling—but then the sender can't be expected to know exactly what kind of nests are used in birds'-nest soup. A well-meant box of rats is emblematic of the widespread Big Nose belief that all Chinese eat rodents. That package is unceremoniously thrown at the head of the messenger who delivers it.

Still, Providence's ladies are thrilled with their genteel Celestial family—that is until, four months after the birth of the son, the diplomat's sister also bears a child. "That's not my sister, that's my Number Two Wife," says the diplomat, or words to that effect. The Providence ladies are paralyzed. Thereafter, the diplomat's social calendar is conspicuously empty.

Meanwhile, back in New York in 1878, Ah Kam and three friends—one of whom, "Ah Foo," may have been the "Ah Fung" he was living with in 1870—are arrested for selling cigars without a license. Despite his past success, the Civil War veteran has found that life has not been so good lately. During the past several years he has become almost blind, forcing him and his wife Kitty to give up their own establishment and move into Ko Lo Chee's boarding house at 62 Cherry Street. And as the darkness closes in, opium has taken over.

Now he is in jail, "suffering greatly," and begging for a fix. A sympathetic white visitor agrees to get him one, and carrying Ah Kam's thimble—the approved unit of measure for the narcotic—makes his way to a Baxter Street hovel.

There he finds an old opium merchant, curled up on a bunk and smoking a long, magnificent pipe with a carved ivory bowl. In an adjoining room, two customers lie in a stupor. Recognizing the thimble that the white man proffers, the man sleepily unlocks a yellow chest and takes out an earthen jar. From this he fills the thimble with liquid opium "of the color and consistency of New-Orleans molasses." Three thimblefuls are provided. The cost: 30 cents. The old man goes back to his pipe and the visitor takes the drug to Ah Kam and his friends in jail. The next day they hope to be released. The opium is barely enough to satisfy them until then.

On Wednesday, March 19, 1879, Wah Kee goes to Pier 17 on the East River to welcome the *Saratoga*, arriving from Havana with a number of Chinese passengers—including a married Chinese woman. It is a momentous occasion, eagerly looked forward to by the bachelors living on lower Mott Street. Wah Kee has even come in a closed carriage for the occasion—not so much because of the celebrity of the lady, but because it is highly improper for a Chinese matron to be seen walking in the streets. As she is dressed in a loose blouse with frog buttons, baggy trousers, and the ubiquitous cork-soled shoes, the Round Eye men at the dock aren't entirely sure that she is, in fact, female, until they get a closer look. She proves to be a "rather pleasant-featured" lady, and wears her hair "in pompadour fashion, with a long needle, with a brass knob at the end, run through it." Wah Kee won't divulge her name, even though she is living with her husband above Wah Kee's store at 34 Mott, but that only enhances the aura of mystery surrounding her.

The arrival of this lady increases New York's female Chinese population by 100 percent—for now there are two. There had been a very few others over the years, most notably Afong Moi, who had been "exhibited" at the Chinese Museum for some dozen years, and one Mary Chang, who came to New York via the British West Indies with her husband and children and ran a boardinghouse on Baxter Street. But Afong Moi was never part of any Chinese community, and at any rate she disappeared from view after about 1848, while Mary Chang seems to have left New York with her family in 1869. It is implied that there may be one merchant's wife hidden away on Mott Street someplace, but no white person has ever seen her. No white person ever sees the new arrival either, after she is spirited away by Wah Kee on this March afternoon. Almost exactly a year later, she will return to Cuba with her husband. With only one virtually invisible Chinese woman in residence—if she exists at all—the men in the Chinese quarter are reduced to seeking out the commercially available feminine companionship among the Irish in Five Points. They decorate their walls with cheap prints carrying titles like "Belle of the East" and "Boston Beauty, No. 6," and dream about the Chinese girls half a world away.

And now it is the week of March 4, 1880, when perhaps 150 Chinese men have taken advantage of low rail fares to escape from California and settle in New York City. It is also the week that the new Second Avenue elevated train line opens. Chatham Square has been entombed by the black steel cage which supports the tracks of the line's terminus, causing the businesses along the streets below to operate in a man-made gloom amid the roar of engines and a steady rain of cinders and dust. It is to two of these establishments, Quong Ching Chung & Co. at 2 Mott Street and Sam Owen's laundry at 19 Park Row, that the new arrivals' luggage, consisting of canvas sacks and one old carpet bag, has been sent. Sam Owen, one of those Chinese who use Western names, interprets for one of his newly-arrived countrymen who wants to tell why he came East. Chinese in San Francisco "get pounded with stones by boys on street," says the man, "He hear he can make money in New York, and boys no pound him with stones. Tickets very low now, so he buy . . ."

The neighborhood these men come to now has anywhere from three hundred to a thousand Chinese, depending on whom you ask. Nevertheless, while that represents a nearly fivefold increase over five years ago, the enclave is still almost invisible, just a cluster of Chinese signs hanging from buildings on the short block of Mott Street between Pell Street and Chatham Square. They mark the half-basement quarters of the tailor, the herbalist, and the curio shop, where the brown-and-white porcelain cow in the window indicates that milk can also be purchased. Cutthroat games of *fan-tan* and *pai gao* take place in little back rooms up and down the block. A bona-fide opium den fills the squalid basement of a back-yard building, its one tiny window so dust-covered that it barely lets any light into the two, grim rooms within.

Nearby, there are at least two legal "dealers in opium," Han Lut, living at 6 Mott, and Wong Gee at 103 Park Street. Wong Gee is a civil-minded individual, however, and has banded together with several others to form a new Chinese benevolent society. Mott Street also has at least one Protestant mission and, of course, the old Roman Catholic Church of the Transfiguration at the corner of Park. The Italians and Irish who worship within view the growing presence of the "heathen Chinee" with increasing alarm.

There is one real Chinese restaurant now, but only one. It is on the second floor of a Mott Street building, over the tailor's shop, and is a simple, no-nonsense sort of place. Designed for Chinese bachelors rather than tourists, it has tall stools at small tables, and a floor littered with the bones which the diners casually toss over their shoulders. Live chickens and ducks squawk in cages, to be selected by customers to be made into a meal. Fish similarly await their fate in nearby tanks. A simple three-course meal for two costs 75 cents. Nevertheless, one can get such rare delicacies as bird's-nest soup, the precious main ingredient of which is bought at the Chinese grocer's for as much as $22.50 per pound. Even though a pound will make enough soup for thirty people, one would only spend so vast a sum for the most important of important occasions.

Chinese can still be found living both south and north of Chatham Square, with isolated "Celestials" even all the way up to Houston Street. Doyers Street is still entirely Irish. Pell is a mixture of white and black, notwithstanding the two Chinese at Number 37. An African-American named Henry Bollen keeps a boardinghouse around the corner at 41 Baxter with sixteen tenants, among whom are five blacks and four Chinese laundrymen.

Park Street, and especially lower Mott, is where the greatest concentration of Chinese live. Yet these men (and one or two women), dressed in their Chinese clothes with American-style hats perched on the fronts of their heads to allow room for their queues, are still hard to spot, overwhelmed as they are by the Irish, the Italians, and the Polish Jews who live all around them. Out of the fifty-two people living at Number 17 Mott, for example, only eleven are Chinese, including one known as "Wily Charly." One hundred and three white people and three Chinese are crammed into Number 15.

It is still a small part of Five Points, just a tiny dot on the map of the great city. But one very important thing has happened. For the first time this year, the press is calling the neighborhood by a brand new name—China Town.

3

.

CHINA TOWN

So it is to China Town that my great-grandfather journeys upon returning from his marriage, "around Christmastime" in 1881. He lives on the first block of Mott, within view of the elevated railway, "the El," in the partitioned basement of a building otherwise packed with Italians and Poles. It is even possible that he comes to live with the illiterate (in English) retail grocer called "Hoar Wo" who is listed in the census as residing in the basement of Number 15. It would be natural for Great-Grandfather, as for any Chinese, to seek out a kinsman upon his arrival, and the common surname makes them "cousins." I suppose it doesn't really matter. All I know is that Hor Poa would be thirty-one years old—and most likely broke.

He has followed the increasing tide of Chinese leaving San Francisco, partially because New York just seems like a friendlier place. The Chinese community in California was probably very aware of the loud protests made by Easterners over Congressional anti-Chinese legislation proposed in 1879, which would have prohibited ships from landing at U.S. ports with more than fifteen Chinese passengers at any one time. "Liberty [can]not be destroyed in any one class and maintained in another!" thundered renowned evangelist Henry Ward Beecher.

It is "an unwarranted assault on the part of the United States to the Chinese Empire!" warned an association of New York Merchants.

"The Anti-Chinese bill is repugnant to every principle of justice and true republicanism!" said the German Republican Central Committee of New York. President Rutherford B. Hayes ultimately vetoed that measure—but spurred treaty negotiations with China that would soon lead to even greater restrictions.

It is true that New York is somewhat more used to foreigners than other places. Besides, there are as yet only a few hundred Chinese in the great city, as opposed to the tens of thousands to be found in San Francisco. But even though there are New Yorkers who find room for more enlightened thinking on the "Chinese Question," it is still not easy for the dozens of "Celestials" now arriving every week.

Even the Imperial Ambassador and his suite are subject to the same harassment as the poorest cigar-peddlers. While visiting New York for the month of August, 1880, they had found themselves virtual prisoners in their luxury hotel uptown, as whenever one of the diplomats ventured out onto the street in his magnificent, aristocratic garb of flowing silk with its embroidered pectoral badge of rank, and with a peacock feather sweeping from his hat, "mischievous boys" would chase him to yank his queue and pelt him with stones. When the Ambassador's secretaries appealed to the police for help, officers only laughed and did nothing.

At least they only had stones thrown at them. Eight months later, a young Chinese man was leaving one of Miss Goodrich's Presbyterian Sunday schools, where he had been receiving lessons in English and Christian charity. A gang of whites taunted him as he walked home along Spring Street and knocked off his hat, whereupon he turned and asked, "Why do you treat Chinamen so?" They answered by beating him to the ground and stabbing him to death.

Still, if the Golden Mountain is where Great-Grandfather wants to be, he has come back just in time. The Republican party, stung by the veto of the 1879 bill, has pushed for even more sweeping restrictions: a ban on Chinese immigration to the United States altogether. However it is not just Californians who are making such noises, but a growing number of lawmakers from other states where Chinese have been gaining a foothold. James G. Blaine, Republican Senator from

Maine, Secretary of State, and future Presidential candidate, argues that the "natural" depravity of Chinese women is enough to threaten the moral integrity of the entire nation. Democratic Congressman (and future Governor) Rosewell Pettibone Flower of New York faults the Chinese for stealing jobs while not assimilating into a society which treats them with animosity at every turn. "Not like the European immigrant who brings us wealth and love of liberty," he thunders in Congress, "He comes to take wealth away, and to stamp upon labor the servile characteristics of his race."

So it is on May 6, 1882, that President Chester A. Arthur signs the first Exclusion Act, which prohibits the naturalization of any Chinese in the U.S., while also banning all immigration of Chinese "laborers, skilled or unskilled" for the next ten years, as well as the wives and children of any laborers who are already here. "Laborers" is a vague term which seems to cover just about everyone who works at a job that could be done by a white person. Excepted are those considered by the politicians to be from the upper classes of Chinese society, meaning merchants (who, it is assumed, will be buying American products, or at least selling only things that non-Chinese wouldn't want), students, and diplomats. Of course in China, where learning and good manners are prized above all else, merchants rank on the bottom of the social scale. But then this is the land of Capitalism, where learning has a dollar amount attached and manners are often considered a sign of weakness. Impoverished scholars must humiliate their family names by going into some kind of trade just to come to this country. And even bona-fide merchants will not have an easy time.

The Imperial Government must now issue "merchant papers" to her subjects wishing to come to the U.S., which requires filing an application at an office outside Canton, the only place in the entire Empire where such certificates for America can be secured. Information such as age, address, and "pedigree" must be supplemented by the seal of a business that not only employs the man, but is willing to put up a bond against any expenses incurred to the shipping company in case he is refused admission at San Francisco and deported. Then officials from the Imperial Customs Office are sent to verify the information, before the papers are elaborately drawn up, affixed with photograph and seal, and signed by the Superintendent himself. A total of some 1,500 passports are issued in this manner.

This is not good enough for the Americans, however. The Pacific Mail steamship line requires a further cash deposit from each passenger against the possibility of deportation costs. And finally Washington tersely informs the Imperial Government that they consider the Chinese documents untrustworthy. Among their reasons is the assertion that photographs are useless in identifying Chinese, because, as everyone knows, all Chinese look alike. So, from October of 1883 onwards, any Chinese subject wishing to travel to the United States must first contact some white American who must then write to Washington verifying the petitioner's innocuous mercantile intentions. Washington considers the matter, and then will inform the Superintendent of Customs in Canton if they will permit him to issue merchant papers. It seems not to matter to the Americans that the Superintendent is a subject of the Emperor. It is a process that takes months, bringing emigration to a virtual standstill.

This new Exclusion Act is also in direct contradiction to the 1868 Burlingame Treaty, which guaranteed free movement between China and the United States. Ambassador Burlingame may have been well-intentioned at the time, but everyone else knew that the real motive behind that agreement was to secure access for Yankee missionaries and tradesmen to Chinese markets, not to encourage the Chinese themselves to come here. However, Anson Burlingame is dead, and the Imperial Government has no power to do anything more than lodge vociferous protests, which Congress carefully ignores while maintaining American merchants' rights to exploit the Chinese on their own soil. A new treaty is imposed, ultimately enabling the Chinese Exclusion Act to be extended at intervals over the next sixty-one years, and then only superficially eased. It comes in an era when there are no restrictions of any kind on the millions streaming into the United States from every other nation on earth. To this day, it remains the only American immigration proscription to be aimed at a specific nationality during peacetime.

Predictably, as soon as the Exclusion Act goes into effect on August 5, 1882, it causes massive confusion. Chinese sailors and stewards who were at sea that summer are detained as soon as they land—

even a sailor who was merely sent by his captain onto the dock to attach a line—because they have not been able to file the proper papers.

Chinese passengers sailing from San Francisco to a destination in Washington Territory are prevented from disembarking when it is revealed that the vessel has touched land at Victoria, British Columbia. They are now deemed to have come from a foreign port and are deported—to Canada.

The Chinese servant of a British merchant who is transiting the U.S. on his way from Asia to England is arrested and deported. A Chinese riding the Michigan Central train route from California to New York, which takes a short cut through Canada from Detroit to Buffalo, is stopped when the train re-enters American territory at the New York State border, and again in Detroit as he anxiously tries to retrace his steps. "It is not reported whether this lost Chinaman ever got out of the Dominion of Canada," the *New York Times* recounts.

Even Barnum & Bailey is affected by the new law. When they try to import a new attraction, one Chang Yu Sin, the "Chinese Giant," they have to accompany Mr. Chang to a special interview with Collector Roberts of the Port of New York to gain permission for him to land. Roberts agrees that as long as Chang can prove that he is "neither a laborer or a miner," he will be allowed into the country. The eight-foot four-inch Chang signs a statement to that effect and departs with an agent of the circus.

In the first four months of 1882, 11,300 Chinese enter the United States at San Francisco, anxious to beat the deadline. But for the first four months of 1883 the number has dropped to 1,560 and keeps falling.

Had Great-Grandfather delayed his return to the U.S. by another eight months, he would most likely never have been able to live here again. However, by the time the Exclusion Act becomes law, Hor Poa is safely established on Mott Street and will not have to worry about its ramifications until he needs to leave the country and then return. That will happen someday, but first there is money to be made. The immediate order of business: find a job.

It would be nice to think he got help from a Family Association. Chinese are accustomed to living in a world where family is everything and Governments are of no practical use. So Chins, Yees, and Hors know that wherever they are, they can always call on other Chins, Yees, or Hors to receive a night's lodging, aid when they are sick, burial for their dead, and a stick of incense for their soul. The Barbarian Government is, if anything, less helpful than the Emperor, for here they create a blizzard of rules to interfere with one's life and then send big, humorless men to see that one complies. It's better to have as little to do with anything Official as possible.

So, starting in San Francisco, and in New York for at least the past ten years, lonely bachelors apply at their own clan organizations to receive anything from free meals to placement in a "cousin's" laundry. The Chins and Yees and others have Associations, for they are enormous tribes, with the Yees claiming to be able to trace their lineage back ten thousand years. There are plenty of rich Chins and Yees who will donate portions of their hard-earned cash to aid their poorer brothers, for they know that the favor will be returned at the earliest opportunity. Some family clans are centered in stores in Mott Street, like the Wongs, who all shop and socialize at Chung Kee, a grocery store at Number 5. Some smaller families band together, like the Quans, Chius, Lius, and Cheungs—descendants of four warriors who swore eternal allegiance in a battle to save the Han Dynasty some 1,700 years earlier—who make up the Four Families Association, and who in 1888 will import a glorious carved Ancestor's shrine from China, gilded and festooned with all manner of dragons, griffins, and creeping vines, to hold the tablets honoring the venerable departed. These organizations are further divided into village associations or *fongs*, like Ning Young, which our family belongs to, where families from the same cluster of tiny villages in Toi-shan maintain meeting rooms in which to settle disputes, play a little mah-jongg, and hold banquets to celebrate just about everything.

They all collect small amounts in dues to offer large amounts in loans for starting new businesses, as well as legal advice and housing assistance. Also, any intra-family disputes that might arise are settled by a council of elders, the senior-most of whom is supported economically by the clan like a petty monarch, for it would never do to allow the head "gentleman" of one's family to actually work for a living. It would also never do to cross him in his judgments. But most importantly, these societies provide companionship, a sense of family to lonely men who are stranded half a world away from their wives and children. There they can find someone to smoke or throw dice with, or maybe a partner with whom to compose a few lines of verse. There they know that someone will provide incense and a little food offering when they die, and make sure their bones are sent back to China where they can be comfortable for the rest of Eternity.

The Hor family is small, however, not vast enough to have their own confederation. Eventually, we will belong to the Sam Yip, or Three Families Society, which represents the Hors, Lais, and Gongs. But until their are enough Hors, Lais, and Gongs in New York to get an organization going, Great-Grandfather has to turn elsewhere for a guiding hand.

Where he ends up is at the new benevolent society, officially registered as "Long We Tong Eng Wi," which supposedly means "The Order and Brotherhood of Masons." It is the same one that had just been founded in 1880 by a group of China Town big shots including the opium dealer Wong Gee, the Cuban-Chinese James C. Baptiste and Domingo de Luce, and Tom Lee, a diminutive man with a German wife and a knowing smile who seems to have at least one hand in everything happening on Mott Street. Mr. Lee (whose real name is Wong Ah Ling) has been throwing his weight around ever since his arrival in New York in 1878. He is prone to making extravagant pronouncements to the press and giving flashy banquets for Tammany Hall politicians, who quickly bestowed upon him the office of Deputy Sheriff. No doubt this title, as well as other forms of friendly influence, were supremely useful when Lee's big gambling parlor at 13 Mott was raided in 1879.

It might never have been discovered if it hadn't been for the large numbers of men—clad only in burlap sacks—seen leaving a supposed grocery store in the wee hours of the morning. (Apparently, they had wagered away all their clothes.) So fifteen officers of the Fourteenth Precinct stormed the den late on a Tuesday and hauled off a couple of rooms full of gamblers and gambling equipment to spend the night in the station house. But the next day, despite the abundance of gamers and paraphernalia, the judge mysteriously decided that there was "no positive evidence" of actual gambling. All the charges were dropped. Tom Lee was obviously becoming a master of influence.

And now he has incorporated "The Order and Brotherhood of Masons," whose stated objects are "mutual friendship, brotherly love, and service to the Supreme Being by mutual succor in distress." It sounds good, but despite the name, it is not exactly what most Americans or Europeans would call a Masonic order. In point of fact, Tom Lee and his cohorts have established a branch of the infamous Lün I T'ong, or "Hall of United Patriotism," a society that looks out for its own not only through giving loans, business assistance, and job placement, but by protecting Chinese interests such as gambling, opium smoking, and other private indulgences from the prying interference of unsympathetic Round-Eyes. Many think of it, simply, as the Chinese Mafia. Within ten years it will evolve into an organization with a name that will be intimately familiar to the next century of China Town generations—the On Leong Tong.

The tongs can trace their origins back to the secret Robin Hood-like organization of "fighting freemasons" founded by the philosopher Mo Tzu some four hundred years before Christ. In the succeeding two millennia, peasant rebellions fed numerous secret societies which were all based on Mo Tzu's dicta of help for the poor combined with ruthlessness towards one's enemies.

It was after the fall of the Ming Dynasty in 1644 when the first Triad Society was founded by the abbot of Shao Lin monastery, who led a band of 128 "warrior monks" sworn to overthrow the newly-established Manchu or Ch'ing Dynasty. "Overthrow the Ch'ing, Restore the Ming" became their motto, and as they were forced even deeper underground these Triads developed a bewildering system of secret handshakes and symbols in dress and movement to identify their rebel cohorts, while simultaneously devolving into little feudal bandit armies, sometimes helping, but more often extorting the peasants who were unlucky enough to live within their reach. Two hundred years later, while still giving lip service to restoring the Mings, Triad power increased dramatically during the chaos of the Opium Wars and the Tai-ping Rebellion, which coincided almost exactly with the first big wave of emigration to California.

In the United States, they offer "official protection" from the oppressive white society, recruiting their members from among the Cantonese immigrant class known as the *Say Yup*, or "Four Towns." These are rural, unsophisticated young men from country villages in Kuang Tung Province—villages like Hor Lup Chui. They know that whether ill, in debt, or in trouble with the law, the Tong will help them, even to the point of exacting revenge for some slight, whether a recent business deal gone bad or the fruit of a family feud going back centuries.

A Tong initiation is a somber, clandestine affair. Candidates, dressed in long cotton robes, assemble in a dim, smoky room to swear utter fealty to the organization.

"Have you a father?" they are asked.

"No!" comes the reply.

"Sisters?"

"No!"

"Brothers?"

"My only brothers are the Patriots!" they cry, before an altar with a drawn sword which symbolizes their fate if they should betray their oaths. They are then provided (for $5) with a thick book which describes the secret signs and signals by which members recognize each other in public. There is a specific way to hold a teacup, a way to button their shirts, secret gestures and coded slang, all encrusted in tradition more than a thousand years old. A $20 fee goes towards the banquet cel- . ebrating their induction. A further $25 to $100 may be charged in annual dues, according to one's ability to pay. One of the chief benefits of membership is no longer being under intimidation to join.

I suppose that Great-Grandfather may have been involved with the Lün I T'ong in San Francisco, where they had been established for at least twenty years. It may have been the Tong which encouraged him and others to come to New York in the first place. All I know for certain is that after its incorporation, Tom Lee and the Lün I T'ong move into 18 Mott Street. And before long, so does Hor Poa.

Not that my Great-Grandfather is some kind of mafia henchman. It is difficult to live in China Town in 1882—or in any other year for that matter—and not be associated with the tongs in some way. If you own a business, you will need to pay "protection" money, so that the tong will take care of nagging problems not only with the competition, but with the local constabulary. And even if you are just an ordinary worker, there is still a bewildering city to contend with, full of white boys throwing stones and officials making trouble. Even finding a place to live in the Chinese neighborhood can be difficult, with landlords regularly charging higher rents than for whites and relegating Asians to the most undesirable spaces in their buildings. Why, just a month after the establishment of the new tong, the United Christian Brethren of the Moravian Church summarily evicted all Chinese from some eight buildings they owned on Mott, even forcing old Wah Kee to move his store over to Park Street. The "Christian Brethren" issued new leases which forbade subletting to "Chinamen or negroes." It is an area where the Tong, for now, is helpless.

But like any populist politician, Tom Lee knows how to work his constituency, and late in the summer of 1881 he stages a massive party, not only to soothe his neighbors' nerves, but to poke the surrounding white society in the eye. "The first grand clam bake on the Chinese plan ever held . . . this side of the Pacific Ocean," is a grandiose affair, announced to the China Town community by means of red posters pasted up on the bulletin board at the corner of Mott and Chatham Streets. It is meant to be a quiet affair, claims its host, one for Chinese alone. Yet, for some reason, the newspapers seem to know about it even before the Chinese in China Town do, and as always, Tom Lee is available for interviews. He tells the papers that he expects 800 people to pay the $5 charge (the posters say $7 in Chinese) for the trip to a beach in Staten Island where there will be food, music, and beer. The latter admission seems to be a relief to one reporter, as white society has long looked with a mixture of astonishment and disdain at the Chinese lack of interest in intoxicating spirits, or at least intoxicating spirits that they recognize. Tom Lee's attendance estimate does seem a little optimistic, however, especially as there are supposedly only 919 Chinese in the entire State of New York.

So, sure enough, on the day appointed for the excursion, it is a mere fifty off-duty launderers, shopkeepers, and Tong idlers who eagerly clamber into the fourteen hired hacks for the drive down to the ferry to New Dorp, Staten Island. All the while they are serenaded by a Chinese band crammed into the lead carriage, which a white observer later says produces "an assortment of sounds which they were pleased to term music." Deputy Sheriff Lee has also requested a contingent of New York City police officers to be detailed to protect the procession from potentially hostile crowds as it boards the boat. New York's finest arrive on the scene forty-five minutes after the party has left the dock.

The first order of business on arrival is of course, eating, the principal Chinese means of celebrating any conceivable event. In the dancing pavilion at New Dorp, specially fitted out with a huge gong for the occasion, is spread an enormous American breakfast. There are ham and eggs, clam fritters, fried eels, potatoes, and coffee. It's not what any of the Chinese would call *food,* exactly, but that is what Mr. Lee has provided. The band has regrouped by this time and scrapes away at familiar Chinese melodies as the picnickers dig into their meal "with knife and fork in a thoroughly Christian manner." Beer and cheap cigars follow, which provide a certain novel festivity, but then there is a creeping uncertainty as to what to do next. There seems to be no gambling, the usual activity of choice, so these men, whose workaholic lives have made them unaccustomed to leisure time, wander aimlessly about. Some listen to the music. Some idly watch the surf, composing poetry and thinking about how much all this fun is costing them. Normally, they would have brought along kites, to engage in savage contests of skill—beautiful tissue-paper birds and butterflies, tails fluttering, strings encrusted with ground glass so as to cut the lines of competitors' creations.

But such time-honored pleasures are banned, as Tom Lee has decreed that today is to be enjoyed in a more Western mode. After lunch, he organizes a couple of American-style foot races, with purses of $2.50 to the winners. The prize money causes a few to turn out, but the attempt at a tug-of-war turns into a complete fiasco. "Too much like work," mutters one participant. It is reminiscent of the comment supposedly made by an early Imperial Ambassador to Washington at a ball given in his honor. Silently observing the swirling forms of waltzing couples, he finally turned to his American escort and said, "Can't those people afford to hire someone to do all that work for them?"

So the men while away the afternoon sitting in the bar and napping on each other's shoulders. At six o'clock they pile into the carriages for the long trip back to 18 Mott Street, where Tom Lee has organized a massive reception, replete with strings of lanterns, firecrackers, and more music. Thousands supposedly turn out to welcome home the fifty sleepy excursionists, but then, of course, this second party is free, and no one has had to miss a day of work. It also allows Tom Lee to pose before the entire community (and the New York press) as the great benefactor, the demi-emperor of the neighborhood. His ham and eggs, beer, cigars, and tug-of-war have allowed him to represent himself as New York's greatest "assimilated" Chinese. It is not long before white New Yorkers start referring to him as the Mayor of Chinatown.

So there is no question that, for a while at least, Hor Poa works for Tom Lee. Not as a Tong foot soldier, exactly, but at something more suited to his family vocation—carpentry. In fact, my Great-Grandfather is one of the first carpenters in the entire New York Chinese community, and Tom Lee has a lot of work for him to do. For instance, there is his store at 2 Mott (described in 1881 as a "tobacco and opium" shop) and his new restaurant next door at Number 4, which is known especially for its dumplings. And then, in 1883, Tom Lee teams up with other "Chinese capitalists" to buy a big chunk of Mott Street in what may be the first purchase of real estate by Chinese in New York. Wah Kee buys Number 8 for $8,500, Kwong Hing Lung gets Number 10 for $8,000, Man Lee has Number 12 for $6,000, and Tom Lee himself secures the Tong headquarters building at Number 18 for $15,000, a princely sum in such a neighborhood. Not satisfied with mere ownership, however, Lee and company promptly post eviction notices for almost all their tenants, Asian and Caucasian alike, although Great-Grandfather continues to live at Number 13. It is a mere two years since the Moravian Church outraged the Chinese with their wholesale expulsions, and now Mr. Lee is following their example. The rumor is that he is consolidating his hold on the neighborhood by eliminating businesses who don't pay their proper dues, while enriching himself by raising rents. Regardless, it certainly provides a lot of work for a carpenter for hire.

Meanwhile at Number 8, the "Wah Kee Company," as it is known, grows into a major import-export business, dealing not only in Chinese groceries but porcelain and silk, while exporting to China everything from American-grown ginseng to art prints to firearms. By 1885, Wah Kee's estimated worth will be $150,000, making him a wealthy man indeed (although not as wealthy as one of his competitors, Wong He Chong, whose estimated net worth comes in at a staggering $1 million in an era when a thousand dollars per year is considered handsome). And speaking of getting rich, working as a carpenter renovating all those buildings is helping Hor Poa put away a tidy little nest egg of his own.

The Tong is not the only influence on Hor Poa's life, however. Anyone hoping to make a success in this Barbarian land must learn its language, and for that, Hor Poa and hundreds of others turn away from the society of secret winks and handshakes to its greatest rival, the American institution quaintly known as the Sunday School.

To any even nominally Christian person, the term "Sunday School" conjures up images of Jesus coloring books and simple Bible stories, and that is pretty much what is offered to New York's Chinese of the 1880s. Various outreach missions had been set up by different Protestant denominations, the very first having been established by the Methodists on Worth Street back in 1854. A branch of the Five Points Mission (built on the site of the notorious Old Brewery in 1852), this "House of Industry" was sufficient to minister to the handful of lonely sailors and hapless members of the Tong Hook Tong Dramatic Society who were then forlornly wandering the rough streets of lower Manhattan. But with the swelling of the Chinese population, Chinese mission schools started springing up all over. Sarah Goodrich opened several other Sunday Schools under the auspices of the Presbyterian Church after her 1870 success on White Street, and by the 1880s Chinese bachelors could attend Sunday Schools at the 14th Street Presbyterian Church, the Spring Street Presbyterian Church, the Seventh Presbyterian Church, the Third Reformed Presbyterian Church on 23rd Street, and the Twenty-Ninth Street Reformed Presbyterian Church, all mostly staffed with earnest young women anxious to "civilize" citizens of the oldest civilization in the world. Elsewhere, one Mrs. Augusta Carto, widow of a missionary to China, became the most outspoken, or at least the loudest advocate of New York's Chinese, browbeating the Trinity Baptist Church way up on East 55th Street into surrendering their auditorium for her to use to preach to the heathen. There were Chinese Sunday Schools in Brooklyn, Jersey City, and even in the rarefied air of Harlem.

In China Town itself, the Five Points Mission opened a school at 14 Mott Street in 1879, with a young Chinese Christian named Moy Jin

Kee at the helm. Moy was the Sunday School poster child—until a few months later when he landed in jail. (It seems that he had been shoplifting goods from his employer's store to impress certain young ladies.) The boy was packed off to China while one of the white teachers, Netta Millwood, took over. Classes were offered every evening, consisting mostly of elementary English lessons bolstered by a few rousing hymns and exhortations to abandon the world of opium and gambling to follow the Christian life.

But while attendance was booming in other neighborhoods, for some reason here in the heart of the dragon Chinese participation was unreliable. Teachers suspected that what students they had were merely coming out of curiosity, and besides, there was a nagging feeling that they were not too welcome on the block, with an increasingly hostile atmosphere emanating from their neighbors. It is hardly a coincidence that scarcely a year after Tom Lee opened his Lün I T'ong two doors up Mott Street, the school quietly moved its operations to the Seventh Street Methodist Church. Tom Lee was notoriously touchy about Christians trying to compromise the fruits of his endeavors.

Still, Sunday afternoons and many evenings were full of opportunities for New York's and Brooklyn's Chinese bachelors to "run to the church" to sing hymns and listen to Bible lessons taught to them by the *sen sheng pao*, or "master's wife." An estimated six hundred, perhaps two-thirds of the Chinese population, were doing so by 1883, although many would attend only as long as the English lesson lasted and then leave before the sermon.

It seemed that genteel white ladies were most often the Sunday School teachers, and they earnestly tried to turn their charges into good Victorian Christians, which usually meant getting them to eat with a knife and fork and wear American clothes, as much as understanding anything about Jesus. One favorite activity was to teach the young men to sing sentimental hymns, and then have them perform before audiences of white people at receptions and fairs. Annual picnics, grand affairs with chartered steamers taking hundreds out to Long Island or up the Hudson, became great showcases for displaying Chinese Christians, especially as white picnickers often outnumbered Chinese three to one. "Some of the Chinamen were attired in the garb of civilization throughout, but most of them wore the [clothing] of their native country," wrote one observer after the first such outing in 1883, "The moral effect of the Sunday School picnic cannot be overstated." It was a little sanctimonious, perhaps, but the teachers' intentions were better than those of the gangs of white delinquents waiting outside the churches with stones and clubs.

Meanwhile, the students expressed their gratitude for kindnesses shown them by bringing their lady teachers little presents of sweets or trinkets. Mostly, these were just innocent, friendly gestures, but there were some men who became smitten with their feminine instructors. After all, they lived in a society without women, and a fellow gets lonely after a decade or so. Rumors of such affections caused periodic scandals, fed by breathless (and totally unsubstantiated) accounts in the press of secret assignations. Trinity Baptist was sent reeling after the New York papers started reporting that one of its teachers was actually engaged to a Chinese man. "The attacks which have been made . . . are purely malicious," an indignant Mrs. Carto retorted, "As a matter of fact, with two exceptions, the teachers in my school are either widows or old maids . . . who have got well beyond the age of giddy girlhood." As for the idea of marriage between teacher and pupil, "nothing of that kind has been even so much as dreamed of." Regardless, Trinity would abruptly terminate the teaching of the Chinese, only to see Mrs. Carto depart in high dudgeon.

There is no doubt of the genuine affection and good will most of these teachers felt towards their pupils, however. One lady, in talking about her charges, admitted that at first she "took up this work as a matter of duty, with a strong prejudice against these people," but soon her heart softened. "I have come to love these Chinamen for their many beautiful qualities of heart," she continued, "And I respect them sincerely for their admirable qualities of head . . . They are exquisitely polite, and in the best sense well bred. Under many a laundryman's blouse is hidden a scholar and artist . . . I could almost say that sometimes they put some of us white Christians to the blush . . ."

Christians weren't blushing on Mott Street, however, as virtually across the street from both Tong headquarters and the former Presbyterian school the Roman Catholic Church of the Transfiguration hunkered down and snarled like a trapped Doberman at its Asian neighbors. "On

Sunday the place swarms with Chinamen from all parts of the city and from out of town, who make of the neighborhood a perfect hell," snapped Father Barry, the church's Irish priest. For the time being, the only Christian church actually located in China Town was choosing not to embrace the Chinese.

Nor were all Chinese choosing to embrace the Church. "We have certainly a right to our religion," protested one Wing Fung. Enlisting the help of his white neighbor to "put this letter into grammar for me," he worried to the *Evening Post* about Chinese children being compelled to attend Christian schools. "How should we force the Dragon to send rain in a time of drought unless our children are taught the ceremonies by which this is done? Then there is the worship of our ancestors: how is that to be kept up unless it is carefully inculcated upon our children in the tenderest years? We cannot consent to the godless education which you would give them." Of course there were no fully Chinese children in New York just yet, but the slight aura of panic in the letter reveals a slipping grip on a life under siege by strange Barbarian forces.

But to Wing Fung and many of his neighbors, the idea of being exclusively Christian is godless, because in the Celestial pantheon there are countless numbers of ghosts and demons and creatures who join with the Ancestors in the underworld to meddle endlessly in the affairs of the living. The Scholar, or Mandarin class, of course, practice Confucianism, which is not a religion at all, but rather an elaborate code of behavior meant to bring order to society and encourage respect for Patriarch, Father, and Emperor, in that order. And then there are Buddhists, worshipping that "foreign divinity" and expounding meditation, peace, and the Four Noble Truths.

But the less-rarified air of country villages in places like Toi-shan teems with Taoist spiritual life, from the Nine Dragons that control the universe, to the Eighteen Saints, the Eighteen Auspicious Members, and a prayer rosary with 108 beads, offering twelve sets of nine prayers, nine being the universal number of wholeness. There is Quan Yin, the Goddess of Mercy, or "The one who hears all." It is she you pray to for the health of your baby or to be blessed by having a lot of sons. Quan Kung, the God of War, can provide victory in business. The Kitchen God watches over the household wok. The Monkey God, the Rabbit in the Moon, and a countless myriad of others—all have to be acknowledged.

Faith, such as it is, means little more than "good luck," and if the Ancestors can talk the Prosperity Dragon into coughing up a loan, then why not do everything possible to keep them happy?

Thus it is that the Christians, the Tong, and the Ancestors battle over the soul of China Town. For the practical Chinese in New York who wants to get ahead, the path is simple: embrace all three.

So Hor Poa takes English lessons in the evenings at one of the Christian "Sunday" schools, while carefully avoiding actually becoming a Christian. Piece by piece, his dress becomes more Americanized, starting with a bowler hat, and continuing with a stout pair of leather shoes, and then some dark woolen trousers. The broad-sleeved blouse with the frog buttons is retained, for a while at least, as it is far more comfortable than the tight jackets and waistcoats that the White Christian Devils wear. It is also not time to dispense with the queue, as Hor Poa is still a subject of the Manchu Emperor, and he would like to be able to visit the Middle Kingdom sometime in the future and keep his head attached to his body. So he winds his braid under his hat while renovating Tom Lee's buildings, all the while paying his Tong dues and keeping the incense burning to the Ancestors at the little shrine in his room.

Early in 1883 he is able to walk down to Chatham Square and buy a copy of the *Chinese American,* the first Chinese-language newspaper published in New York. It is a scant four pages, put together by Wong Chin Foo, a handsome young Chinese scholar who has been earning quite a reputation for himself on the American lecture circuit. Delivering speeches in flawless English to white audiences, he tries to explain Chinese philosophy and customs, while dispelling some of the more outrageous myths about the Chinese themselves. "I never knew rats . . . were good to eat till I learned it from Americans," he quipped at Steinway Hall in 1877. "Mr. Wong Ching [sic] Foo . . . has no occasion to be quite so smart and flippant," snapped *Harper's Weekly* in reply.

And now, in a rapidly growing China Town, he publishes the first edition of his newspaper, the masthead date bearing in Chinese both "The 27th Day of the 12th Month of the Eighth Year of Emperor Kuang Hsü" and "February third in the one thousand, eight hundred and eighty-third year after Jesus came." The front page carries just three items: a breathless story of panicked Chinese villagers confronted with a "fire dragon in the sky"; an account of the recent gift of a giant elephant, "powerful and mean, but looking like a human," from the King of Burma to Emperor Kuang Hsü in Peking (Court officials killed the unhappy pachyderm after one of their number was fatally injured while trying to ride it—and then, realizing they had just destroyed a valuable gift to their Emperor, dug a huge hole to "hide the evidence"); and a reprint from a New York paper entitled "Romantic Dreams," a titillating tale of a seventeen-year-old's revenge on the seducer who had fathered her illegitimate child. "After a prison term, the offender was mad at the witness who helped to put him away," Wong dryly observes.

Inside, amid a myriad of ads for everything from laundry equipment to English lessons, Wong provides an intimate peek at life in the China Town of 1883. "[T]here are over ten grocery stores, five or six pharmacy stores, numerous restaurants, and sewing establishments [garment factories] . . . trade is brisk with Hong Kong—a great improvement from last year's prosperity. People now can buy everything in New York without trading with other cities." One store is even displaying a 26-foot-long fish in a tank protected by an iron gate. "Several thousand people" have paid 10 cents apiece to view this "strange and wild" creature.

Commerce is not the only way to make money, however. Wong illustrates the Chinese love for gambling when he tells how a street martial-arts display was broken up by police as a huge crowd gathered to place bets on the outcome. When it was learned that the fighters themselves were battling for a vast purse of supposedly $10,000, the police hauled them off to the station and fined them $500 each.

Then there are the problems of coping with America's modern conveniences and pressures. One Chinese had a fancy new gas heater in his room. When he didn't appear in the morning, however, neighbors broke down his door to find him dead, and his Caucasian wife unconscious. Apparently their faulty heater had filled their room with noxious fumes. "Please be careful in using gas heaters," Wong warns, "which can also create fire hazards."

And a Chinese was arrested for shooting to death a woman named "Precious Gold." If indeed Precious Gold was a Chinese woman, as Wong's prose seems to indicate, this raises more questions than answers. Weren't there supposedly only three or four Chinese women in New

York? What was Precious Gold doing in the presence of a man who wasn't her husband? Could Precious Gold have been a prostitute? A slave?

Wong's newspaper venture is a little shaky from the start. First of all, he rather grandly prints a weekly run of 50,000 for a China Town community consisting of some 700, of whom perhaps 200 can read his mix of classical Chinese and colloquial Cantonese prose. But the biggest problem comes in his issue of June 14, where he publishes a blistering editorial against "a riotous Chinese named Tip, or Chin Pun Tip, a cousin of the man who keeps a low den of infamy on Park Street, Number 94." Mr. Wong accuses Mr. Chin of all sorts of transgressions, which include promoting illegal gambling in New York, grand larceny ("night after night he would stuff his wide and spacious pantaloons [with] the finest silks and satins . . ."), and finally with the attempted murder of the righteous Wong Chin Foo himself. Wong has definitely cast himself in the role of a crusader against the Forces of Evil.

Unfortunately for him, certain Forces of Evil can read. Within a week of the editorial, "gamblers and joint-keepers" visit the *Chinese American*'s office and terrorize the staff, who immediately decamp for Panama—with the newspaper's bank balance in their pockets.

Mr. Chin sues Mr. Wong for libel. Accusations and denials are flung around a New York courtroom without any proof on either side, while the plaintiff and defendant burn sticks of incense to influence various gods in their favor. Another kind of man-made influence seems to be wielded, however, as the jury awards $1,000 in damages to Chin. Six months after it first appears, the *Chinese American* is out of business. But Wong Chin Foo knows when he is licked, and before too long he joins forces with the gamblers and joint-keepers. By 1888, he will be the official secretary to Tom Lee at Tong headquarters.

Wong will have more journalistic success when he revives his paper in 1893—in Chicago.

But meanwhile, Wong Chin Foo remains a prominent voice in New York, and with Hor Poa and the rest of China Town he celebrates the advent of the Year of the Monkey, the 10th year of Emperor Kuang Hsü, or 1884. Some of his countrymen make the journey out to the steam laundry in Belleville, New Jersey, where the laundrymen can be a little freer with their firecrackers, setting off a string at a time. New York's municipal government—composed of silly Round Eyes who don't understand the importance of noise in frightening away evil spirits—has tried to ban firecrackers on Chinese New Year ever since street urchins got tangled up in the celebrations of 1881. But China Town's merchants manage to set a few thunderous bombs off at midnight anyway, just to give a proper kickoff to the week-long festival.

All over China Town, tiny bachelor cubicles are scrupulously swept and cleaned. Incense and offerings of sugary *lin goh* dumplings are left to encourage the Ancestors to send good fortune, while honey is smeared over the mouth of the Kitchen God before it is burned, so that the worthy demon will deliver a sweet report to his superiors when the smoke arrives in heaven.

Larger celebrations are held at the "Joss House" at Tong head-quarters, the word "Joss" being the American slang for what is per-ceived as being the pidgin-English way of saying "god." At any rate, it is a room dominated by a gilded statue of General Quan Kung, the God of War—who is also the patron god of gamblers—making his favor especially valuable to the Tong. Accompanying him is Quan P'ing, his son, and most importantly, Un T'an, God of Wealth, all imported from China and surrounded by mountains of fresh oranges, flowers, and pots of sand stuck full of sticks of fragrant incense. The advice of the spirit world is sought from these and other worthies, with the attendant being paid a small fee to pour a libation and then cast two curved blocks to get a yes or no answer to some specific question about the future, depending on whether they land with their curved sides up or down or in combination. Others shake a box filled with numbered divining sticks. When one falls out, its number is matched to a page in the *Book of Changes* or *I Ching*, which will foretell the for-tune of the petitioner for the coming year. Those hoping for especially good news bring roasted chickens or suckling pig, which the humans will consume after the deity has had his fill.

Outside, all work has stopped, and feasting and entertaining are the order of the day. China Town teems with people crossing back and forth, making calls, leaving small New Year's gifts of money sealed in bright red envelopes. The whole block is dressed up with strings of beautifully painted lanterns and huge bouquets of paper flowers from which hang long red streamers covered with paeans to prosperity and good luck. Hor Poa is dressed up also, the cotton blouse replaced by one of silk brocade, with brightly-colored silk trousers hanging in luscious folds and gathered tightly at the ankles by brilliant, white socks. Decked out in this magnificent costume, he first pays calls upon all of his creditors to settle his debts, as every good Chinese tries to do at this time. He then visits all his friends and acquaintances, enjoying tea and other traditional refreshments—oranges to promote sweetness in life, grapefruits for prosperity, honeyed *jin dui* dumplings and stalks of sugar cane—before going on to the next. There is a Chinese band at 11 Mott, whaling away on gongs and wood blocks in a further attempt to create noise that will keep the evil spirits at bay; later, the Lion Dance will take place, with its papier-maché creature of poetic ferocity, snapping and yawing and snaking down the street, collecting money for the poor.

A commotion erupts when closed carriages pull up in front of 14 Mott and disgorge the city's Chinese women—there may be as many as four of them—who try to hurry quickly inside on their tiny bound feet, for it would be terribly brazen for them to pause long enough to allow themselves to be subjected to public scrutiny. Indeed, even though they all probably live mere yards away, they still must travel to Number 14 in sealed coaches to protect their modesty from prying eyes. Yet the crowds of Irish and Italians, who actually outnumber the Chinese in China Town and have come downstairs to watch the fun, rush to gawk at the sight of these delicate ladies in their long tunics over shimmering silk trousers. "Them women!" they shout, "Look at their pants!" and as the unruly throng jostles for a better view, "them women" in question squeal in alarm and disappear inside.

There are banquets given this week, at Tong headquarters and at all of the four or five China Town restaurants. The tables groan with lotus-root soup, steamed seaweed known as *fat choy* (happy prosperity), suckling pig symbolizing abundance, and chickens to represent the phoenix and rebirth. There are dishes of steamed clams and oysters cooked with seaweed, called *fat choy ho see* (prosperity and good business). Oranges, seemingly whole, but mysteriously hollowed out and filled with a variety of brightly-colored sweets, await every guest, as well as eggs, similarly filled with meats and nuts. There are candied watermelon rinds and watermelon seeds, dyed red, sugar-coated lotus seeds, and lotus roots. And after every course, tea and plum wine or rice brandy drunk in round after bleary-eyed round from tiny cups.

A very few of the socially prominent—refined Mandarin scholars who in New York work in shops or in laundries—don their peacock-feather hats and drive in carriages up to the Chinese Consulate on Eighth Street. The Consul, for his part, doesn't expect many visitors. He is, after all, the representative of his Imperial Majesty, and the mere peasants who make up most of China Town's population are not worthy to be received by him. As for the celebrations on Mott Street, they represent nothing but ignorant superstitions, he says, and so will not be graced by his illustrious presence. Meanwhile, back in China, the Emperor whom he represents rolls up his sleeves and turns the earth with a plow, in a ceremony meant to guarantee fertility of the soil by virtue of his personal intervention.

The Year of the Monkey is an important one for China Town. It is in this year that the *Chung Wah Kung Saw,* or The Public Assembly of the Chinese, will be founded at 10 Chatham Square. This is a government within a government, applying for recognition not with the New York Municipality, but with the Imperial Court in Peking. The *Chung Wah Kung Saw* is formed with the intention not only of aiding the poor, but as a foil to the growing power of the Tong. Led only by "respectable," educated men, they will mediate disputes, shepherd new businesses, and eventually regulate just about every aspect of China Town life. A president is elected annually from among the "gentlemen" of the community (often against their will), as well as Chinese- and English-speaking secretaries to act as liaisons with the outside world. In 1890, the same year that the Tong will officially become known as the On Leong, The Assembly of Chinese will also adopt a new name—the Chinese Charitable (later, Consolidated) Benevolent Association. As the CCBA they will finally register with the State of New York, while their headquarters at 16 Mott Street (where they move in 1888) will become the hub of China Town life.

This particular Year of the Monkey is momentous for another reason as well. In the cold pre-dawn hours of January 31, 1985, a young, shirtless Chinese man races in a panic across Mott from his room at Number 17, to rouse the white doctor living across the street. The young man, one Fung Cham, had originally ignored his wife's complaints of pain, but not long after the arrival of Dr. Ten Eyck, Mrs. Fung is delivered of a healthy baby boy. It is the first fully Chinese baby born in the City—or at least the first recorded. The news spreads like wildfire, and soon Chinese bachelors are crowding the Fung home to see the child. A white reporter also wants to see him, but Fung Cham, just leaving his job at Wah Kee's store, demurs. He is afraid that the white man will just make fun of him in his newspaper, or, as Fung's comments appear in the *New York Times*, "No dlam Melican me let in. Make flun me. Me no mlake flun plapers. Me no dlam fool." Mr. Fung, it seems, knows whereof he speaks.

The Year of the Monkey is an important one for Hor Poa as well. He has done well in China Town, regularly sending money back to his parents and bringing great face to his Ancestors. He has a dutiful wife, a growing daughter, and money hidden in a box under his bed. But now it is time for him to render one more service to his family. For later this year he will be joined on Mott Street by yet one more resident of little Hor Lup Chui in the Toi-shan district of Kuang Tung Province, southern China—his younger brother, Hor Sek. This second son will also attempt to make his fortune in America, while back in the Middle Kingdom, old Hor Jick Wah sits in front of the village Ancestors' Hall and complains loudly about his two worthless boys who are wandering in the Golden Mountain, knowing full well that his friends are green with envy.

The year 1884 is not the optimum time for coming to America. On July 4, President Arthur signs a law which makes the Exclusion Act even more restrictive than before. Chinese laborers from "any and every port," regardless of residency, are now barred, meaning that Chinese genes alone will hereafter keep travelers from places like Cuba, Peru, or Borneo out of the Golden Mountain. In addition, the definition of "merchant" is tightened, and illegals will be punished with one year in jail or $1,000 in fines, although so few merchants have been getting through that the point seems somewhat moot. In 1885, the first full year that the new law is in effect, exactly twenty-two Chinese citizens will legally immigrate to the United States.

So, while he may have arrived in New York in 1884, it's hard to believe that Great-Great-Uncle first came to the United States any time in the previous two years. Perhaps he was already living in San Francisco. Perhaps he came over with Hor Poa when he returned in 1881, only to join him in New York three years later. Or perhaps Great-Great-Uncle took another, increasingly popular route, one that would enable him to avoid American customs officials altogether.

Back in Hor Lup Chui, during the seventh year of Kuang Hsü, rumors were rampant that soon the Golden Mountain's borders would be closed forever. As Hor Poa, not even able to wait long enough to sire the son the Ancestors required of him, made ready to depart, others around him were desperately looking for a way out. They found one much the same as their brothers of a generation earlier had done, as Barbarians, also known as Red-Haired Devils, turned up looking for workers to construct the Transcontinental Railroad—the Canadian Transcontinental Railroad, running from Vancouver to Montreal. Passage to Canada would be provided in exchange for years of hard work in even harsher conditions than had met the builders of the American route. The weather was colder, the snow deeper, the mountains more rugged. A total of 15,701 Chinese were imported to do this work, and at least six hundred died during construction, although the popular legend is that for every foot of track laid through the Canadian Rockies one Chinese succumbed to exposure or accident. The one thing that makes it easy to think that Great-Great Uncle was among this group is the dates—construction commenced in 1881, the year Hor Poa returned from China, and the railroad was completed in June of 1884, when Hor Sek turned up in New York. Indeed, it is the prospect of 15,000 suddenly unemployed Chinese poised to rush over the border from Canada which probably motivated Congress to push their Sinophobic legislation through one month later. I like to think that during that month some barely made it through—among them, a ragged small-town boy out to join his prosperous big brother in New York City.

Of course, even if he was stopped at the border, there were other, not strictly legal ways to get into the U.S. Merchants returning to China for good were known to sell their merchant papers to those who were willing to change their identity. For those already in Canada, $30 can hire a man to smuggle one into a boat sailing down Lake Champlain, or guide one to a spot where it is possible to merely walk into New York State or Vermont. One could buy forged merchant certificates for $25, or even foreign naturalization papers at rates ranging from $5 for Peru to $10 for Chile, for before July 1884 even the U.S. Congress won't keep out citizens of a friendly power, even if those citizens have a name like Hor Sek. At any rate, regardless of how he does it, sometime in 1884 Great-Great-Uncle takes up residence with his older brother at Number 18 Mott Street. He went through a lot to get here. Unfortunately, all that trouble may not have been worth it.

At first, Hor Sek's new life looks promising, as there is plenty of work available. Chinese servants are becoming something of a vogue for New York hostesses, and the irrepressible Augusta Carto is enthusiastically promoting her Trinity Baptist Sunday School boys as candidates. One potential employer expresses the sentiments of many when she huffs, "We want Chinese and won't take negroes!"

For those less presentable, or less willing to deal with Caucasian housewives, there is the tobacco trade. Indeed, there are something like four hundred Chinese cigar-makers working in the City, enough to have their own trade union at 30 Pell Street. They are preferred over Europeans and children for the dexterity in their small hands, and a skilled worker at one of the Cuban cigar factories in Maiden Lane, or at the Cuban-Chinese Miguel Atak's place at 91 Chatham Street, can make $35 to $40 per week, an absolutely enormous sum.

But as with a growing number of Chinese, it is a laundry job that is Hor Sek's for the asking, and it is to a laundry he goes. Unlike the cigar and servant fields, which are controlled by whites, Laundry Associations (which cost $25 to join, and without membership in which a laundry won't be permitted to open) help to regulate the location of new operations, to reward loyal owners, and also to make sure that there is no unhealthy competition. They keep the prices profitable—shirts, 10 cents; underwear, 7 cents; handkerchiefs, cuffs, and collars, 2 cents— and deal rather heavy-handedly with those who try to undersell their brethren. But the ironers and washermen belong to their own unions, and when they band together to demand higher wages in the summer of 1884, the owners respond by not only refusing to pay, but actually lowering the prevailing wage from between $3.50 and $4.00 per day to a mere $3.00, or $10.00 per week plus food and lodging for those who live in. Still, with a six-day work week, Hor Sek can make $18. That's not bad in the New York of 1884.

Wah Kee, the preeminent shopkeeper in China Town, says that there are over 200 Chinese laundries in New York by 1880, growing to an estimated 1,000 by 1885, all founded since the first sixty-eight laundrymen were secretly smuggled into that Belleville, New Jersey, laundry in 1870. They are most common on the East Side, especially in the streets near China Town like the Bowery and Canal Street. But there are a few farther afield, such as Hing Mow, serving the blacksmiths and carriage factory workers on the part of Broadway that will someday be known as Times Square, and Hop Kwong, a lonely business way, way up amid the farms and country houses of Third Avenue above 110th Street.

If Hor Sek is employed in an especially busy enterprise, his fellow workers might not all even be Chinese. A laundry could have up to ten employees, with Irish and black women often hired to do the grunt work. Some whites, ever suspicious of mixing genders and races, are certain that pretty Irish girls are especially employed for extracurricular reasons. They do not seem to care what happens to the black women who work there as well.

It's a hard life. Work starts at dawn and goes hours past dark. Washing, ironing, starching, labeling, and packaging for delivery are all done on the premises, often just two or three rooms. A huge stove kept going in the drying room, and tubs of boiling water in the washroom, make the quarters unbearably hot in the summer. Deliveries are made to homes in white neighborhoods invariably hostile to the "heathen Chinee." Stone-wielding punks soon develop the sport of using laundry windows (and workers) for target practice. If they don't smash the windows, they just smear them with filth. Older Barbarians will get a friend to "steal" their laundry by making a false claim—and then force the laundryman to pay them for the supposedly lost goods. Not to do so would mean instant arrest, so the Chinese always pay.

The laundrymen often live right at the laundries themselves, sleeping on narrow bunks in rooms next to the blistering drying stoves. Newcomers are subjected to a six-month apprenticeship, first at the steaming washtubs, then wielding the eight-pound irons, then on to finish work. And after a year or two of backbreaking toil, a thrifty laundry worker like Hor Sek could become a laundry owner.

It didn't take much money to open a laundry. A store in a good location could be had for $35 a month; a crank-operated washing machine was $15; a newfangled collar-washer, $45; a hundred pounds of soap, 95 cents. Hor Sek and my great-grandfather might have had some money laid by, or they could have gotten a loan from the Tong. More often, prospective laundry owners posted a notice on the community bulletin board, inviting potential partners to form a *whey*.

A *whey* was a group of twenty individuals each desiring to borrow a certain amount of money, say $200. Each *whey* member would put down $10.00, along with a sealed bid with the amount of interest he is willing to pay for the use of that total amount of money for one month. The member offering the highest interest—often as much as 40 percent—is awarded the $200 first, less the interest, which in the case of a 40-percent rate would mean that each of the other members would give him $6.00. The recipient is then pledged to pay the others the full $10.00 in one month's time. In other words, for $10 down, the 40 percent borrower receives the use of a total of $114 (16 from each of the other 19 *whey* members), for which he will pay $190 at the end of one month. The 20 percent borrower will receive $8 from each member and so on. Month after month, *whey* members take turns using the capital, until finally the one offering the lowest interest obtains the money. Having survived in the *whey* for twenty months, he also reaps a handsome profit in interest. If everyone pays on schedule, everyone can make a bundle. But if one person defaults, the whole structure can collapse.

Starting this year, the Laundry Association declares that a prospective buyer of an established business must put 50 percent down, with one month to come up with the balance. At that time, buyer, lender, and all other creditors meet at the laundry to settle the debts, and then the title to the business is clear. Fail to pay, and Tom Lee's henchmen will be employed to make sure that you don't leave town until you do. A profitable laundry could be sold for $350, although the one right on Chatham Square was supposedly worth $2,500, affording its owner numerous trips to China and untold other luxuries. For an owner, the profit could be worth the trouble.

But for Hor Sek, living right in the middle of China Town provides too many facile opportunities for forgetting his sweat and loneliness. There are a lot of vices within easy reach, and as Exclusion Laws and zealous immigration officials heat up, and Chinese everywhere are herded into their little ghettos, they become increasingly insular and self-contained. There are virtually no Chinese women. There are few family members. After the laundry work is done, about ten o'clock at night, dimly lighted doorways on Mott, and Pell, and Park, and Chatham Square beckon to tired men trudging the pavement. Great-Great-Uncle falls in step, seeking escape through the indulgences available to him.

Prostitutes. White people seem convinced that China Town is riddled with brothels, with young white women held as sex slaves in lieu of Chinese ones. Father Barry of the Church of the Transfiguration loudly claims that "little girls" are regularly "enticed away," by means of opium-laced candy, to engage in "bestial practices that cannot be mentioned," which of course he proceeds to describe at every imaginable opportunity. What he doesn't say is that in 1880s New York State, the legal age of sexual consent for girls is all of ten. That's 1, 0. Perhaps the State Government in Albany should be blamed for encouraging "bestial practices" of its own.

Certainly there are prostitutes in China Town, as there would be in among any large concentration of single men with money on their hands. Additionally, any white woman cohabiting with a Chinese man tends to be viewed as a prostitute by self-righteous Victorians, but a Chinese man with a good income, strange though he may seem to society's eyes, is still a safe refuge for a destitute white girl with few options. Some women are even said to love their half-Chinese children "as much as if the blood in their veins ran pure." Respectable gentlemen and ladies just shake their heads in disbelief.

But we are still in Five Points, after all, and desperately poor women—white, black, and even Chinese had there been any who were unattached—do what they need to do in an era without social services or many job opportunities for members of their sex. There are girls who visit the laundrymen for a quick session on a cot in the drying room, while in China Town proper you will find working women set up in rooms by themselves. There are also a couple of brothels (some supposedly paying dividends to Tom Lee) on Pell Street, which is still far more Irish and Italian than Chinese. The fact that these cater very largely to the swaggering swells of the Bowery goes unnoticed. But let Chinese men pay a visit and it is trumpeted as evidence of their degradation. As for the women, a dollar per visit is a lot of money if it's managed carefully. If not, it is at least enough to provide the drugs or alcohol for escape from a life of loneliness, squalor, and untreatable venereal disease.

Gambling. Everyone likes to gamble. It is not demonized by the Chinese in the way that Christians would have them do. It is just some fun, some excitement, a way to win the fortune it would take so long to earn. And when one loses, as happens more often than not, there is a sigh and a shrug and another roll of the dice, for a nest egg can always be re-earned. To stop the Chinese from gambling would be like stopping the Chinese from eating. "The Chinaman will gamble with his last cent," says Wong Chin Foo. If arrested, "he will feel for his companions in a dark cell in the Tombs, and bet with his toes if all other conveniences are taken away."

In basements and back rooms, family association parlors and dormitory rooms, the games go on. Men in restaurants place wagers on the number of buttons on the next stranger's coat. In temples they use their fingers to bet on "stone, paper, scissors." And then there is mah-jongg, with its little walls of ivory tiles to be removed, one by one, only to be slammed down on the table with a noise like a gunshot accompanied by shouts of triumph when a set is won. The rules are actually very similar to gin rummy, with betting conducted by means of piles of little ivory sticks which act as chips, making the game seem even more exotic to the uninitiated. The tiles are kept in little drawers of beautiful wooden boxes, often painted red and carved with the Dragon of Prosperity to tilt the odds in the owner's favor.

But there is gambling and there is Gambling, and China Town provides ample opportunity for its residents to indulge themselves to well beyond the fullest extent of their little cash hoards. Gaming rooms are set up like any other business, with partners coming together and pooling their money to buy the necessary equipment and rent the necessary rooms. A payment to Tom Lee—$5 per table per week—is an absolute necessity to keep the police (and Tom Lee's henchmen) at bay. By 1891 there will even be Gambling Associations or Guilds, one for each different type of play, which operate just like the Laundry Association, regulating the various games—and providing a unified voice to keep Tom Lee's graft at a manageable level.

First there is the lottery, or the "Hundred Letters Game," with betting shops set up on Mott Street. There, a steady stream of runners arrive with bets collected at laundries and cigar factories, while other participants carefully scrutinize betting sheets before taking a brush and marking their bets with daubs of red ink. This is a game played not with numbers but with classic eight-line Chinese poetry, written out on slips of paper—eighty characters, eighty choices. Even when the police seize betting slips, their translators solemnly inform them that they have merely confiscated snatches of a poem. The bewildered Round Eyes usually let the suspected gamblers go free.

So twice a day, at four in the afternoon, and then ten at night for the workers, the individual characters from that day's poem are written on slips of tissue paper, wadded up and thrown into white bowls to be mixed together so that the thirteen winning words can be drawn at random. Hopeful players display no emotion when they lose; they merely reach for the red ink to start the process again.

Another variation of this is the *tsz fa*, or Riddle Game, in which there are thirty-six possible answers to each of six riddles posted throughout the day. Thus, "The bright light shines over the shadow valley" could refer to "pretty woman," or maybe "bird," or "money." Actually, all thirty-six choices could probably apply. Meanwhile, Tom Lee allows the lottery agents to keep a portion of the handsome profits from the games which they supposedly own.

Then there are the gambling parlors, the larger ones resembling Tom Lee's 1879 operation, the one where he so graciously provided burlap sacks to those patrons who had gambled away all their clothes. *Han ton*, or steerers, are paid $5 per week to stand in the street and beckon in soft voices to tired men just having completed a day of intense hard work. "*Fan tan* within," they murmur in Chinese, "Go and make your fortune." Each green laundryman lured inside earns the *han ton* a bonus.

Two rooms, always hung with scrolls and lanterns in vivid red, the lucky color for money, are situated behind an innocuous-looking store or business. In the first chamber, *fan tan*, or "spread and turn over," is played. A croupier sits on a stool, shaking a large container of Chinese copper "cash." A banker waits with his scales to weigh the silver and gold coins being wagered, making sure none of their value has been shaved off. Another banker stands ready to seize the pot or pay the winners.

The play starts with the gamblers placing their bets on one side of the board set on the high center table, each side numbered 1 to 4. In one movement, the croupier slaps the open end of the container down on the board, leaving a pile of "cash" behind. Then, with a long black wand, he deftly removes four cash at a time, each movement increasing the tension in the room, until there are no longer four cash left to remove. If there is just one coin remaining, then the wagerers on that number win, and so on, although the stakes placed on losing numbers are left intact. Those who bet on corners, or two numbers at once, can also win a reduced amount. However, if there are no "cash" left, all the bets are forfeit to the bank. No one ever bets on the number 4, as there could never be four "cash" remaining.

The inner chamber is where the real power gambling goes on, the stakes so high that there is not actually any money present, lest some overeager participant or police raider should sweep it away. Winners are presented with an I.O.U. which is later rewarded with cash from the safe, while losers are honor bound to send their losses to the bosses by sundown the next day. Not to pay would mean a great loss of face. When dealing with a cheated Tong gambling-house owner, it may also mean a great loss of limb.

This second room is where *pai gao* can be found, the poker-like game played with dominoes. Here there are also croupiers and bankers, and an assortment of professional Hong Kong gamblers, out to make a killing. Then there are the ragged *ton san*, the "pull-coat-tail fellows," who lurk by the tables, hungrily watching the play, but wise enough not to wager any money of their own. They wait to give the uninitiated the benefit of their experience, often playing a few hands for the novitiates, and receiving a handsome tip when they win. At the bottom of the heap are the idlers, the opium addicts, who hang around the rooms, hoping to scrounge a few nickels from winners who always give out "good luck money." After their fantasies of riches are exhausted for the evening, they wander out into the night in search of more guaranteed ways to dream.

Opium. A drug for relaxation known to the Chinese for centuries, but ruthlessly forced on them in quantity by nineteenth-century British and American traders who know that addicts make the best customers. Opium is not illegal in the United States in 1884, and despite popular opinion, there are far more whites than Chinese who are hooked on the narcotic. Still, there are many Chinese users, who, along with the desperate and forgotten poor of Five Points and the Bowery, make ideal customers for Tong entrepreneurs. Tom Lee makes sure that China Town has more than its share of outlets in which they can indulge, and opium dens, or "smoke houses" can be found on Baxter and Mott Streets and the tiny, swarming alleys off Mulberry such as Donovan's Lane and Bandits' Roost. There is even one in the back of Tong headquarters, where two teenaged white girls are found by the police one night in the spring of 1883. Father Barry of the Church of the Transfiguration has encouraged the raid, not so much because of the presence of drugs, but to rescue the "innocent" white girls he is certain were being lured to their ruination by the wicked Chinese. The fact that these girls are apparently Five Points prostitutes does not reduce the censure he reserves for his pagan neighbors.

The smoke houses are fairly similar. They are often in backyard buildings for added quiet and privacy, but the locations of many of them are well known, the addresses casually reported in the papers without, apparently, any ill effect. Still, there is usually a lookout, a door with a peephole and a heavy chain. A second door and a second guard, who murmurs the question, 'How many?" before letting the guest into the inner sanctum.

A room, low and dark, is lined with bunks fitted with woven mats and a lacquered leather or porcelain Chinese pillow, to be placed under the head as the users recline in their torpor. There are two to a berth. The pungent smoke saturating the air has a slight glow from the tenuous light of a single oil lamp hanging from the ceiling.

A "layout," the array of strange tools for smoking the drug, is provided in the *yen hop*, a large box on a wooden tray. Inside, the *yen tsiang*, or pipe, also called a *gong*, is the principal article, a two-foot-long tube of bamboo with a delicate and beautiful ivory bowl mounted on top. These pipes are imported from China, and can be of great age and value, the chew marks on the business end denoting generations of languid use. A delicate wire wand, the *yen hock* is used to extract the *yen pock*, a nugget of opium, black and glutinous, from the *ow*, the little decorated jar in which it is kept. It is then heated over a *yen dong*, a tiny spirit lamp, turning into a morsel of honey gold before it is inserted carefully into the pipe. The user lies sideways on his pallet, holding the pipe-bowl with its precious contents over the flame to keep it warm, and greedily sucks its anxiety-numbing vapors into his lungs. Then sleep, or rather deep languor, during which all the world seems peaceful and soothing and warm, so warm.

Before another round, there is a little scraper, the *yen she gow,* to remove the residue, or *gee yen,* that has collected in the pipestem, which is then carefully preserved for future use in another wooden box, the *yen shee hop.* A tiny sponge, the *sui dow,* is used to clean the pipe for the next dose, and scissors, *kiao tsien,* are there to trim the lamp wick so the process can start all over again. At dawn, the sluggish shopkeepers and launderers, prostitutes and businessmen, both white and not, rouse themselves to somehow struggle through another day. Dedicated users, or *yen she kwoi,* can keep smoking for days at a time.

"Banging the gong" can be expensive. One can buy brand names such as *Fook Yuen* ("Fountain of Happiness") and *Li Yuen* ("Fountain of Beauty") which come in different doses and qualities. Flashy white men and Tong big shots favor the *Li Yuen,* big opium pills which cost as much as a dollar a hit, although ordinary users can buy the smaller *pen yen* for a quarter or less. The poorer, more needy smoke a cheap concoction made from the *gee yen,* the preserved dregs, while the truly desperate, the hopeless addicts who cannot even manage to earn enough for a *gee yen* mixture, merely hover around the smoke house as *bunk yen,* those who can only hope for a free whiff of opium smoke to ease the pain from the degradation into which they have fallen.

One lasting effect that opium has on New York is the new phrase that has entered Bowery slang. From now on, when people "have a yen" for something, everyone will instantly envision a certain kind of sharp hunger which must be satisfied soon, very soon. "Joints" are places where opium is openly sold.

So, it seems Great-Great-Uncle falls into the mire of poverty and isolation that New York has to offer him, and he is ground down until there is nothing left to grind. On September 3, 1886, a white doctor is called to a room on the second floor of the old wooden building at 18 Mott Street to attend a certain weak and wasted Chinese laundryman. Two days later, at one o'clock in the afternoon, after two years in New York, the laundryman, my Great-Great Uncle-Hor Sek, breathes his last.

The listed cause of death: "general dibility (sic)." He is not yet thirty-five years old. Back in China, a wife and son and aged parents await news from their great hope for the future, a sojourner who was searching for the key to their fortune, but, has detoured and ascended the dragon from a mountain shining with a counterfeit gold.

Hor Sek's body is delivered to Naughton's funeral home at Number 37 Mott. Foreign Barbarians are always enlisted to handle Chinese dead, as no civilized person would want to run the risk of bringing a possibly unhappy ghost under his own roof. It is even considered unlucky to have someone die in one's home, and people have been known to evict the dying so as not to bring misfortune to their rooms. Perhaps it is only a coincidence, but within eighteen months of Great-Great-Uncle's death, the Tong quits number 18 Mott and moves around the corner to a loft on Pell Street. Hor Sek has left his mark after all.

So, the Irish Joseph Naughton places Hor Sek's body in a handsome walnut coffin, and his Hibernian employees load and drive the fancy glass-sided hearse pulled by a team of horses with tall black plumes. The body of Great-Great-Uncle thus departs China Town in Victorian splendor, followed by a line of hired carriages carrying Hor Poa, Tom Lee, and various others wearing mourning armbands of red, white, and black. Next to the driver, high on the hearse's box, a Chinese majordomo throws fistfuls of red ceremonial paper money into the air. He would prefer to set off firecrackers or bang shrill gongs to frighten evil spirits away, but the Municipal Police make such noisy displays difficult to perform. So it is hoped that the money will divert any pursuing demons into losing sight of the funeral procession as they stoop to collect the fluttering cash, for if they can't find the burial place, they won't be able to torment the deceased. It works, to a large degree, as the everpresent white boys hurling epithets and stones from the sidewalks break off their abuse and chase after the glittering spirit riches hanging in the wake of the funeral cavalcade.

Naughton's driver, in his tall black hat, ignores all the fanfare as he sullenly guides the team. He is used to these Chinese processions rumbling slowly around the bend in Mott Street, under the El at Chatham Square, down Park Row, past Pearl Street, past rooming houses and laundries, to join the clamoring traffic thronging over the new Brooklyn Bridge to Flatbush Avenue and then Fulton Street leading out of the City of Brooklyn and into the suburbs, mile after lonely mile lined with vegetable plots and marble yards, the horses clip-clopping in quick promenade.

At Cypress Hills Cemetery, in a bleak corner bordered by the wall of a factory, the party halts and the Irishmen wrestle the heavy coffin onto the struts spanning the open grave. Sticks of incense and decorative red candles are immediately lit, to provide a sweet fragrance to lighten the spirits. When they are spent, they are added to a roll of the dead man's best clothes and burned in a pyre by the grave. The smoke carries the wardrobe to heaven so that the new arrival will be properly attired at his presentation to his Ancestors.

A grass mat is laid for the mourners to step upon as they reverence their friend with three standing bows and three bows kneeling, touching their foreheads to the ground. Each tenders an offering of tea, poured from a delicate porcelain cup directly into the grave. It is one last brotherly drink to go with the feast set out by the Majordomo—a roasted chicken, rice, oranges, and sweets—meant to fortify the traveler on his long journey to the Spirit World. They would normally like to leave the meal at least overnight, but there are those unpleasant white boys hovering nearby to consider. So the meal is hastily gathered up and packed away while the friends and relatives pause for one last look. But before they climb back into the carriages for the trip back to New York, they are each handed a piece of brown rock candy and a penny, tightly wrapped in white paper. The candy is to wash away the bitterness of the occasion. The penny is to buy more candy to keep sweetening the pain. As the carriages leave, the sextons commence lowering the coffin, while the cloud of howling Barbarian adolescents descend on the site, spitefully flinging the artifacts of death into the air.

Just over a year later, in December of 1887, Hor Poa makes his second trip back to the land of his Ancestors, carrying his brother's body with him. It is one of the most important familial obligations a man can have, to see that his brother's soul is properly interred in his native soil. No amount of incense and roasted chickens could put Hor Sek's spirit to rest as long as he lay in this foreign place.

Hor Poa could have saved himself the trouble and expense if he had waited another six months, for in the summer of 1888, the Six Companies in San Francisco decide to use their budget surplus to send home the body of every dead Chinese that remains buried in the United States. A team of specialists is sent to every American city with a substantial Chinese population, where they locate the graves of Chinese dead. In the cemeteries, the men set up a little bamboo shack at gravesides, as they dig up the bodies and scrape or burn away any remaining flesh. They are cheerful, singing as they clean and polish the bones, finally packing them into small tin boxes for bulk shipment back to China, with the name of the deceased painted neatly on the outside. The cost for this service: $6.50, not including postage. Meanwhile, friends and family members at home faithfully burn incense and roast chickens to help the bones' owners make this posthumous terrestrial journey.

But by the time the bone-retrieval team arrives in New York, Hor Poa has already brought Hor Sek home, sailing out of San Francisco in the *Gaelic*. Since he is not a merchant, he does this with a laborer's identity certificate, which documents that he was resident in the United States when the Exclusion Law was passed in 1882, and is thus entitled to leave and return. His papers must be scrupulously in order, however. After all, 1888 will be a year when only twenty-six new Chinese immigrants manage to enter the country, and returnees must withstand ruthless scrutiny of their papers or else they will be deported forever.

Indeed, it would be easier to believe that Hor Poa's later recollections of this trip were fabricated for various reasons to impress future immigration officials, were it not for one factor in the equation—Tom Lee. Tom Lee has no trouble obtaining the necessary documents. He can provide a white man to testify that the good Hor Poa is known to him as a merchant who has never been seen doing manual labor. Or a payment to the right official—there were several to choose from—could result in the appropriate seal. However it is done, the two wandering Hor brothers arrive in their ancestral village late in the 13th year of Emperor Kuang Hsü, a.k.a. 1887. Hor Poa unwinds his queue and proceeds to mourn anew.

This time there is much more noise—gongs are pummeled, firecrackers exploded, hired professional mourners wail and bellow as the bones are finally installed for good in the family tomb just outside the village. The pursuing evil demons don't have a chance.

For eleven months Hor Poa honors his father with his presence, and tries to become reacquainted with his wife and with his adopted daughter, Hor Yee Sum, whom he may have never actually met before. He also has the additional burden of providing for his brother's family, which includes at least one son. Hor Jick Wah's five-roomed house is just not large enough for daughters-in-law, grandchildren, and who knows what other relatives. But since Hor Poa is, by Chinese standards, quite well-to-do, this may be the time he chooses to buy the house next door to his father's. And with all this extra room, a son is just the thing to cap off the family prestige.

So before Hor Poa departs for New York in October, he apparently adopts a boy. Although he will later try to say that this is his natural son, it is a hard claim to uphold. For Hor Mei Wong is born in the seventh month of the year of the Ox. In other words, the child arrives in the world a minimum of eleven months after his father has set sail for San Francisco. Within weeks after the father's return, Congress passes the Scott Act, which revokes all previously issued Chinese identity papers, thus preventing any laborers temporarily out of the country from ever returning to their American lives. It looks as though Hor Poa may never be able to leave the Golden Mountain again.

4

"FAVOR PAPERS"

It is a Chinatown on the verge of taking off that Hor Poa returns to in the fall of 1888. The census indicates that there are around 2,000 Chinese living in New York City (which still consists only of Manhattan Island), of whom a grand total of four are women. Despite the Exclusion Act, they have filtered in from Cuba and Peru. Chinese living in California and in rural American towns, where hostility against them has been growing increasingly shrill, have taken refuge in the great city, where they still form only a tiny fraction of the immigrant population. However many there are, all of them covet merchant status. They can try to get it from their own Family Association, for if offered the right bribe, the "Gentleman" of the clan can try to pull strings and get all sorts of "favor papers" which might include everything from business registrations to fraudulent immigration documents. But the easiest (and safest) way to obtain a Merchant's Certificate is to actually become a merchant, and there are all sorts of businesses in Chinatown in which to invest the money required to obtain that exalted station.

By now these businesses, their facades a riot of bright reds, greens, and golds, and hung with a towering jumble of Chinese signs and silk lanterns bedecked with giant red tassels, have filled Mott Street from Chatham Square to the Transfiguration Catholic Church, and a little beyond. They are edging out the Italians on Pell and almost entirely taking over tiny, crooked Doyers Street, where eight years before there wasn't a single Chinese to be found. The smell of fish and incense hangs in the air.

In Chinatown now there are over thirty groceries, which on Saturday nights are thronged well into the wee hours by Chinese from all over the region, who carefully fill their twists of brown paper with the delicacies that will help them through another grueling week. Many stores are patronized only by natives of the proprietor's home county, the small differences in dialect setting these shops apart almost as much as the more formalized Village Associations nearby. Tuck High has been at 19 Mott Street since 1879. Yuet Sing is on the second floor of 10 Chatham Square, the rear of which has been, for the past few years, the headquarters of the Chinese Charitable Benevolent Association, or CCBA. And Wah Kee's at Number 8 Mott is still one of the most important stores in the neighborhood. It is the telegraph pole outside his store that has become the official community bulletin board. Here, plastered around its circumference, the CCBA can announce judgments they've handed down in local feuds, or the Lün I T'ong can post the percentages they expect to be paid by gambling operations. Hopeful businessmen advertise for partners, laundrymen offer establishments for sale, and Chinese missionaries post notices of new classes in English and the teachings of Jesus Christ. Here also, Tom Lee continues to advertise his elaborate picnic excursions with one proviso: no Christians allowed.

This is the year that the Lün I T'ong, soon to be renamed On Leong, moves itself to new headquarters at 10 Pell Street, while Tom Lee's old two-and-a-half-story wooden house at 18 Mott is torn down along with its neighbor. As his new brick building rises, late this year, the CCBA also erects its new home right next door at Number 16. "Skilled Chinese mechanics, carpenters, masons, and woodworkers," which must include Hor Poa, have been hired to build this, "the first genuine Chinese building in New York."

The CCBA takes its mission of looking after the people seriously, its brick building, three stories tall (it will later be raised to five) with flamboyantly carved wooden balconies that are festooned with lanterns and banners on festival days, housing not only meeting rooms, but a few hospital beds, for Chinese are often turned away from Caucasian institutions and need a place away from home where they can go to die. With a restaurant on the second floor and a "Joss house" on the top floor, the CCBA building accommodates three of the essentials of the Chinese universe—stomach, health, and the hereafter.

The Joss houses are gorgeous things. There are at least three in Chinatown now, Hor Poa probably having helped build the particularly beautiful one in the new Tong headquarters. One climbs a narrow stair to the converted loft space on the top floor, where, amid "colors numbering more than the raindrop ever thought of" sits the elaborately carved and gilded statue of General Quan Kung, which was imported from China at great expense some years before. From the ceiling hang exquisitely painted silk lanterns, as well as long silk banners inscribed with sayings of the great warrior. Before his image are silver vessels holding smoldering incense and ceremonial paper money ready to be burned. Red tapers flare in silver candlesticks, and offerings of tea, in tiny porcelain cups, wait on a red altar-like table draped in a dazzling embroidered fabric. Teak stools interspersed with small square tables, high, like pedestals, and all richly carved and inlaid with marble and mother-of-pearl, line the walls. Delicate lace curtains filter the light streaming through the south-facing windows.

It is a wondrous, alien place, which serves a greater purpose than as a setting for divining the future. It is the principal meeting room for the Tong, and also for the Laundry Association. Here they meticulously regulate the placement of new laundries and set prices, while the Tong's close proximity makes it doubly convenient for them to receive their cut of the action.

The Tong's position on Pell Street also allows them to keep a beady eye on the machinations of their subjects, for this is also the year that Yee Kai Man, who calls himself "Guy Maine," teams up with his closest friends, all prominent Chinese Christians like the Reverend Huie Kin, Jee Man Sing ("Joseph Singleton"), and Dr. Joseph C. Thoms to work with police to try to stamp out gambling in Chinatown. They put on workmen's clothing and "infiltrate" gambling parlors. They lead police raids. They testify in court. And after about a year of these shenanigans, Tom Lee runs them out of Chinatown. From then on they find it more prudent to operate from rather less conspicuous locations.

Joseph Singleton involves himself in politics, Dr. Thoms goes to work with a church in Brooklyn, while Huie Kin carries on at his Presbyterian Chinese Mission on Clinton Place, eventually becoming New York's first ordained Chinese Christian minister in 1895. But in 1889, Guy Maine is tapped to run the "Chinese Guild," the Sunday School of St. Bartholomew's Episcopal Church, a rich, socially prominent parish located way up Madison Avenue at 44th Street. None of the Christian Sunday Schools operates in Chinatown proper at the moment, but that doesn't stop St. Bart's from making its presence felt.

The Guild building at 23 St. Mark's Place—two stops away from Chatham Square on the Third Avenue El (and a respectable distance away from the church itself)—is open every day from nine in the morning to ten at night. In the visiting room, laundrymen and cigar-factory workers are taught popular Victorian parlor games. The library is stocked with Bible tracts, the works of Confucius and Mencius, and a "Syllabic Dictionary" in Chinese and English. In the music room, Guy Maine leads his countrymen in singing hymns, "while also teaching them the meaning of the words they sing." There is a smoking room (in the basement—no opium, please), and even some bedrooms set aside for sick members. Only the large gymnasium is not as popular as the organizers had hoped. ("There is plenty of physical exercise in our place of business," sniffs one tired laundry worker.)

"The characteristics of the people who join [The Chinese Guild] are termed 'queer' by the public at large," Mr. Maine writes in 1890, "When they set foot on this land they are unkindly treated, they are abused, they are stoned in the streets, they are killed in their mines, they are robbed in their shops. Such treatment would make 'queer' any immigrant that comes into this country. It is our aim to gain their confidence first, then religion follows."

St. Bartholomew's not only teaches English, it offers assistance in landlord negotiations, interpreting in courts, drawing up leases and legal documents, translating, finding doctors and lawyers, and "procuring police protection." When there is trouble from "The Master Laundrymen's Association," a group of white steam-laundry owners whose stated goal is to eliminate Chinese competition by encouraging people "not to give any work or trade whatsoever to this heathen race, who are . . . a disgrace to our free institutions," Guy Maine steps in to defend his brethren. During just one year, 1891, he seeks justice in the courts in

217 cases of crimes against Chinese—everything from thirty-six assaults-and-batteries, to eighty-seven laundry windows smashed, to eighty-five instances of "boy annoyance in various ways." His efforts bring about all of nineteen arrest warrants. As for Christianity, "We make it a point in every case to give them a homeopathic dose of religion after each assistance rendered."

Still, to benefit from this assistance, one must become a member, and the St. Bart's Chinese Guild (whose name in Chinese means "The Society for the Protection of the Good") does cost money: $2 to join and $1 per annum thereafter. By 1891, membership has to be cut off at 612 to keep the place from being overwhelmed.

There are eight restaurants in Chinatown now, for while a Chinese laundryman will save his pennies by sleeping in his shop and wearing a hodgepodge of clothing culled from uncollected laundry orders, he will happily pay a week's wages for a blow-out meal to celebrate some event, like New Year's, or a first son's celebration, or winning a poetry tournament, which, even to ordinary Chinese workingmen, is as exciting as his white counterparts would find a World Series baseball match involving the New York Giants or the Brooklyn Bridegrooms.

Hong Ping Lo Restaurant at 16 Mott is on the second floor, like all the other restaurants in the neighborhood. Hanging from the ceiling are big banners, with poetic utterances from classic Chinese philosophers on the subject of eating.

"It is only the superior man who knows what he eats and what he drinks."

"It is here that heroes met and sages drank; why should we abstain?"

Lining the walls, high up, are the little red slips covered with calligraphy that constitute the menu. The requisite silk lanterns and baskets dripping with flowers dangle above high, square tables for four, with stools instead of chairs around them. It is still a bachelor society, not yet given over to tourism, and the great, round family tables of my own childhood are not yet needed. The kitchen, at the rear, is open to the dining room, and people regularly stroll back to inspect the freshness of the pork or select a live duck from one of the cages stacked up against the wall. Different chefs have different specialties, and devotees of the place know that when so-and-so is cooking, they should order the eels, whereas his partner might have a special squab dish that would be a crime to miss. Talented chefs are much sought after, earning perhaps $80 a month, plus room and board. A meal can cost anywhere from 15¢ to $50—but then the former price is for soup, rice, and stir-fried chicken, while the latter buys a forty-course banquet for twelve that takes two days to eat.

The cooking is done in great iron woks set into specially-constructed brick stoves, fed never with coal but with sweet-smelling woods. A roasting pit has a pig turning on a spit, future fish dinners swim in a tank next to the fowl cages, while their fresh-killed brothers hang from the ceiling. Even white people have to admit that a Chinese kitchen is scrupulously clean, although they can't seem to get past the persistent legend that among the meats being prepared for stir-frying are the remains of neighborhood puppies and stray cats.

Another luxury Chinatown residents indulge in is a good barber, of which there are six in 1888. Customers expect to spend about an hour on the barber's stool, where a haircut and a shave are the least of the services rendered. The Chinese barber provides a total body experience, starting with a careful washing before the shaving starts (sans soap), first high on the forehead moving the hairline way back to emphasize the long queue behind, followed by the entire face—chin, cheeks, neck, even eyelids, which are carefully scraped clean of any stray hair or down.

Then it is on to the ears, with the barber laying the customer's head in his lap as he works with a whole array of specialized tools to cleanse them of wax, and then to shave the insides of them too. Likewise the nose has a fine, sharp razor applied to take care of any unsightly growths in the nostrils. Then the whole face and neck are washed again with fine oils and wrapped in hot towels.

A sip of tea, and the massage starts, the barber tugging at the head, squeezing the shoulders, pummeling on the back, adjusting the spine like a chiropractor. The arms and neck are rubbed, kneaded really, until at last the fingers and toes are each individually pulled until they crack. The body tingles, the skin glows, and the treatment is over. It costs 75 cents. On Sundays, the laundryman's day off, and Mondays, when the shopkeepers can take a breather, the lines outside the barbershops trail out into the street. If the itinerant dentist is in town, one can then go and have that painful tooth pulled—which the dentist does just with his fingers.

On other fronts, Wong Chin Foo says that, "there are now two tailor shops, five cigar stores, three hundred sailors, four thieves, twenty-five highbinders [Tong thugs], eight doctors, sixteen fortune-tellers, one professional spiritualist, and one solitary drunkard" in Chinatown today, although he may be exaggerating about the drunkard.

There is one person he has missed, however. Hong Yen Chang, alumnus of Yale College and Columbia Law School, has become the first Chinese admitted to the New York State Bar. Although he had passed all the examinations, he was turned down on his first attempt in 1887 by Judge Van Brunt, who gave no reason other than "the Court's discretion." So the State Legislature in 1887 passed a special measure which allowed Hong to reapply, and this year he is accepted. An African-American named William M. Randolph ("his face is of a bright mulatto color, but his hair is kinky") is admitted at the same time, and when he and Hong step forward to receive their parchments, the roomful of white students breaks into applause.

These lawyers will soon be needed, it seems. "It is a year of anxiety and persecution," writes Guy Maine, as members of the Chinese Guild grow discouraged and give up their studies. In Chinatown, laborers are scrambling to buy merchant status. An old man doggedly seeks to be arrested for some reason. A fearful and disheveled laundryman wanders the streets in a distracted search for the Chinese Consul. Gripped tightly in his hands are two stolen taxi licenses that he seems to think will protect him from his oppressors. He is finally locked in a padded cell when it becomes apparent that in his derangement he may try to kill himself.

The cause of all this dismay is the hated Geary Chinese Exclusion and Registration Act, passed by Congress in May of 1892. Everyone had expected the 1882 Exclusion law, originally only supposed to last ten years, to be extended, especially with people like Samuel Gompers, as head of the American Federation of Labor saying things like "The racial differences between American whites and Asiatics [will] never be overcome. The superior whites [have] to exclude the inferior Asiatics, by law, or if necessary by force of arms."

But instead of merely prolonging it, Representative Thomas Geary of California has pushed through draconian rules that would make Exclusion even more oppressive than before. Now Chinese laborers will face stiff penalties unless they are carrying special identity papers, a sort of internal passport, and if they leave the country intending to return, they may do so only if they have left substantial financial commitments or close relatives behind. It is strikingly similar to the rules the future Soviet Union will apply during the Brezhnev era. Some could compare it to the South African pass laws of the 1950s.

So, by May of 1893, every Chinese laborer in the United States will be required to pay a fee for the privilege of filling out a stack of forms stating, among other things, that he legally entered the country before 1892, and then provide two white men who will testify before the Collector of Internal Revenue to that fact. Two photographs (supplied at the applicant's own expense) are then attached to the resulting document, despite the old whine that photographs are useless because all Chinese look alike. "There is as wide a variance in the physiognomies of Chinamen," huffs New York's Internal Revenue Collector, General Michael Kerwin, "as there is in the features of any strongly marked race. Except in their lack of facial hirsute adornment."

These identity documents don't allow greater freedom of travel or any other prerogatives. They must simply be carried at all times to be shown upon demand as evidence that the bearer is not one of the suspected thousands being smuggled over the borders every year. Any Chinese laborer found without one will summarily be sent to prison for a year without trial, and deported without due process. Once again, the Chinese are denied the basic rights given to any immigrant from any other country in the world.

Tom Lee gives a reporter his assessment of Geary:

"[The Chinese] are most heartily in favor of it," the Tong leader says, smiling through his whiskers, "True, it prevents many of their relatives and friends from coming to this country; but they have long ago gotten over the bitterness of that, and they profoundly appreciate the protection it gives them and the right which is bestowed upon each one of them to uninterrupted and peaceful residence in the United States."

He seems to be alone in his thinking.

The Chinese community is not quite as helpless as it was in 1882, and quickly mobilizes what resources it has to protest Geary. Chinese leaders such as Dr. Joseph Thoms, Thomas Singleton, and Wong Chin Foo form a political alliance called the Chinese Civil Rights League, and thunder against the Act in speeches at Cooper Union. They join forces with the Six Companies of San Francisco to convince the nation's 100,000 Chinese to boycott the registration. The New York Chamber of Commerce roundly condemns the Geary Act as "unjust, unwise, and inexpedient." Forty-three Episcopal bishops declare it "in violation of the most venerable traditions of our Government." Even General Kerwin seems to be dragging his feet about the law he is charged to enforce. He talks at length about "the remarkable honesty of the Chinese" and their "eagerness to obey the law" while at the same time muttering that he can't yet take any action because he doesn't have the proper forms. Meanwhile in California the Chinese servants of Representative Thomas Geary quit en masse, leaving the Congressman's family to cook their own food.

As the May 5, 1893, deadline for registration approaches, the boycott is proving remarkably effective. In Greater New York, only one Chinese has come forward to register, but he was turned away because he hadn't supplied the required white witnesses. Newspapers start calculating how much it will cost to deport the entire Chinese population of the United States (at $35 a head, excluding rail fares); there are predictions that Chinese warships will attack San Francisco; and a handful of laundry workers volunteer to be arrested for not registering, in order to test the constitutionality of the law. The arrests occur. Their case is argued, and the Supreme Court upholds the validity of Geary. When Congress extends the deadline for registering, Chinese laborers reluctantly line up to fill out the forms.

Meanwhile, my Great-Grandfather neatly sidesteps the whole issue by following the lead of many of his neighbors. Late in 1893 he invests $200 in a two-year-old grocery-import business called Quong Yuen Shing (Great and Unique Prosperity) & Co. at Number 5 Mott Street, thus officially becoming a "merchant." An individual store might have dozens of merchant-partners (Quong Yuen Shing has seventy-four). Even Chu Fong, the famous actor who has just opened a new, permanent Chinese Opera house at 5 Doyers, has qualified as a merchant by owning operating shares of the theater. He also has dozens of "partners," including some of his actor-employees, who would otherwise be known as laborers. Even though all these merchants are hoping for (but rarely receiving) regular dividends, the driving motivation behind it all is that merchants are exempt from having to register under the Geary rules.

For now Hor Poa is secure—although like many of his fellow merchants, he may register as a laborer also, just to be on the safe side.

"A merchant is a person engaged in buying and selling merchandise, at a fixed place of business, which business is conducted in his name, and who, during the time he claims to be engaged as a merchant, does not engage in the performance of any manual labor, except such as is necessary in the conduct of his business as such merchant." Thus Representative Thomas Geary defines what Great-Grandfather claims to be from this time on, although in truth Hor Poa stretches the definition just a bit. He does the carpentry at Quong Yuen Shing as well as at other budding mercantile enterprises throughout Chinatown, making money to be sure, but putting himself at risk if some spiteful white person should testify to the immigration officials that he has been seen working with his hands.

Unfortunately, the man appointed by President Cleveland to the newly-created post of "Chinese Inspector" for New York is a humorless, racist former Confederate Army colonel by the name of J. Thomas Scharf. Adept at inventing nefarious conspiracies when he can't find any other evidence to support them, Colonel Scharf works under the basic assumption not only that most of the "little brownies" (as he is wont to call Chinese) are in this country illegally, but that their presence is due to the corruption and incompetence of the deputy inspectors who work for him. This does not make him popular around the office.

He bombards his immediate superior, New York's Collector of Customs James T. Kilbreth, with accusations that these deputy inspectors are accepting bribes from Chinese laundrymen, from the Tong, even from the Canadian-Pacific Railroad (which he supposes is trying to avoid the cost of sending deportees back to China). When Kilbreth doesn't respond, Scharf dispatches fat packets of complaints to the Secretary of the Treasury in Washington, who merely routes them back to Kilbreth's office again.

When he's not trying to get his co-workers fired, Scharf is tearing around his district, arresting Chinese, their lawyers, or anyone else whom he fantasizes is trafficking in illegal immigrants. "Shut up! Get out of my way, you damned Chinaman, or I'll throw you overboard!" he is quoted as saying in a typical exchange on the deck of an arriving ship. In one spectacular stunt, he has every Chinese on a train in which he is riding—fifty-two in all, including one terrified woman—arrested when they arrive at Grand Central Terminal. All will eventually be released, although the young woman, who is the newly-arrived bride of one of the men, will be kept for days on the groundless suspicion that she is a prostitute. It is a commonly held belief among people like J. Thomas Scharf that all Chinese women are prostitutes.

Meanwhile, at the police station, he shouts questions like "Where is City Hall?" at the bewildered crowd in an attempt to determine if they are, in fact, New York residents. "Why don't you, John and Lee over there, start a university and learn these fellows to talk English?" he then bellows at a group of English-speaking Chinese trying to help with interpreting.

"We might teach them. Can't 'learn' them," comes the sardonic reply. It is unfortunate that the Colonel doesn't have a sense of humor. It is also unfortunate that he doesn't have his own staff interpreter with him, but the man he originally hired for the job, a Chinese named Worry S. Charles, was soon arrested for trying to extort money from prospective immigrants. It seems that not only did this man work for the Chinese Inspector's office, he was also a valued employee of some of the shadiest Tong bullies in Chinatown.

Worry Charles will not be the only person whose character Scharf disastrously misjudges, however. When he targets the spotless Chinese Christian leader and Government interpreter Joseph Singleton, publicly accusing him of being the head of an immigrant-smuggling ring, the gentleman has the Colonel arrested, bringing a libel suit against him for $10,000. Never having been on that side of the iron bars before, Scharf appeals to his Customs House co-workers to help him raise the $500 bail. They happily decline. It is left to three Treasury Department officials to pool their money to win Scharf's release—on condition that they remain anonymous. As for the lawsuit, "the inspector got down on his knees and begged off.

"I do not think that Mr. Scharf means any harm," sighs Collector Kilbreth for the umpteenth time, "He is merely irresponsible, and utterly lacking in judgement and discretion . . . No one who knows Mr. Scharf would attach any importance to any charge that he makes." Still, despite Kilbreth's best efforts, the federally appointed Chinese Inspector remains in office for the remainder of President Cleveland's term, and beyond.

Hor Poa remains unmolested, however, and in the first month of the twentieth year of Kuang Hsü (a.k.a. March, 1894), and armed with a certificate identifying him as "Ho Pook, a person other than a laborer," he returns to China. This time, instead of sailing out of San Francisco, he follows the new trend of taking the train across Canada and sailing out of Vancouver. The Canadian-Pacific steamship and railroad line offers a package deal that the American companies can't beat, about $110 each way, complete. From 1891 onward, this becomes the preferred way for East Coast Chinese to go home.

So now, about once every three weeks, trains full of China-bound passengers leave Grand Central and crawl up the banks of the Hudson, past Lake Champlain, to arrive after twelve hours at some tiny border-crossing town—Malone or Ogdensburg in New York, St. Albans or, on this particular trip, Richford, Vermont. There they disembark to be grilled by a Deputy Chinese Inspector—one of those whom J. Thomas Scharf is so fond of debunking in the press. The Deputies check the Chinese travelers' documents and then, for those declaring that they wish to return, subject them to a battery of questions: Where are you employed? For how long? How much money do you have invested, and where? Are you married? Do you have children? Parents? Siblings? Have you been back to China before? When? From which port? With a merchant or a labor certificate? Can you show us documentation? They are asked to describe their home villages and New York businesses, down to minute descriptions of their houses and the names of their neighbors. They must describe their wedding ceremonies, define their wives' feet (bound, natural, or "released"), and respond to anything else that might come into the Deputy's head. The answers are carefully filed away for later use, and Hor Poa proceeds on to Montreal, to Vancouver, and then to the *Empress of India* for home.

Great-Grandfather is now forty-four years old, and has a very big face in tiny Hor Lup Chui. He has been married for fifteen years, out of which he may have spent two with his wife, who has been living her silent, lonely, servile existence in Hor Jick Wah's house along with her adopted son and daughter. (The latter may by now have been sold off in marriage.)

It can't have been a good life for Moy She. The adopted son, Hor Mei Wong, does give her some face, but not as much as if he were the product of her own body. Hopefully, her husband has provided money for servants so that the burden of caring for the old man is not too great. But what might have been a joyous reception for her husband is marred by the death of her own father in Chung On village, fifteen *li* across the fields. Perhaps it is because she is in mourning, which if she were a man would mean that she couldn't have sexual relations for a year, that prompts Great-Grandfather to take another wife. More likely it is that the rich returnee from the Golden Mountain is beset by old ladies offering their pretty granddaughters in marriage. After all, Moy She is old—she's nearing forty.

In any event, Hor Poa adds insult to injury by taking Yau She as his Number Two wife and installing her in Hor Jick Wah's household. About her I know absolutely nothing—except that she also fails to give birth to a living child. So Hor Poa adopts a son for her as well—Hor Mei Fun, Mei being a name that all the boys in this generation—Hor Poa's China-born sons—will have. He also adds a house for her to the compound, and leaving a large framed photograph of himself behind to remind his family what he looks like, Hor Poa is soon off to New York once again. Meanwhile, Moy She continues to wither on her branch. She will never see her husband again.

Canadian-Pacific takes him back across an ocean and a continent. For first-time travelers, it is a confusing, frightening trip. A relative related the sensations of this journey to me once. He was ten years old, and being sent to meet his father in New York. The country seemed huge and empty. Hour after hour passed of desolate mountain or deserted prairie. And then, a miracle. There in the middle of wilderness were Chinese men on horseback, racing alongside the train. They rode close, they waved. The boy waved back, smiling, feeling a little better to see that there were some of his own kind in this Barbarian land. It was only later that he learned who these mysterious Chinese horsemen were. They were called—Indians.

Hor Poa's train takes him back to tiny Richford, Vermont. It is a bucolic place, perched astride the rushing Missisquoi River amid the verdant green hills that give Vermont its name. The travelers from Canada arrive at the little depot on the north side of the Missisquoi, where their papers are checked by Customs officials before they are sent on to Boston. If they are going to New York or points south, however, they must trudge over the little bridge and past the mill, past the pristine white Congregational church and the imposing, mansard-roofed mansions of the principal citizens, to the other little depot on the south side of the Missisquoi to pick up another train to St. Albans City and south. That is, assuming they are white, or black, or Japanese.

If they are Chinese, however, they are taken next door to the Inspection Station, which looks like a one-room schoolhouse, and raked over the coals. New arrivals have the most trouble. They must somehow convince Deputy Inspector Halstead that they have the right to enter the U.S., by virtue of being merchants, students, diplomats, or transients. Telegrams are sent back and forth to New York and Boston— "Chinaman Wong Feng Sang claims to be a merchant with Wing Wo Chung & Co. of 34 Pell Street. Please investigate,"—and the Customs office in New York will dispatch an agent to see if it's true. Or the applicant will claim to be the son of a bona-fide merchant, resident in New York, who then must be found and interviewed.

For a returning Chinese, all that mountain of paperwork left behind on departure is dragged out, and they are grilled all over again. *How* many children? Why did you say *three* last time, but now you say *two?* You first came to the United States in 1873? Didn't you say *1879* before? Why do you say there are *thirty* houses in your home village when you said *fifty* a year ago? How much money do you have invested? What is the address of your New York business? What are the names of the white people who know you? And back to one very, very important point—why do you say the village well is in the *tail* whereas last time you said it was in the *head?* Isn't it true that you are *lying?*

Those who survive this gauntlet are sent on their way. Those who trip up on some point are jailed, often for weeks, pending further investigation. In Richford or St. Albans there could be dozens of Chinese locked up at any given time; in Malone, hundreds, stuffed into the county jail with common criminals behind the courthouse. And those who fail all the tests and appeals are finally deported back to China at Canadian-Pacific expense. But not to worry. After all, the company had collected a bond from each Chinese passenger before embarkation, to pay for just such an eventuality.

Hor Poa has been a resident of the United States for twenty-two years. He speaks tolerably good English, is respected, well-to-do, and a leader in his community. He is also treated like a leper at every turn. It is after the humiliating experience of this trip to and from China that he decides to make a drastic change.

When he gets back to New York, Great-Grandfather cuts off his queue. From now on there is no going back.

5

.

THE BELLE
OF
CHINATOWN

His now-short graying hair is parted on the side. He goes to Louis Levy's—they specialize in small sizes—and buys a business suit, with a vest, a white shirt, a stiff wing collar, and a silk necktie. He is remarkably handsome in his new getup, distinguished even, his regular features having a distinctly Caucasian cast. But most important, Hor Poa, with his two wives and three children 10,000 miles away, is sick and tired of enforced bachelorhood. Within a year of his return to New York, he marries again.

I think my great-grandmother is mentioned in an 1898 book called *New York's Chinatown* by Louis J. Beck, a newspaper reporter whose workmanlike prose exhibits all of the breathless revulsion so common among uptown white residents at this time. He describes a beautiful teenaged girl living at 19 Mott Street as "the Belle of Chinatown." I like that, because I know for a fact that Gon She, my great-grandmother, lived at 19 Mott before she got married. She was just sixteen years old, and judging from her photograph she was a classic, moon-faced Chinese beauty, one of the forty or so Chinese women in New York, of whom perhaps five were unmarried and eligible.

Louis Beck also writes that a year or so previously, a Chinatown merchant paid $1,200 for the privilege of marrying her. That fits too, for

I know for a fact that when my merchant-Great-Grandfather married Gon She in 1896, the absolute minimum bride-price for a Chinese woman in New York would have been $800, and for one as young and pretty as my great-grandmother, the price would have been considerably higher.

But that's not all Louis Beck has to say.

He also insists that this particular Belle of Chinatown was a prostitute.

Prostitute? Oh dear. Perhaps I should say *slave.* No, that's not any better. Concubine? No. Number Three Wife? Well, yes, but . . . It is so frustrating trying to pin down my great-grandmother's origins exactly. No one in the family seems to know anything much about her, and any source written by a white person of this period is just hopeless. If it is learned that a man has paid a bride-price for a woman, she immediately becomes a "slave" or a "prostitute." A non-Judeo-Christian wedding is viewed with grave suspicion, and the fact that the groom has usually never even conversed with the bride before the event complicates matters further in those highly censorious Victorian minds. Of course, it also doesn't help matters any when it is known that a man has two or three wives simultaneously.

There certainly were Chinese women who had been forced into, well, compromising positions in America. Hakka women—those from the northern clans who had settled in Kuang Tung in the 18th century— were sometimes kidnapped by Chinese pirates and sold to the Triads, who then resold them in the Chinese expatriate, bachelor communities of south Asia and California. Poor Chinese peasant-farmers would sell unwanted daughters to other families—like Hor Poa's—to be raised as minor daughters or servants. "Sell," of course, is the American word. "Adopted" would be how the Chinese would have thought of it. These girls would, in turn, be "sold" into marriage when they reached the appropriate age, as opposed to the European custom of bribing desirable sons-in-law with fat dowries of cash or land. At any rate, raising a daughter was an investment with an expected return profit. Sad to us today, but normal in Chinese society.

Frequently, boatloads of these women might be married off to the highest bidder in places like San Francisco or Vancouver. It often wasn't terribly different from Scandinavian farmers in the Midwest ordering mail-order brides from Norway, or frontiersmen importing a wagon-train-load of ladies for the purposes of matrimony.

Unfortunately, however, many of these women often *were* forced to work as prostitutes, especially in California, where squalid brothels were kept full of small-footed captives to serve the pleasure of tens of thousands of lonely Chinese "bachelors." Sometimes these prostitutes had been legitimate wives of Chinese Californians and had been kidnapped away from their husbands, so desperate were men for feminine companionship. After all, Chinese men in America outnumbered Chinese women some two hundred to one.

After her "useful" working life was exhausted, such a woman might be resold as a wife, or maybe just a personal sex slave, to a former customer. One such young woman was brought by her captor, an On Leong member, from Oregon to 17 Mott Street, where she was forced to earn money in a manner which she later declined to specify. Soon, however, she fell in love with the grocer next door at Number 19, who eagerly arranged to pay her posted bride-price of $900. My Great-Grandfather was in on this deal, and went with the couple over to On Leong headquarters to officially witness the transaction—and see that Tom Lee got his cut. Unfortunately, when the woman married her new husband at City Hall her original captor had her arrested for bigamy. The lady ended up in the Tombs prison, trying to explain her plight to a judge.

"Normal" as it may have been, all this was just more evidence of the vulnerable roles Chinese women were born into. At home they accepted their lot, not seeing any possibility of change. Once on the Golden Mountain, however, some began to sense that they might finally have the means to change their destinies, at least a little.

In San Francisco, three captive young women managed to dictate a letter to the police, "We are three poor girls, kept by an old man . . . and an old woman . . . as slaves to make money for them by prostitution," it began. "Will the authorities of this city aid us, poor victims, to escape this disgraceful life? We will be grateful." One of the three then managed to get away on her own and find her way to City Hall, where officials sent her to Dr. Gibson's Christian mission. It is not clear how much her lot was improved, however, as all the good Doctor did was immediately marry her off to a Chinese Christian who attended his school. From Dr. Gibson's point of view, the lady's virtue was saved. No one seems to have asked her opinion.

In New York in 1890, a Chinese woman actually *sued* the man to whom she had been sold in marriage against her will. When the Court suggested another Chinese husband, supposedly more to her liking, she vehemently declined. For the time being, she would live as a single woman with the white lady Sunday School teacher who had snatched her from his clutches. The would-be husband was fined $2,500.

One cannot deny that there were at least a few Chinese prostitutes in Chinatown by the later 1890s, but very few. Even Louis Beck had to admit that while there were forty Chinese "women of respectable families" there were only three "slaves and prostitutes." These the missionary ladies were fond of rescuing, teaching them to say the Lord's Prayer and ABC's by rote, after which they seemed to think that their duty was done.

Still, the vast majority of "working girls" in Chinatown would always be white; many of them were kept by Chinese pimps—like Tom Lee who received $3 a week from each of the women under his "protection." Most of these were opium- or alcohol-addicted, renting their bodies for a dollar or two per customer to support a habit born out of desperate poverty. They would hang out in places like McNally's in Chatham Square, where women would "pull their clothes up to their knees, whirl around, and expose their limbs using vulgar and profane talk." The brothel at 11 Mott Street had nothing but white girls for sex, but for a nominal fee the madam would get a Chinese girl to come in and take off her clothes, so that the johns could "see what a Chinese woman looked like." But even white women who were the bona-fide wives of Chinese men living in Chinatown were often assumed to be prostitutes, and missionary ladies were always trying to get these women away. It was common for them to express open-mouthed astonishment when the wives opted to stay with their "heathen" husbands.

Gon She was not my only relative accused of being something unsavory. Hor Poa's cousin Hor Yin raised a huge commotion at the Chinese Inspector's office when he tried to bring Tso She, his wife of sixteen years (whom he hadn't seen in fourteen) and their adolescent daughter from China. He had made sure that the ladies traveled in style, in cabin class, well above the hoi polloi on the *Empress of Japan* to Vancouver. They managed, just barely, to survive the inquisition at Richford, even though Tso She was obviously flustered: "If your father and mother were dead at the time of your marriage, who arranged for your marriage to your husband? What was her name? Where did she live? Was it before or after dark that you first saw each other on the day of your marriage? Can you name the persons who were present at your wedding? Can't you remember *any* of them? Was there *anybody* present at your wedding? How do you reconcile these statements?"

The trouble was that someone in the Inspector's office had heard a rumor that this thirty-four-year-old woman and her child were "bought" in Hong Kong for $500. But it is rather more likely that Hor Yin just sent over his agent with money for traveling expenses and a few personal luxuries not obtainable in New York. Men buying sex slaves did not usually include thirty-four-year-olds in the package, and then give them cabin-class steamship tickets to boot.

But Deputy Chinese Inspectors flew into a blizzard of activity, spending days in trains tracking a single laundryman to a tiny town in Pennsylvania on the suspicion that he was the source of the gossip. Once found, they put him on the grill.

> *Q. Is it not a fact that you told Chin Willie that Louis Fong bought the women in China for $500 and brought them here?*
>
> *A. That is all a lie! I did not tell him that at all! Some people are always trying to get others into trouble by telling lies!*
>
> *Q. Do you know Hor Yin, one of the owners of the 'Oriental Restaurant' in New York City?*
>
> *A. I do not know him.*
>
> *Q. What are the names of the two women who came on the same ship with you, and were admitted at Richford?*
>
> *A. I do not know their names.*
>
> *Q. Is it not a fact they are slave women, that a Chinaman by the name of Hore Lew Sang, alias Hor Yin, purchased them in China and brought them here?*
>
> *A. I do not know anything about that.*
>
> *Q. Can you give me the name of a Chinaman or anyone, who knows anything about the women?*
>
> *A. I do not know anyone who knows about them!*
>
> *Q. Are you sure of this?*

White witnesses were called who cast into doubt the merchant status of Hor Yin, who, while being a partner in an import business, seemingly worked elsewhere—with his hands: "Wallace states that he . . . went to the restaurant in company with Stenographer Horton and saw [Hor Yin] there assisting in the cleaning of the restaurant. From the foregoing I believe it is clearly established that the applicant does not come within the meaning of the term 'merchant' as defined by the regulations."

Hor Yin, Tso She, and their daughter are all arrested on charges ranging from perjury to keeping a woman for immoral purposes. They are jailed in lieu of $3,000 bail—several years' salary for the average worker. Two years go by before Inspector Sisson reports to Washington that he has been "unable to secure any evidence tending to show that the alleged relationship does not exist." The family is finally released after Hor Yin pays a fine. By now his daughter is of marriageable age herself.

So where does this all leave me with Gon She? Years later she will tell the Chinese Inspector that she came to this country as a three-year-old with her parents in 1883. But that year was the first year of Exclusion, and immigration was very difficult, although as her alleged father, Hom Mon Wai, was a merchant, it is possible that they were among the few hundred that made it through. Still, it would have been extremely unusual for a merchant to emigrate with his wife and *daughter*. "I remember the ship in Hong Kong," one woman would say, years later, "I was the only Chinese girl. A girl! All the old-timers . . . said my father was a stupid man. Whoever want a daughter to come to the United States? They always bring sons. They don't bring daughters!" Of course, Hor Yin did bring over a wife and daughter some twenty years later, so . . .

Whatever their relationship, in 1894 Hom Mon Wai and company arrived in New York, where Hom was a partner with the Choy Chong Wo store at 19A Mott Street. They lived upstairs in that building, which seemed to have an unusual number of Chinese women residing there—four in 1890, three of whom were teenagers, among twelve adult Chinese men and some children. It is not clear from the records if they were married. But even Louis Beck doesn't go so far as to call Number 19 a brothel (as he does with several other Mott Street addresses) and anyway, by his time, even the rich Wah Kee dwelt there with his Caucasian wife, children, and servants, and Wah Kee was stolid respectability itself.

So, did Hom Mon Wai buy an adolescent girl and bring her to New York in the hopes of selling her? And why does Louis Beck use—*that word*—in connection with that address? Is Hom Mon Wai, in fact, my great-great-grandfather?

The truth is in the names. Hom Mon Wai is not my great-great-grandfather for one inescapable reason. If he was, then my great-grand-mother's married name would be Hom She. What Gon She most likely was was a *moi ji*, or indentured servant, which Louis Beck would most certainly define as "slave" or "prostitute." She was indeed sold as a very young girl to a merchant of the Hom family who was emigrating to America, but not to earn her master money through prostitution. For *moi ji* were raised to serve in a more domestic role, usually as a maid to the lady of the house. They were not paid, but it was understood that their masters would care for them and raise them and see that they found a husband. A *moi ji* was often like a daughter, frequently so much so that outsiders didn't realize that she wasn't a blood relation. When Gon She told the Chinese Inspector that Hom Mon Wai was her father, she was being perfectly truthful. He was, in fact, the only father she had ever known.

Hor Poa and Gon She have a traditional Chinese wedding, New York style, which means four red gowns worn by the bride during four different sections of the massive wedding banquet held at some Mott Street restaurant. The Tong is there in force with their womenfolk—sitting separately, of course—and there are the rounds and rounds of increasingly woozy toasts, accompanied by the requisite off-color remarks, before Hor Poa takes his prize home. By all accounts, he is happy with his lot, and Gon She probably feels that she could have done a lot worse.

Immediately after the ceremony, Hom Mon Wai takes his $1,200 and returns to China for good.

The forty-six-year-old groom and his sixteen-year-old bride don't waste any time. Scarcely a year later, in 1897, Gon She gives birth to a son, my grandfather. He is born with the aid of a midwife, like all other Chinese children, at their apartment in 21 Mott. Number 21 is home to some fifty Italians compared to only twenty-five Chinese, but it is considered a fairly prestigious place to live. It is an "old-law" tenement, with long, narrow flats, the darkness of their interiors relieved by only the tiniest of air shafts. Still, for 1897 it isn't bad, with gas lighting, and in around 1900, new housing codes will dictate that a bathtub be installed in every kitchen, and a real flushing toilet on every floor.

Of course, the rumor is that the Italian neighbors utterly refuse to use any hallway toilet that a Chinese family might share. They prefer to visit one of the old leftover backyard privies, for it is common knowledge (among them) that Chinese are notorious carriers of syphilis and leprosy. At the same time, it is also said that they scoff at the Asians' liberal use of the kitchen bathtubs, as it is also common knowledge (among them) that full-body bathing is grossly unhealthy.

Living in a real apartment is probably a step up for Hor Poa, as he has probably been staying in a tiny cubicle at the dormitory in Tong headquarters since his arrival in New York. Most of the single men in Chinatown live in dormitories or *gon see fong,* usually supplied by their family associations. Dozens of Chins, or Lees, or Wongs will live crowded together in converted loft spaces, or several adjoining tenement flats, or in rows of bunks in the back room of some family-owned grocery. They share expenses and responsibilities for such essentials as the family shrine and the maintenance of the Kitchen God. The sum total of each man's worldly goods is kept in a canvas sack under the bed. When someone becomes mortally ill, he is often made to leave so that his death won't bring bad luck upon his roommates.

But then at the other extreme would be the residence of Mr. Chu Fong, the owner of the Chinese Opera House, said to be the wealthiest man in Chinatown. He holds court at his luxurious apartment at Number 34 Mott, dressed in the sumptuous silks of a gentleman of leisure, and surrounded by obedient wife, children, and servants. His is the Victorian fantasy of the Chinese home, full of carved ebony and satin brocade. It is often cited in the press as "ideal of what an American domestic establishment should be in all its appointments."

September 7 is the date that Grandfather's birth is officially registered with the city ("Hoeh—male") but for the rest of his life, his birthday will always be observed on September 28. You see, if one advertises the actual date of one's birth too loudly, a demon could come by on that day and snatch you away. Better to keep him off balance by claiming another date. But then, birthdays aren't really celebrated anyway, which accounts for why so many people aren't sure how old they are.

By Chinese standards, this boy baby may not be considered Hor Poa's first son, but nevertheless he receives all the lavish, traditional First Son attentions that the father can afford. For a month, Chinatown is buzzing with news of the birth, for Chinese children are still somewhat rare, and a first son is thought of as a special blessing. He doesn't make his official appearance, however, until one lunar month after birth, when he is brought forth at a great First Son's banquet held in the best restaurant the family can afford. It is a grand party, which features such delicacies as bright red hard-boiled eggs, to assure prosperity, and long-life noodles, which are wound around and around chopsticks before eating, because to break one might bring bad luck to the birthday boy.

A First Son's Banquet was one of those rare social occasions where it was proper for Chinese women to appear, although for the trip from 21 Mott to even the nearest restaurant, directly across the street, a closed carriage is still a strict necessity for propriety's sake. Gon She sits with the other ladies at a table of their own, while at a propitious moment, Hor Poa takes the baby from her to present him to the male guests.

Naturally the baby is dressed in red. Normally his head would have just been shaved for the first time, leaving a patch for the beginning of the queue, which would be wound in red silk. But since Hor Poa doesn't have a queue, his son won't have one either. He does, however, wear the traditional First Son's "crown," a red skullcap topped by a gold ornament in the shape of the Genius of Longevity. As the baby is carried through the room, the guests all stick lucky red envelopes full of money into his clothes, for while it is good luck to give children pennies and nickels, it is especially so to grace a newborn boy with silver. The father then lifts up the baby, now jingling with coin, and for the first time declares his name—Hor Ting Pun. He hasn't been named until this time, again to fool those (apparently very stupid) demons. Ting is the generational name that all of Hor Poa's American-born sons will carry.

So, Hor Ting Pun was born in America in America's greatest city. Even Chinese Inspector J. Thomas Scharf won't make trouble for him, as one month after the baby's birth he is forced—kicking and screaming—to resign. The trouble is, despite the fact that everyone else born in the United States is supposed to be a citizen automatically, Scharf's former superiors in Washington don't consider Hor Ting Pun to be one— because his parents are Chinese. It will take a special Act of Congress in 1898 to grant citizenship to American-born children of Chinese heritage. Even Congress senses that there are limits.

Meanwhile, back in China, old Hor Jick Wah has died. For Hor Poa, this should dictate a lengthy mourning period which, among other things, forbids sexual relations. But it also means that at the age of forty-three Moy She finally has some measure of control over her own situation for the first time in her life. Indeed, as the Number One wife of a rich overseas Chinese she presides over an enviable domain consisting of a two- or three-house compound, with sons, a daughter, in-laws, servants, and even a junior wife to boss around. With money sent to her by her husband, she is duty-bound to finance projects to enhance the village—a new school, a brick wall replacing the old one of bamboo, perhaps an elaborate new shrine dedicated to the Hor Family Ancestors. She is honored and respected at last; life is as good as it is going to get for her. Two years later, Moy She is dead.

Informed by letter, Hor Poa doesn't mention the event to anyone, but then it is considered very bad manners for a gentleman to discuss his family's females in polite company. However, when forced to bring it up during an interview in the Chinese Inspector's office a few years later, he reveals that he is even unsure of the month of his wife's demise. What could one expect? He never really knew her.

In that same year, 1900, Gon She will give birth to a daughter, to be named Yee Yut. There will be no party for her.

As a Chinese boy-child, Grandfather led a charmed life. Everywhere he went he was viewed as a lucky charm, and thus plied with pennies and sweet buns by the proprietors of restaurants and shops. Even his little sister would be petted and fawned over as she took her walks with her father, for there were at most 150 children out of the perhaps 7,000 "Celestials" in the five newly created boroughs of New York City in 1900—a year in which 142 women were also counted. As toddlers these two wore brilliantly-colored padded clothing in cold weather, layer upon layer, until they looked like little beach balls waddling down the sidewalk.

Sometimes their father would drop them off at the new Christian Kindergarten at 11 1/2 Mott, leaving Gon She alone at home to tend the Ancestor's Shrine and tackle the endless round of piece-work that the garment-factory bosses brought her every day. Chinese women were trained from childhood in embroidery and other needlework, and the bosses were only too happy to exploit this talent. Despite having an attentive husband all to herself, she was still only the Number Three Wife, and as such, her own children would have called her "Stepmother," as a way of deferring to the distant, and now departed, Moy She. At any rate, no one would ever have used her name. She was the Wife of Hor Poa or the Mother of Hor Pun. Her world now consisted of whatever view was framed by her window as she tediously plied her needle and waited for her husband to bring home some restaurant food for dinner. As a dutiful wife she would serve her husband first, only eating after he had had his fill.

As for Yee Yut, there is a little two-year-old girl described in a newspaper story about the Kindergarten, who could be her. "[She] is about as big as a good-sized doll," the reporter writes, "Wear[ing] lavender trousers that come down over her little white shoes, and . . . trimmed with broad bands of black and white at the bottom. The upper part of her roly-poly person is clothed in a loose shirt of brightest green. Over this is tied a short, bright pink bib apron, a pocket in which contains [her] playthings, including a large pipe of her father's and other impediments of travel. On her head is a soft silk cap, shaped something like Napoleon's, with the flat front edge, covered with Chinese embroidery, coming down to her eyes. In this ensemble, with her perfectly stolid little almond-eyed face, with scarcely any nose, and with her mouth round and puckered like a small cherry, [she] is altogether ravishing." Whoever this little girl may be, she is also reported as having a five-year-old brother, possibly named George (which is the English name my Grandfather is given when he starts school), a big brother whom she fiercely defends when he gets into a scuffle. "With immense dignity and determination she walked up to the offender, hit him back, and then stood and said things to him in Chinese, which were probably too awful to print."

Poor Yee Yut. Like most Chinese girls, this was the only period in her life when she would know any freedom. After the age of twelve, girls were securely locked away until they married, and then their husbands shut them up in their apartments. But that point would prove to be moot, for about a year after the family's return from a trip to China in November of 1902 Yee Yut would be dead from pneumonia. She was three years old.

It's odd, but when one looks at census and other records of the time, there seem to be significantly fewer Chinese girl children than boys. It could be because Chinese fathers were importing lots of young sons from China, or that they didn't consider girls important enough to mention to the census takers. Obviously, the late Yee Yut wasn't discussed in the family, because when her older brother was asked by the Chinese Inspector in 1911 to recall her name, he said he had no idea. But that doesn't mean that she wasn't loved. A Western doctor was in constant attendance on the little girl for the last week of her life, when many Chinese would have considered herbal medicine sufficient. And it wasn't indifference that kept the parents from going to her funeral, assuming she had one. Ancient tradition dictated that mothers and fathers did not attend their children's funerals, because when a child dies the natural order of the Universe has been disrupted and so the death cannot be acknowledged. Just as with other suffering, mourning must forever be kept inside and never let out.

So life was tough for Chinese men, and virtually intolerable for Chinese women, by the American standards of the late 20th century. Okay, it was intolerable by the American standards of the late 19th century as well. Still, if I had a time machine, this is the period in which I would visit Chinatown, just for a week or so—as a tourist to the past.

In a way I do experience time travel every time I walk down Mott Street in search of a moon cake or the perfect roast pork bun. For there is one place left where I can go straight back to 1899. It is a store where time has stopped. A store where in fact, time never really got up to

The Ancestral Hall, like this one in a village south of Canton, was the spiritual center of Hor Lup Chui, my family's home village. (*Photo by Author, 1994*)

A Taoist Shrine in Chinatown, New York, in 1888. This may be the one in the Chatham Square headquarters of the organization that would eventually become the Chinese Consolidated Benevolent Association, or CCBA—the unofficial Government of Chinatown. (*From "Cosmopolitan; a Monthly Illustrated Magazine." June, 1888. Courtesy New York Public Library*)

"The Chinese Lady," Pwan-ye-Koo, and suite. "Exhibited" by P. T. Barnum in New York in 1850, she was renowned for having two-inch-long feet. (*Courtesy Museum of Chinese in the Americas*)

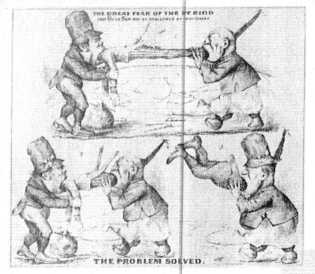

Early cartoon, showing the prevalent paranoia over the idea that the Chinese would swallow up not only Americans, but even the Irish. (*Courtesy Museum of Chinese in the Americas*)

Even fellow immigrants showed no sympathy, as shown by this 1933 letter to the Immigration Department. (*Chinese Immigration Files, National Archives, Northeast Division*)

This may be my great-grandfather, Hor Poa, in the 1880s, next to an early "Chinatown Bulletin Board"—the base of a telegraph pole opposite 8 Mott Street. Behind him, Mott Street is so thick with horse manure that it is hard to tell it is paved. (*"Chinatown. The Official Organ of the Colony." The Jacob A. Riis Collection, Museum of the City of New York*)

My great-grandmother, Gon She (standing, at left), in what appears to be a Chinese young women's evangelical band. The Caucasian lady may be Miss Helen Clark who specialized in "rescuing" Chinese women and children from paganism— whether they wanted to be rescued or not. (*Author's collection*)

The rich Chu Fong and family pose for a photographer in his luxurious Mott Street home in 1906. (*Courtesy Museum of Chinese in the Americas*)

A far more typical bachelor's cubicle. Note the board-and-trestle bed. (*Museum of Chinese in the Americas*)

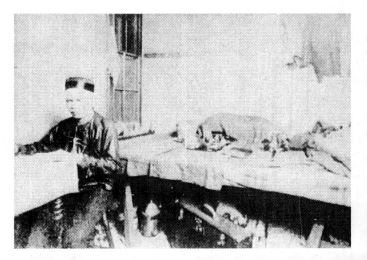

Hor Poa and Gon She at the time of their marriage in 1896. *(Author's collection)*

Fan Tan players, Circa 1870. *(Courtesy of Sinotique, 19-A Mott St., NYC)*

Lottery ticket, seized in a 1901 gambling raid on Mott Street. Instead of numbers, gamblers bet on individual words from classic Chinese poetry. (*Committee of Fifteen Records, Box 4, Manuscripts and Archives Division, New York Public Library*)

联泰日厰

Long Fee Establishment a place where the sale and drawing of lottery tickets is carried on, hours 5 to 5/6 P.M. 9 to 10,15 evening #13 Mott S, front

6

Chuck Connors in one of his fake "opium dens," around 1906. A chop suey lunch would be included in his famous Chinatown vice tours. (*Courtesy Museum of Chinese in the Americas*)

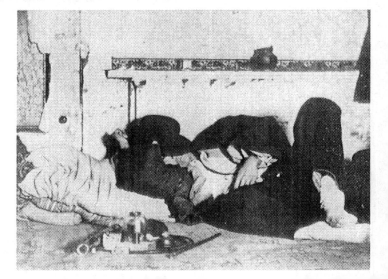

The real thing, photographed by Jacob Riis in the 1880s. Note the "works" on the tray. (*"Smoking Opium in a Joint" The Jacob A. Riis Collection, #F, The Museum of the City of New York*)

Tom Lee in an undated photograph. At the turn of the century, he had one hand in every vice racket in Chinatown, while the other slipped "protection money" into the pockets of the local constabulary. (*Courtesy of The Museum of Chinese in the Americas*)

Brightly colored, fancy balconies festooned the fronts of most Chinatown buildings, like these at Nos. 20—14 Mott Street, photographed circa 1905. The Hip Sing Tong long complained that the On Leong wielded an unfair influence over the CCBA. It is easy to see why, since 14 and 18 Mott were On Leong buildings, and the CCBA was wedged in between, at No. 16. (*George Hall Collection, The New-York Historical Society*)

ENVOYS OF THE WARRING TONGS WHO AGREED ON TERMS OF PEACE FOR CHINATOWN, AND JUDGE WHO PRESIDED.

'NEVER TOUCHED ME,'

Hor Poa should be among these pictured at the signing of the 1906 Tong War Treaty. The truce barely lasted 18 months before bloody fighting broke out again. (*The World, Feb. 3, 1906, courtesy New York Public Library*)

Viewing the Chinatown Bulletin Board at the corner of Doyers and Pell, around 1900. Here, among commercial notices and local gossip, the Tongs posted the percentages they expected to get from various gambling tables in the neighborhood, while some merchants nervously proclaimed their neutrality in the Hip Sing and On Leong conflicts. *(Courtesy Museum of Chinese in the Americas)*

The St. Bart's Chinese Guild, when it was at 4 Mott Street, 1897. This popular Sunday School was known for offering a myriad of social services, plus a "homeopathic dose of religion." The white child in the front row is probably the son of a teacher. *(Courtesy of St. Bartholomew's Episcopal Church)*

Inside the Chinese Opera House on Doyers Street. Even semiliterate laundrymen knew many of the classical Chinese dramas by heart. *(Courtesy Museum of Chinese in the Americas)*

This train station in Malone, New York, was built with a special room for examining Chinese entering the United States from Canada. Detainees were taken to a jail a mile away. (*Courtesy of the Franklin County Historical Society*)

This former school annex in Richford, Vermont was meant to house up to 125 Chinese detainees, sometimes for months at a time. Prisoners sold homemade kites through the barred windows. The cheaper trans-Canada passage became the route of choice for east-coast Chinese traveling to and from China after 1891. (*Courtesy Mrs. Rhoda Berger*)

My Great-Uncle Sun's identity card (using an alternate spelling of his name) obtained for a family trip to China. (*Courtesy Dr. Alison Ho*)

The interior constructed by my great-grandfather for Quong Yuen Shing, soon after it moved to 32 Mott in 1899. It was known both for its herbs, fancy groceries, and its sumptuous silks. (*New York Tribune, March 5, 1899. Courtesy New York Public Library*)

. . . and in 1997. The lanterns and drawers are gone, but little else has changed. (*Photo by author*)

Inside the Port Arthur, the Best Restaurant That Ever Was, around 1920. The family says that the decorative woodwork was also created by my great-grandfather. (*Courtesy of the Museum of Chinese in the Americas*)

The view up Pell Street in the 1920s, as seen from the window of the family apartment at *Sun Lau* or the "New Building" at 33—37 Mott. Note the elevated train looming in the background. (*Courtesy Karen Fung*)

My grandparents in 1920. My grandfather holds Uncle Everett, wearing his First Son's crown, while Aunts Constance (left) and Thelma sit in front. This is the only image I have of my grandmother, who would bear two more children before dying at age 29. (*Author's collection*)

Great-Uncle Sun (front row right) and his Boy Scout Troop, 1918. (*Courtesy Dr. Alison Ho*)

Edmund and Betty Wolff Wong at a celebratory banquet before his fatal flight. (*Private Collection*)

The aftermath, in Brooklyn. (*Private Collection*)

Hock Shop and Frances Wolff, at the time of their marriage in 1927. (*Courtesy, Richard Hoe*)

Helen Wing (right) dances with her brother, Paul, and Dorothy Toy (Takahashi) as Toy and Wing, among the most popular Asian-American performers of the 1930s. (*Courtesy Museum of Chinese in the Americas*)

At Bradley Beach in 1928, my Aunt Thelma is entertained by an Al Jolson impersonator. A Chinese, disguised as a white man, doing a bad imitation of a black man. Go figure. (*Courtesy Karen Fung*)

Miss Chinatown, 1958. Just 35 years earlier, no respectable Chinese lady would allow herself to be seen in public. (*Courtesy Mrs. Anne M. Chan*)

Stiltwalkers were once a fixture of New Year's celebrations. (*Courtesy Mrs. Anne M. Chan*)

The family at the marriage of Great-Uncle Sun to Dorothy Doshim in 1944. (Standing L—R: Bickie, Dorothy's sister, Constance, Ruth, Dorothy's sister-in-law, Frances, Thelma, Everett, and Fong. Seated L—R: Dorothy's brother, Sun, Dorothy, and Hock Shop. *(Courtesy Dr. Alison Ho)*

Shavey Lee leads the happy couple in the obligatory toast to Chiang Kai-shek. Dorothy's father was Wu Do-shim, but immigration officials confused his family and given names. Thus the "Doshim" family was born. *(Courtesy Dr. Alison Ho)*

Madame Chiang Kai-shek speaks at the Chinese School on Mott Street in 1943. Standing next to her is the teacher known to his students as "Fat Chester." An uncomfortable-looking Mayor Fiorello LaGuardia is seated at far left. *(Courtesy Mr. Jip F. Chun and the Museum of Chinese in the Americas)*

My mother, around 1939. *(Author's collection)*

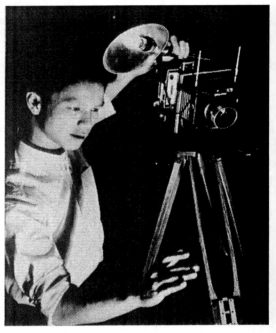

My father, around 1941. He earned extra money in college as a portrait photographer. *(Author's collection)*

Auntie, around 1923. *(Courtesy Karen Fung)*

Hock Shop and his LaSalle, circa 1941. (*Author's collection*)

The "new" On Leong headquarters. (*Photo by Author*)

The Sun Wei Village Association in 1993. Chiang Kai-shek and Sun Yat-sen beam down on a room where time seems to have stopped. (*Photo by Andrew Garn. By permission*)

A Lion-Dancer ushers in the New Year. (*Photo by Tim Lee, with permission*)

speed. A store which, from my childhood, older relatives have solemnly pointed out and said, "Your great-grandfather did this." I speak of Quong Yuen Shing, the "Chinese General Store" at Number 32. Inside, the Ancestors still breathe.

Hor Poa had been a "partner" since the place had opened at 5 Mott in 1891, but when they moved across the street in 1899 he was hired to do all the carpentry and renovations. Even today, when one enters through the old wooden door in the center, flanked by the original 19th-century plate-glass display windows, the eye is immediately drawn to the arch in the back, fantastically carved into a myriad of shapes. There are peacocks and dragons and lucky animals squirming around the branches of two leafy trees which frame what was once the pharmaceutical counter. In those days, traditional Chinese doctors sent their patients to Number 32 to get a piece of the stag's antlers hanging from the ceiling to relieve their "internal wind." Or, from the dozens of distinctive square drawers filling the wall behind the arch, the clerk would measure out dried sea horses to strengthen the kidneys, rhododendron blossom for asthma, cicada shells for joint pain, and the ever-popular *luk mai* or Six Flower, a mixture of dried almond, lotus nut, shaved lily bulb, and a little root called *wai shan,* which is not only a cure for sore throat, but also great in soup. They and any number of the other six thousand dried herbs, roots, berries, and nuts held in the drawers were wrapped in mysterious little twists of paper stamped with red seals, all waiting to be mixed together and brewed into steaming potions that would balance the warring forces in an ailing body and restore health, vigor, and well-being. They also frequently gave off an odor that seemed strong enough to strip paint.

The drawers and the herbs are gone now, but that is the most obvious change. Above and next to the arch hang plaques of Chinese poetry, along with delicate old watercolor portraits of Chinese ladies, seated demurely on European-style chairs. The old pendulum schoolhouse clock still ticks on the wall, the click of an abacus still accompanies every sale, and the pressed-tin ceiling looks as though it hasn't been painted for a hundred years—possibly because it hasn't. In the corner, the same square oak table still squats where the founding owner, old Lee Yick Dep or his younger kinsman Lee B. Lok would proffer a cup of tea and a smoke of tobacco on a water pipe to honored customers.

Twice a day—at mid-morning and mid-afternoon—the workers dragged out the table to eat hasty meals run in on huge trays balanced on the heads of waiters from one of the neighboring restaurants.

At other times they might sit there, writing brush in hand, while lonely temporary bachelors dictated letters to family in China or had some confusing American document translated into Chinese. The letters sent home contained return envelopes self-addressed in English, which were only marginally helpful to the poor beleaguered postman, who would wander up and down Mott Street looking for a particular Lee or Chin among the dozens of Lees and Chins who, unfortunately, moved within the quarter a little too often. A bamboo rack by the door still holds mail for the itinerant waiters and laborers who then, as they do still, required a more stable mailing address. Mail could be there for weeks or months, but it will find its owner in the end. In a glass case, high in a corner, is a tall blue-and-white vase which for most of my life was marked "Not for Sale." It is the collateral for a many-decades old loan which has yet to be repaid, the details of which no one can quite remember anyway.

However, it is the arch that dominates, still bearing traces of its red-tinted gilding, the color of prosperity enhanced by the glimmer of gold. My elders always told me that Great-Grandfather carved this arch, but more recently I have come to the reluctant conclusion that in fact he probably only installed it. By 1899, Chinatown merchants were importing crates of fancy decoration for their stores and restaurants. Elaborately carved Ancestors' altars, statues of the gods for the new Joss Houses, furniture encrusted with marble and mother-of-pearl were appearing all over Chinatown, spurred by the fact that the neighborhood was increasingly becoming a tourist destination for white New Yorkers who wanted to believe that a visit there was a walk on the exotic wild side.

But not only did Great-Grandfather install the arch, he built the square drawers, the venerable counters, the shelves that still groan with merchandise. In the back room he constructed an elaborate system of cubbyholes and offices, for Quong Yuen Shing was more than a post office, a translating service, and a place to buy fancy Chinese groceries and sumptuous silks. The Lees conducted a thriving international business from those rooms, not only in importing and exporting, but also in banking. Those Toi-shan farmers didn't trust American financial institutions, and when they were sending money back home, they would take their cash to someone like the Lees who would convert it into Mexican dollars and send it to their representatives in Hong Kong or Canton, where the families could pick it up. Silver Mexican dollars were preferred because of the purity of the metal—although, once in China, each company that handled the coins would stamp its own firm name in them with a steel die. Eventually, the contents of a typical Hong Kong safe "resembled nothing so much as battered bits and scraps of old tin." The only way the money's value could be determined was by weight. The two Victorian safes at Quong Yuen Shing are used for more mundane storage now, but millions of well-used dollars have passed through them to support honored parents back in the Middle Kingdom.

Also in the back room, Great-Grandfather built a series of sleeping lofts—hard wooden bunks, some single, some double, crammed into spaces over and between the office cubicles and safes and piles of merchandise. Here slept the store clerks and the packers and the occasional homeless Lee relative looking for a temporary place to stay. Down at the end of the long line of the narrow aisle between the bunks and cubbyholes is a sink, a toilet, and a tiny window. It's cramped and airless and chaotic—and for those Chinese sojourners, just like home.

So the men of Quong Yuen Shing toiled away all day among boxes and baskets stuffed with the exotica of another continent. From Asia they imported dried mushrooms and salt fish, sea cucumber and boned ducks' feet, birds' nests and big pieces of dried sharks' fins. For the launderers they kept collar-crimpers and boxes of starch. For the restaurants, there were stacks of simple yet beautiful rice bowls. Yet oddly, despite the herbs and dry goods and fancy groceries, Quong Yuen Shing was known primarily for its sumptuous silks and brocades, bolts and bolts of which lined the shelves on the right-hand side.

Well into my adulthood, there was another place from which I could visit the 1890s. Grandfather was born at what I consider the dawn of the Golden Age of Chinatown restaurants. China's, after all, was a culture where the natives greeted each other not with "Hello," but with "Have you eaten yet?" Eating palaces such as the Tuxedo at 2 Doyers, the Oriental Restaurant on Pell, and its neighbor, the sumptuous Chinese Delmonico's, officially opened by New York Mayor Strong himself in 1897, were awash in dragons and lanterns, teakwood and mother-of-pearl as the Chinatown tourist industry got into full swing. But the restaurant Grandfather probably had his First Son's party in was probably the same one in which our family would have parties for generations—decades and decades, until the old place seemed eternal, although it proved mortal in the end, alas. I am speaking of the Port Arthur, at 7–9 Mott Street, the Best Restaurant that Ever Was.

It was on the second and third floors, and opened in 1897 or thereabouts, named for a city on the northeastern Chinese coast where the Japanese defeated the Russians in their 1894 war. It was the first victory of an Asian power over a European one, and the Port Arthur Restaurant reflected pan-Asian pride. Family elders have always believed that Hor Poa helped build the interiors there as well. None of them are exactly sure, although since it was next door to Quong Yuen Shing before it moved, it's a perfectly logical conclusion. Besides, the Port Arthur was just as magical as that store would be. To my mind, the Ancestors breathed in there as well.

We'd go through the street door to the left of the Chinatown Fair and up the tiled stair with the big brass rail. At the top was the little lobby with the big goldfish tank, shining in the gloom. Goldfish weren't, and still aren't, merely decorative. They keep out the evil spirits, who, as all the world knows, have a tendency to rush through doors and straight up staircases to wreak havoc with whatever is found at the top, like sleeping children—or cash registers.

I remember the Port Arthur as all carved dragons and huge, six-sided glass lanterns, adorned with delicate paintings of ladies and landscapes. Wooden fans spun on the ceilings. Rows of stiff-backed teakwood chairs with marble seats stood in a line, while if one peeked under the starched linen tablecloth, one would find that the big, round table for twelve—normal chair height, no stools here—was merely a piece of plywood slapped on top of an equally exquisite piece of furniture with little carvings in the corners and the gleam of mother-of-pearl. The floor was all geometric design done in mosaic tile. Up another staircase, carefully closed off to keep those pesky demons at bay, there were private meeting and banquet rooms that I only ever glimpsed from a distance. But I knew that those were the rooms where deals were made, where Tongs hammered out concessions and Big Shots were paid homage to.

At the Port Arthur I was first introduced to those long-life noodles, which would be trotted out for every elder's birthday and would be so long that by the time I wound one around my chopsticks it would barely fit in my mouth. Here also we got the sickly-sweet almond juice, another good-luck substance that we Cousins would dare each other to try before one would bravely knock it back. We also always seemed to get a wonderful chicken dish, a bird seemingly roasted whole with its head intact—until you sliced it open to find that it was merely a shell of skin full of glutinous rice, the bird having been somehow completely boned from the inside. We had delectable steamed sea bass, and savory duck, and crabs, and spare ribs, and platters full of lobsters dripping in black-bean sauce. And then occasionally some hapless non-Chinese guest of ours would timidly ask for an egg roll or some other such aberration, only to be fixed by a withering stare from my father's side of the table along with the snide growl. "I thought you wanted Chinese food."

Ah, tourists! Back in the 1890s they would be handed a menu in Chinese and a pair of ivory chopsticks, neither one of which was any use to them at all. For the adventurous, a waiter would bring small samples of each dish so the diner could make a selection. Birds'-nest soup or steamed squab cost a hefty $2; sweet-and-sour chicken, pork lo mein, or stir-fried lobster with Chinese vegetables, 75 cents; egg foo young, 50 cents; stuffed bean curd, 15 cents; or a whole variety of *yum cha* dumplings, what we call *dim sum* today, 5 cents apiece.

But the average Big-Nose would just demand a fork and follow the example of those of their friends who were smug in their supposed knowledge of Celestial cuisine. "I have introduced many to the delights of chop-suey," wrote one such gourmand in 1898, "A standard dish that stands the test of time much as does the roast beef of Old England."

The test of time? Never mind that in 1904 a Chinese restaurant cook from San Francisco tried to claim royalties on this "standard" dish, which he said he invented. And never mind that when Prince Pu Lun of the Imperial Court toured Chinatown in that same year, one of his American escorts said, "And now, Your Highness, we will eat some of your national dish—chop suey."

"What is chop suey?," asked the Prince.

Tourists called their visits to Chinatown "slumming," and would often combine a trip to the Port Arthur or the Chinese Delmonico's with a peek at an opium den and a visit to the "priest" of a Joss House, where they would light incense and toss some divining sticks around. And then, also, Chinatown was full of "lobbygows," non-Chinese toughs who would gladly accept a fee to steer the slummers to rendezvous with an opium pipe or a (white) prostitute working above some squalid Chatham Square joint.

Well, they weren't *entirely* non-Chinese. George Washington Appo was the half-Chinese son of Quimbo Appo—the same Quimbo Appo who had been so infamous before the Civil War for killing his landlady in a drunken brawl—Quimbo Appo, who had been the first Chinese New Yorker sentenced to death, but who was eventually committed to an insane asylum, where forty years later he was still consumed by delusional ramblings. His son, George Washington, had been beautiful once, but after his father had been put away and his mother abandoned him, he had grown up on the rough streets of the Five Points with nothing more than his wits to feed him. Now he was fifty and he had lost an eye in one of his many fights with the lowlifes he worked with to swindle tourists—a sad wreck of a man, prowling the streets looking for a sucker to finance a drink or an opium pipe to help dull his memories.

George Washington Appo was smooth, though, very smooth, able to charm the cash out of the pockets of rube and sophisticate alike. During the time that he was giving evidence at a citywide corruption hearing, he went up to the famous Christian reformer, the Reverend Dr. Charles Parkhurst, and purred, "I beg your pardon, Doctor. Could you let me have two tens for a five?" "Oh, certainly! Certainly! To be sure!" replied the flustered Dr. Parkhurst, caught completely off guard. He dug into his pockets and handed a smiling Appo $20 as change for a five-dollar bill. And when soon afterwards, Appo appeared in court for the stabbing assault of one of his cohorts, his laconic defense was, "I was drunk, and don't remember anything about it." Soon, like his father, he will disappear into an asylum, where he lose himself to his ravings forever.

This was also the heyday of Chuck Connors, the self-described "Mayor of Chinatown," the "Sage of Doyers Street," and the "King of the Lobbygows." He was a flashy Irish ex-boxer and Bowery barfly who spent his days swaggering amongst Tong runners and sightseers, concocting stories and bumming drinks. He could usually be found, dressed in his trademark bowler hat and row after row of pearl buttons, at some of the more notorious Chinatown watering holes like the Chatham Club on Doyers Street or Tom Lee's establishment, quaintly known as "The Dump," at Number 9 Bowery, which was patronized by "the dirtiest specimens of humanity to be found." Make that "the dirtiest specimens of *white* humanity," as not only did Chinese tend not to drink much alcohol, they weren't generally welcome in such lively haunts, even in their own front yard.

Connors had no obvious means of support but lived rent-free in an apartment at 6 Doyers Street supplied by Richard K. Fox, publisher of the *Police Gazette*. Like the editors of the *Sun* and the *World*, he delighted in profiling Connors's adventures in his rag, so much so that Chuck became a celebrity in his own right. He was featured on the vaudeville stage, courted by politicians, and even formed his own society, the Chuck Connors Club, which boasted such illustrious members as the boxers John L. Sullivan and Jim Corbett, the actor Richard Mansfield, and Al Smith, later Governor of New York.

But Chuck's real claim to fame was his Chinatown "vice tour," during which he would make up lurid stories about white slavery and hatchet murders to titillate his uptown patrons. He would even toss in an opportunity to view in person the evil degradation of an opium den, which was really just the apartment of a Chinese friend named Georgie Yee and his white wife, Blonde Lulu. These two would obligingly pose in a carefully rehearsed opium stupor while one of Chuck's minions would deliver a Sermon Pathétique to the shocked but enthralled tourists. "These poor people are slaves to the opium habit," he'd bark through a megaphone. "And whether you came here or not to see them they would have spent this night smoking opium just as you see them doing it now!" He then would trot his charges off to a restaurant, giving Georgie and Lulu a breather before the next group was due.

Once a year, Chuck and his girlfriend "Pickles" would host his famous Chinatown Ball, which, although not actually held in Chinatown, still attracted the elite from the highest and the lowest of New York Society. At the 1903 Christmas Ball, "there were Chinamen dancing with white girls, negro women waltzing with white men in evening dress, pugilists from the Bowery, well-known theatrical folks from the up-town theaters, society men and women who had come in their carriages just to look on, and a raft of humanity from the Chinese quarter." Stage stars Anna Held, Maxine Elliot, and other uptown swells fox-trotted to such numbers as "Chinatown Voted the Laundry Ticket" and "I Don't Care if It Snows in Bed." Pickles reduced a society matron to scandalized gibberish by publicly asking her for a cigarette. And to complete the picture, at about midnight, temperance crusader Carrie Nation showed up with her hatchet. "I came here to stop this ball!" thundered the old lady as she scolded the young men for smoking and threatened the young women with arrest as she dashed the cocktails from their hands.

"If yer don't git downstairs in a minute," shouted Pickles as she grabbed Miss Nation by the arm, "I'll push yer t'rough de back of yer neck!"

Meanwhile, the fifty-year-old Chuck Connors himself, resplendently unshaven in ill-fitting evening clothes, stood at the bottom of the stairs to welcome his guests. "Der are udder automibiles up stairs wid loose wheels," he said, "Jist step in and help yerself to a twist."

On the other side of the coin were the Missions. The Rescue Mission on Doyers Street was founded in 1893 specifically for the "recovery and reformation of fallen [white] women." The Evangelical Band met in a tiny room at 8 Pell Street and often supplied speakers to uptown churches. Under their president, Chin K. Kiu, it had grown from twenty-four to 224 members in only three years.

The Evangelical Band was partially supported by the St. Bart's Chinese Guild, which in 1897 moved its Sunday School to a couple of crowded rooms at 4 Mott Street. Guy Maine and the Guild really distinguished themselves that year when they stood up to the Laundry Association and the Tong in defending a laundryman who had dared to lower his prices without permission. Based on the questionable testimony of a Tong member, this unfortunate man had been suddenly arrested and imprisoned on charges of grand theft, while his laundry was stripped to the bare walls by a wagon-load of mysterious Chinese men who arrived in the night. The Guild was able to prove his innocence and gain his release, but not without raising the ire of Tom Lee and company. Guy

Maine soon found it expedient to move his operations once again, this time to St. Bartholomew's new parish house on East 42nd Street.

And then there was the Morning Star Mission on the second floor of 17 Doyers, its rooms "made attractive by several spiritual young Chinamen, who, arrayed in dress suits in good American style, ranged themselves about a cabinet organ and sang Moody and Sankey's hymns in seductive falsetto, to the delectation of a crowd which gathered about the door."

It had been established in 1892 by Miss Helen Clark, "a beautiful, charming, cultivated young woman, who, in the pursuit of her duty, goes without hesitation into every house and every room in Chinatown, coming in contact with its most disgusting forms of vice, preserving her sweetness, and carrying with her to the heathen a veritable incarnation of the Christian spirit." She was fond of breaking up unions between Chinese men and white women, and did not hesitate to snatch children away from adults whom she—occasionally correctly—suspected of abuse or worse. Of course, this didn't make the Tongs too happy with Miss Clark either, and it was they who were suspected of setting the fire that drove her out of her Doyers Street quarters. Obviously, she was doing something right.

So Miss Clark branched out on her own, creating the Evangelical Mission Day School at 21 Mott while leaving the Morning Star in the able hands of the Mission's preacher, Fung Y. Mow. His Chinese wife was considered shockingly immodest by many of her male countrymen—mostly because she held a degree from the American Medical College in Canton. While Reverend Fung saved souls downstairs, Dr. Fung patched up bodies upstairs.

As for Miss Clark, she would daily canvass the neighborhood for children, many of whom she assumed were slaves (but they probably weren't), to bring to class, managing to pry about thirty away from their parents at a time. Yet even while she was teaching at school, "other teachers visit the homes to try to show the Chinese women the Christian way of living."

She almost certainly snared my great-grandmother and her children, who, after all, were virtually a captive audience since they lived just upstairs. It wasn't all bad, since Miss Clark and her staff would sometimes assemble small groups of Chinese mothers and take them on picnics. Yet even in the height of the summer, these respectable Chinese matrons would insist on travelling in closed carriages with every window and blind tightly shut for propriety's sake. Only thus, in these stifling conveyances, would they allow themselves to be transported to the Barbarian entertainments.

One of my favorite possessions is a photograph of Gon She after her marriage, posed with three other young women in a semicircle around the seated figure of a primly-attired missionary lady, who may be Miss Clark herself. Whoever she is, she seems to have assembled them in a sort of Chinese Christian Girls' Band. The "women of the Flowery Kingdom" are all identically dressed, like a collection of China dolls, playthings to be collected and put on display when important company is expected. But at least Miss Clark gave my Great-Grandmother an excuse to get out of the house. It was more than her menfolk would do.

But I have digressed. Why do I want to visit the Chinatown of the 1890s? Because, back when my Grandfather was a toddler, all of Mott Street seemed to simmer with the mystery of the Port Arthur and Quong Yuen Shing, the shop exteriors glittering with fantastic carved balconies, gilded and painted in all the lucky colors of prosperity—red, gold, and rich, vibrant green. Lanterns swayed in the breeze. No new store could officially open for business until strings of firecrackers were set off to scare away the evil spirits. Silk banners, covered with beautiful, complicated characters that took years to master, blazoned messages of congratulations, or good luck, or wisdom four thousand years old. It was a place where the New Year was ushered in by a lion, the hours and years were named after the creatures that control the universe, and goldfish kept the demons at bay.

Baskets of fresh vegetables from bean sprouts to hairy melons, spilled onto the sidewalks. These were obtained from little Chinese truck farms that had recently begun to sprout up in the suburbs, like Shen Ho Joe's new place in Long Island City. He lived in a shack and was the laughingstock of his white neighbors, but his judicious applications of liquid manure stored in barrels yielded "beans as large as an ordinary-sized radish." Shen Ho Joe eventually returned to China a rich man.

There were the fishmongers, with live eels writhing in shallow tanks. In the butchers' windows hung geese and ducks and strips of sweet roast pork, dark red and juicy. And in every store, the household god presided with sticks of incense and a benevolent smile. It was a place where the smell of perfume and pig snouts filled the air.

The men crowding the sidewalks still largely wore traditional frog-buttoned blouses of blue silk or cotton, and long, braided queues hanging nearly to their knees, only now, instead of the thick-soled shoes and leggings bound with brilliant white socks, they largely sported American-style trousers and shoes, with felt hats perched on the fronts of their heads. On festival days like New Year's, or for the visit of a V.I.P. like Prince Pu Lun, the somber blue would be replaced by radiant embroidered silks of all hues, sometimes even yellow, which in China was reserved for the innermost circles of the Imperial Family.

This was a sensuous Chinatown, where men took their gorgeous and rare songbirds for early-morning walks in their cages—for they knew that the birds would be happier, their songs sweeter, if they got out in the light and air. So they sedately walked them up and down, up and down, or hung them outside of the windows of their rooms, where they tempered the clatter of the street with their mellow voices. After 1895, the men could have taken their birds to the newly-created oasis of green known as Mulberry Bend Park (Columbus Park after 1911), built when social reformers such as Jacob Riis finally prevailed upon the City to demolish the squalid heart of the old Five Points and give the local residents a place to breathe amidst trees and flowers. However, Mulberry Bend Park was on Mulberry Street, and firmly in Italian territory. Chinese men and their dulcet friends were not welcome in this foreign domain.

So they sat on Mott or Pell with their avian companions, over fragrant bowls of tea. Fine teas were appreciated in the same way that Europeans treasured fine wines, and precious blends were carefully brewed in delicate pots, to be poured into big bowls so the exquisite aroma could be savored before being transferred to the tiny cups for careful sipping.

Chu Fong's Chinese Opera House was in full swing in the basement of 5 Doyers Street. It was a plain room, with rows of wooden benches and an unadorned stage. The stage manager sat in full view, idly smoking cigarettes until required to saunter into the action and hand one of the players a prop. During battle scenes, he placidly added to the din by exploding plates of flash powder at the right moments— and by placing cushions under fallen warriors' heads. There was no scenery, no curtain, but somehow on this little platform four thousand years of Imperial splendor marched out night after night.

The orchestra sat in the center of the stage, up against the back wall. Westerners invariably used words like "cacophony," "din," and "noise" to describe Chinese music, but then we are talking of people used to the oom-pah uniformity of John Philip Sousa. But even for them, it was just possible that after a spell of listening to "Autumn Moon on a Placid Lake," or "Praising the Plum Flower" the barriers could be broken down, allowing the ancient strains to curl through the brain like the smoke from a stick of sandalwood incense, or the steam from a bowl of stone-flower tea.

Twenty-five notes make up a Chinese octave, played on delicate, lute-like instruments which are bowed or plucked, the *ching-hu, erh-hu, chüeh-hu,* their bodies made of bamboo and snakeskin, the tops of the necks carved into the heads of dragons or bats.

The *p'i-p'a* is two thousand years old, pear-shaped, with four strings and as many as twenty-six frets made of ivory or buffalo horn. The *p'i-p'a* player of my grandfather's childhood would have grown his nails long and sharp, to pick the fragile music seemingly out of the air.

The *ch'in* was just as ancient, a long, narrow zither with layer after layer of hard, shiny lacquer on the Tung wood surface, a patina of tiny "wave cracks," "ice cracks," and "serpent cracks" formed with age adding beauty and value. There were the flutes, like the *ti-tzu* and the *xun,* the shrill gongs *(lo),* the crashing cymbals *(po),* and the all-important *tan-pi ku,* the barrel drum which dominated all, and set the tempo for the entire experience.

And then there were the actors—the gods, the heroes, the fluttering ladies—all played by men in wild and fantastic make-up and wigs, their heavy silk costumes blazing with embroidery and appliqué. They could move with majesty or vault like monkeys, but their singing seemed as atonal and bizarre as the instrumentals did, to the untrained ear.

Once again, familiarity brought an appreciation of the sounds—the sopranos bell-clear and pure, the basses rumbling like thunder. The Opera was singing, tumbling, kaleidoscopic poetry, telling epic sagas that could last days or weeks. It was wildly popular with both merchant and laundryman, scholar and peasant. On Sundays, the one day they were released from their toil, they all thronged the Opera looking for escape, and found it in spades.

An evening's performance would last for six or more hours, but the ticket prices edged down as the night progressed. So while a customer might have paid 50 cents for a seat at six forty-five when the play was starting, by ten o'clock it would be 10 cents, and after eleven o'clock it would be free. Thus, the audience swelled as the time went on. Yet to the Western observer, they seemed strangely uninterested. The men never applauded or reacted beyond a grumble of recognition. Indeed, throughout the performance they would be wandering around, eating, smoking, talking with their neighbors, while somehow remaining connected to the action. But after all, these were the same classic verses they had seen on the threshing floors of their home villages as children, and they all knew long passages by heart. One play might be a simple Ming Dynasty drama about a man forced to choose between greatness and duty; the next might be the epic tale of knights and emperors; in the next, a fairy king offers his daughter's hand to whoever can tame a magical horse. It would have been almost like hearing a familiar nursery rhyme or bedtime story all over again—only in this instance it was a nursery rhyme told in classic eight-line poetry over a period of six days.

As usual, the White Devils interfered. Whenever Chuck Connors ushered a party of his society "slummers" to the conspicuous box, right next to the stage, all action in the opera stopped as the orchestra scraped up a tune and the more acrobatic company members dashed onstage to perform impromptu gymnastics. Sometimes, when the interruption was a lengthy one, a placard written in Chinese was placed on a pole. It explained that because the actions of this particular section of the opera might offend the Barbarian guests, it would be skipped, and the audience was requested to imagine what they were missing. The near riot that ensued would be quelled by a fierce note sounded on the *ti-tzu*—which an obsequious guide would explain away to the American ladies as an expression of the joy the company felt at the presence of their exalted guests.

The white patronage would prove valuable, however. For in 1897, the Reverend Charles Parkhurst mounted his famous morality crusade, and the City cracked down on violators of the Sunday blue laws. Public performances given for any but religious purposes were banned, and while Chu Fong tried to justify Chinese opera as a spiritual experience, he was arrested and the theater forced to close on Sundays, after which he sold out his interests and made money in other ways. After all, the theater must not have been allowed to compete with the Morning Star Mission just up the street. While the Sunday ban continued, the Chinese Opera was engaged in an ultimately losing struggle to get by on the meager ticket sales made to those few patrons who were free on week-day evenings, and f slumming parties, at a dollar a head, wanted to interrupt an ancient classic, who would complain?

One didn't need to attend the Chinese Opera House to hear poetry, however. It was all around, recited in a language that was and is more sung than spoken. It was the basis of the lottery. It was on placards in the eating houses. It was a thing of such high value that one Ah Fong had been hired by the rich merchant Yuet Sing to come to his private office every evening from eight o'clock until midnight to read to him from the Classics. It was the thing which, more than anything else in Chinese society, separated the high from the low. It offered flight from the darkest prison.

Around the time of my grandfather's birth, Wang Sing gave a grand banquet to celebrate his winning of the annual poetry competition. It was something that everyone who could, participated in—businessmen, launderers, lackeys who chopped vegetables in restaurant kitchens. In that particular year the rules were these: it would be a four-line poem with eight words per line. The first word must be "dragon," the last word "ship." In English, Wang Sing's poem read:

> *Dragon, who rules the shoreless sea of death,*
> *When I lie dreaming on my loved one's lip*
> *And thou dost come to take her parting breath,*
> *Oh, take me with her on thy spectral ship.*

The Belle of Chinatown

Not every "heathen Chinee" was prostrate over an opium pipe or a gaming table, it seems.

I wish I could stop here, and leave Chinatown in a sweet-smelling haze infused with the delectable tones of a love poem or a bird in a cage, but that wouldn't be entirely correct. The Chinatown at the time of the 1890s was still a narrow space, made all the narrower by the relentless grind of backbreaking toil. Its residents' isolation was made even sharper by the hostility of the world around them, which had to be endured in an enforced solitude, mostly without wives, without children. The gilding and the incense sometimes just served to mask the passions seething under a placid exterior. For in September of 1897, the month of my grandfather's birth, an event occurred which would radically change the timbre of life in Chinatown for decades, to this very day, in fact.

It was the first battle of the Tong Wars.

6

.

TONG WARS

Saturday, September 25, 1897. A group of five or six young Chinese men step into the night air of Pell Street from Number 12. It is the home of their twenty-year-old leader, Mock Duck, a cherubic young man who enjoys a reputation at odds with the prevailing popular image of the Chinese as sinister gamblers and opium fiends, white slavers and purveyors of illicit puppy meat. He is known to be, instead, a nice Christian boy, one who works closely with the New York City Police Department on behalf of a group whose stated goal is to "crush out all vice in Chinatown." They are the Hip Sing Tong, or Hall of United Virtues. "Hip Sing" is about to become a household term in New York City.

The Hip Sing Tong, which the On Leong disdains partly because it is made up mostly of rough-hewn launderers whereas the On Leongers are wealthy men of commerce, had been officially incorporated with the State of New York in November of the previous year, but in fact had been sniping at Tom Lee's heels since its members first arrived from San Francisco in 1887. J. Thomas Scharf's trusted interpreter, Worry Charles, was one of its operatives, as was Charles "Tong" Sing, both of whom had petitioned the Police Civil Service Board in 1895 for appointments as undercover officers in the fight against the evil gambling empire of Tom Lee and the On Leong. Sing, also known as "Scar-faced Charlie," was convicted later that year for robbing a Chinese man in Newark of $101. Scar-face offered to pay back the money. The judge sent him to jail for ten years.

As for Tom Lee, he is rich, very rich. And he is getting richer. His On Leong Tong, also known as the Chinese Merchants' Association, has a tidy income from dues paid by merchants who seek his protection—partly from unfair competition, mostly from his own henchmen. In addition, in the late 1890s he and his kinsman Lee Toy are receiving a $16-per-week kickback from each of Chinatown's hundred or so gaming tables—the lion's share of which goes to the gentlemen of the Sixth (eventually known as the Fifth) Precinct to keep them off his back. It is unfortunate for him that in the last few years Police Commissioner Theodore Roosevelt has been under increasing pressure from both the reformist Mayor William L. Strong and the Reverend Charles Parkhurst's Society for the Prevention of Crime to wipe out such corruption. And Chinatown is a prime target.

But it is nearly impossible for any of Roosevelt's detectives to get past the lookouts posted at the door to every gambling room on Mott Street. As any white man approaches up the stairs, an unseen warning in Chinese results in the sudden slamming of doors and the sounds of things being hastily stashed away. If the door is broken down, nothing more may be found than a peaceful poetry society sparring over verses, or perhaps contemplating a steaming bowl of noodles.

So the police and the Parkhurst Society have grown more and more dependent on Hip Singers such as Mock Duck, who profess Christianity and are ever so anxious to stamp out immorality in their adopted city. Lawmen and Christian leaders alike hail the new Tong as "a benevolent corporation . . . expressly designed to aid the Chinese to learn American ways, and to advance them in religion and mutual helpfulness." Of course, the man who wrote those words was Frank Moss, a racist fathead who in the same chapter expressed his opinion of Chinese in general by saying, "As a body, they are a dangerous, useless and disgusting lot of people." He is also the longtime lawyer for the Parkhurst Society, Worry Charles, and other Hip Sing crusaders.

There is just one small voice questioning Moss's assessment of the Hip Sing. It is that of Miss Helen Clark of the Evangelical Mission Day School, downstairs from my great-grandparents' home. True, Miss Clark sees "highbinders" around every corner, but in the case of the Hip Sing, she may be onto something. After all, wouldn't the best way for one gambler to get rid of another gambler be to let the police do it for him? Frank Moss declares Miss Clark's ideas to be "amusing." Tom Lee, however, is not laughing.

There have been hints of trouble before. In 1894 an admitted gambler, Wong Get, had gone before the Lexow Commission, which was investigating police corruption, to expose the cozy arrangement between Tom Lee and the Sixth Precinct. By 1895, the Say Yup (or Four Towns), the regional association from which the On Leong drew most of its members, and a rival group, which seemed to be from the Hip Sing ranks, were already boycotting businesses owned by the opposition, with tensions growing to the point that Commissioner Roosevelt issued a stern warning against any contemplated violence. And in 1896, when the Hip Sing Tong officially emerged, the name of their new president seemed familiar—Mr. Wong Get. However instead of being the outraged gambler of two years earlier, he had somehow transformed himself into the founder of "a permanent place of meeting . . . away from the baneful influences of the opium den and gambling joint, where religious observances, social amusements, recreations, and intercourse may be enjoyed and the study of the English language may be pursued." And finally, in 1897, the On Leong got wind of Mock Duck's nocturnal research expeditions into Tom Lee's little realm. Enough, as they say, was enough.

So we are back at that September Saturday in 1897, when a group of men waits in the darkness near the foot of Doyers Street for Tom Lee's young nemesis to appear. When Mock and his friends step out onto the sidewalk, they are immediately set upon by men armed with hatchets and knives. Lee Hung Tai receives an axe blow to the shoulder, but the attackers' main target is Mr. Mock, who manages to produce a weapon and slash one of them in the leg before he himself is felled with a cut from what appears to be a butcher's knife. Tourists flee from the tiny intersection as the mêlée continues with knives and blackjacks. Meanwhile, at least six police officers, who are conveniently (and suspiciously) nearby, arrive in time to catch one Chu Woy slipping his deadly hatchet down his trouser leg. The ambulances that are summoned have difficulty negotiating the narrow lanes, now clogged with hundreds of slummers and other rubberneckers who have run to see the fun. Eventually eight men are hauled off to the Elizabeth Street police station after their wounds are dressed. The neighborhood remains in an uproar for nearly an hour.

There are similar disturbances near the corner of Pell and Doyers over the next few years. On Leongers challenge Hip Singers and vice versa, and a few heads are knocked around. In one 1899 free-for-all, some twenty Chinese and at least five policemen battle it out, in which one Chinese is stabbed and one officer is shot through the thigh. But it is from a very unexpected quarter that tensions will be heated right to the boiling point.

Back in China, the old Dowager Empress, Tz'u Hsi, is causing trouble again. This de facto ruler of the Empire has always been contemptuous of Barbarians, also known as Red-Haired Devils, and she has become increasingly resentful as her realm has become more and more infiltrated by Christians, and Inventors, and Military Men with their silly steamships and cannons. The Emperor, Kuang Hsü, tried to introduce some new, progressive ideas into his Government in his "Hundred Days of Reform" of 1898, but his xenophobic Aunt ruthlessly repressed them. She imprisoned the hapless young Monarch and executed all of his advisors that she could catch.

So now she has somehow manipulated a rebellious rabble called the Society of the Harmonious Fists, or the Boxers, into turning their rage against the ineffectiveness of her own Manchu Dynasty into a ferocious war against all foreigners and Christian influence. Suddenly, in the summer of 1900, European missionaries are attacked all over northern China. Fathers are hacked to death before their wives and children, who are then beheaded one by one. When the Boxers botch the job, Imperial soldiers might step in to finish it for them. Other missionary wives are doused in kerosene and set alight, or dragged out to have their breasts sliced off and left to bleed to death. Some Christians are even sacrificed in temples as offerings to the gods. And as

Europeans frantically barricade themselves inside the British Legation in Peking, Chinese Christians ("second-class Red-Haired Devils") are massacred by the thousands. A multinational military force finally fights its way a thousand miles cross-country from Shanghai to relieve the beleaguered foreigners in the Capital, forcing the Dowager Empress (with the captive Emperor in tow) to flee to the far west of China. But this is not before two hundred Europeans and some sixteen thousand Chinese Christians are killed. Many think this is the end of the Empire. Within a year, however, Tz'u Hsi will be back in the Forbidden City as if nothing had happened.

The reaction throughout the West is one of horror and revenge. In New York, most Chinese aren't even sure what the Boxers are, but that doesn't keep drunken white mobs from surging into Chinatown from the Bowery, smashing windows and slapping the faces of Chinese they meet. Near-riots erupt uptown as laundrymen all over the City are hauled into the streets and beaten bloody while their shops are torched or smashed. Restaurant owners hire security guards, the Laundry Association offers rewards for information leading to the arrests of vandals, and Guy Maine at the Chinese Guild is kept busy pursuing them in court, even while Sunday School attendance drops drastically because his students are afraid to venture outside of Chinatown.

At least no one is killed. But then, just as it looks as though the white rage is subsiding, the Tongs turn on each other once more.

Mock Duck is beginning to compete with Wong Get for power at the Hip Sing, and Tom Lee wants to show him who's boss. Again it is on Pell Street, between the roar and gloom of the Bowery El and the corner of Doyers, that trouble erupts on Sunday, August 12, 1900. Shouts and the sounds of cries and a scuffle have drawn a small crowd to the front of Number 9 when a cocky white passerby, Thomas Herlihy, pushes through them to find the fun. Inside, the dark and narrow hallway is nearly bursting with at least a half dozen men grappling desperately together. All of a sudden two shots ring out and a member of the Hip Sing Tong falls, bleeding profusely from his side.

Immediately the struggling group breaks up, most fleeing into the rear courtyard. But Goo Wing Chung, brandishing a .44-calibre Colt pistol, dashes for the street, with Herlihy in hot pursuit. He almost catches him across the way at the door to Number 8, but Goo smashes Herlihy in the face with the butt of his revolver and escapes inside.

Meanwhile, John Phillips, a black man who lives upstairs, has seen the commotion and starts heading down to see if he can help. But with a now bruised and very angry Thomas Herlihy snarling at his heels, and Phillips heading him off in front, Goo darts into the first room he comes to on the second landing and locks the door. When the policemen Phillips summons finally break it down, Goo is waiting impassively. His revolver, which he has rather clumsily hidden under the sofa, is found to have one chamber empty.

A paddy wagon pulls up and a whole squad of policemen swarm into Number 9, where they find the Hip Singer, Lun Kin, nearing death on the floor. The rest of the party hovers in an adjoining courtyard where they had become trapped after scaling the fence. At the police station, they are all found to be heavily armed with a variety of nasty long-bladed knives, snub-nosed revolvers, and lethal slingshots, the likes of which the police had never seen before. One of them carries a bar of solid iron, eighteen inches long, which he dangles from a cord attached to one end. Another has a hunk of pear-shaped metal, something like a plumb bob, which can be swung overhead, bolo-like, to be brought crashing down on an opposing skull. But through it all, the six arrested On Leong fighters display the same nonchalant indifference as their murderous companion. Goo Wing Chung never breaks a sweat.

The City learns more about the methods of Tong warfare when, five weeks later on September 21, Mock Duck retaliates. This time the battle takes place on Mott, almost in front of the Transfiguration Catholic Church. Two laundrymen are walking down the street when someone runs up and throws hot pepper in their eyes. Panicked and partially blinded, the two try to run, but a fusillade of shots rings out. One of them strikes Ah Fee in the heart, killing him. Ah Fook, a bystander, is gravely injured. And most tragically a little Italian boy, sitting on his mother's lap on a neighboring stoop, is struck by a stray bullet and dies.

Mock Duck and four others are soon arrested and indicted for murder while Wong Get, the ruler of the Hip Sings, escapes to China. Mock also flees the city when released on bail, but he's soon returned in irons. He hadn't counted on the extent of Tom Lee's web; it is the old On Leong leader who has informed the authorities that young Mr. Mock is hiding in Buffalo. Twice in the ensuing weeks Tom Lee has hot pepper thrown into his eyes, but his police bodyguard forestalls any actual assassination.

Chuck Connors now has a new item to add to his Chinatown Tour, the gory scenes of Tong battles-to-the-death. Daytime slummers tremble at Connors' heavily embellished tales, while in reality Hip Sing headquarters at 12 Bowery is an armed fortress, jostling for power with that of the On Leong at 14 Mott. Doyers is, for the moment, no-man's land, connected by tunnels and an arcade to both Mott Street and Chatham Square.

Hor Poa is caught in the middle. As a Say Yup, he is an On Leonger, and has been for nearly twenty years. On the Tong's behalf he is called upon to witness legal matters and negotiate deals, his respectability making him ideal for such tasks. Unfortunately, this also means that he probably sits on the councils that decide how to avenge Hip Sing strikes, a fact that I have to acknowledge. However, as long as Tom Lee is alive, he seems to be the driving force behind Tong violence, whereas the only time Hor Poa's name ever appears in direct connection to the On Leong is as a conciliator. That, at least, can offer me some limited consolation.

At any rate he, along with all the rest of Chinatown, is feeling jittery. The Mott Street murders of Ah Fee and the little Italian boy were plainly visible both from Quong Yuen Shing at Number 32 Mott, where Hor Poa works, and from the Hor family apartment at Number 21. Hor Poa has little children running up and down the street when not in their kindergarten. Gon the is frantic. So, in 1902, when the opportunity presents itself, he gathers his family and runs to China.

This ten-month trip will consist mostly of conducting business in Hong Kong. Most merchants wouldn't take their Chinese wives on such a journey, because the Authorities make it so difficult, and laborers are forbidden to take wives either into or out of the United States. Still, Hor

Poa won't leave his family alone and unprotected in Chinatown, and manages to get them through. While in Hong Kong, he takes the Number Three Wife and their children back to the home village for about a month, where he visits his other, somewhat scattered family.

My grandfather, now five years old and having never experienced anything but the hard streets of the City, finds this alien world immensely unsettling. There are great frightening beasts, like chickens and pigs, running around loose, and the streets aren't paved but thick with mud. Perhaps for the first time in his life my grandfather is left to run barefoot outside. Many decades later, he will still shudder at the unpleasant memory of that mud oozing through his toes.

Number Two Wife Yau She, who I suppose has now been promoted to Number One, and her son Hor Mei Fun are living in the old family compound, where Hor Poa and Gon She take up residence. The two wives have never before met each other and the tension is relieved only slightly by the fact that the rivals are lodged in two different houses.

But the older son, Hor Mei Wong, is living across the fields at Chung On Village with the late Moy She's widowed mother. When his glamorous father arrives home, the boy is dutifully packed off to Hor Lup Chui to pay homage to a man he has seen only once before. He finds a fifty-two-year-old dressed in a gentleman's gown, with his short hair covered by a Mandarin's hat with a fake queue attached that he bought especially for the trip. (For safety's sake, it's best to remember that while the Emperor may be kept in opium-addicted captivity by his dragon Aunt, the Empire still has the power to behead those who don't show him proper respect.)

Hor Poa receives his children formally, inquiring politely as to their health and education. He has been sending money to them via cousins or business associates—up to $100 per year, plus stock in a Chinese railroad—and in return he receives occasional letters from Hor Mei Wong in the careful handwriting of a young scholar. ("Please do not worry, but hope Father in America prospers, and family, the large ones and the small, are all well. Then we two brothers have nothing to worry about. If you make enough money, come home soon, and Father and his boys will have a good time together.")

One child is not there, however, the adopted daughter, Yee Sum.

She is long married or dead or something; yet in a way she may be the most important member of Hor Poa's household at the moment. For just before her father left for China, he went down to the Chinese Inspector's office in New York to file papers to admit his oldest child to the United States—a son named Hor Yee. It seems that someone had bought his daughter's name and Hor Poa's services as a father, so that whoever this boy was, he could immigrate legally as the son of a merchant. A "paper son." Actually it is pretty obvious, because "Hor Yee" doesn't use the middle name Mei, as should all the sons of this generation. Futhermore, "Yee" is a girl's generational name, not a given name at all. Lucky for him, the immigration officials don't seem to know that.

Hor Poa would have received a hefty fee, not only to lie to the Chinese Inspector, but also to supply a detailed prompt-book so that "Hor Yee" could pass the grueling examination at the border. There was a whole network supporting paper-son-smuggling, known as the *how gung*, which would supply paper fathers as well as something known as a "Commissioner's Discharge"—better than a birth certificate. The Commissioner in Malone would share in the fee paid by the *how gung* to the paper father and other go-betweens; this didn't amount to much per person, but then the Malone Commissioner made up for it in volume.

Apparently in "Hor Yee"'s case, the deception was successful (despite the fact that Hor Poa didn't recognize his supposed son's photograph) and "Hor Yee" would eventually join his paper father in business. Among friends, he would be known by his birth name, but if any white person was around, his paper name was used as a shield. It was always a struggle to keep them straight.

I have the picture of "Hor Yee" that Great-Grandfather didn't recognize; not surprisingly, he doesn't resemble anyone in our family. This is good, because he looks like a delinquent. I expect that the fee Hor Poa got paid was enough to cover the family's trip to China. At any rate, the two parted when they quarreled after a couple of years working together in New York. Hor Poa would later hear a rumor that the boy had died in Singapore.

The family moves into an apartment at 3 Doyers Street upon the death of little Yee Yut, which has made it inauspicious to stay in the old place. The new one is not a particularly pleasant place to live, with the El looming over them on one side, and loud white drunks staggering back and forth to the brothel at Number 8 or dives like Scotchy Lavelle's at Number 14, Barney Flynn's across the street, and the Chatham Club at Number 6, where the adolescent Irving Berlin sings and waits on tables when he isn't working at "Nigger" Mike's around the corner on Pell. But Hor Poa imagines that this is a safer place for his family, separated as it is from Pell Street by the Chinese Opera House, the Morning Star Mission, and Tom Noonan's House of Rescue. Evil spirits and Tong bullets will be stopped by the sharp bend in the tiny lane, and Hor Poa can avoid the dangerous Pell Street intersection altogether by using the arcade that runs from about Number 15 Doyers straight through to 12 Mott, right next to On Leong headquarters. Or he can even use the tunnel that opens up right in between his building and the Opera House, following a serpentine underground path to both Mott and the Bowery.

Things seem stable enough so that in 1904 Great-Grandfather decides to open his own business, called Quan Yick Lung & Co. It will be at 39 Mott Street, just across from the foot of Pell, and next to the old wooden buildings to the right of the Transfiguration Church that make up Naughton's Funeral Home and livery stable at 35–37. On the right side, at Number 41 Mott, is a saloon which, even though owned by Lee Chung, is still a hangout for "crooks of the Italian type, guerrillas, vamps, procurers, and young dissolute women." The smarmy action doesn't get started until around one in the morning, when there is dancing and loud "hoochy-coochy" music. Between the smell from Naughton's stable and the noise from Lee Chung's saloon may be found the reason why Great-Grandfather's rent is only $32 per month.

Rent isn't the only expense, however. There is the Chinatown institution quaintly known as *p'o tai*, or "boycott money" to consider. In their capacity as the supreme regulator of Chinatown businesses, the CCBA has granted the "sole right of use" to any Chinese business tenant anywhere in their jurisdiction. This means that he alone has the right to operate a store in that particular space, a right which lasts for his lifetime, even if the store has long been shuttered and out of business. For a new Chinese tenant to move in, a hefty fee must be paid as "basic rights" to the original proprietor. Theoretically, this keeps businesses from changing too easily, and helps the original owner recoup any losses. In reality, it means that some stores stand empty for a long, long time.

I don't know if he pays "basic rights" for Number 39 Mott, but Hor Poa devotes a hefty chunk of change to his new enterprise, $23,000—twenty-three thousand *1904* dollars—in addition to having about eighteen partners who have invested anywhere from $200 to $1,000 apiece. For Quan Yick Lung is to be a top-of-the-line purveyor of silks and fancy groceries, elegant and beautiful, like Quong Yuen Shing. In fact, Hor Poa imports much of his stock through his friends at the older company.

Great-Grandfather spends months renovating the space, which includes all the refined decorative touches of the Port Arthur. I have a ornamental panel from Quan Yick Lung hanging on my wall, or at least I'd like to think so. I found it in the trash outside of Number 39, only just recently. It had obviously been in their basement for decades, as it was encrusted with cobwebs and filth. I ruined a pair of pants carrying it home, but even through the grime I could see magic. It's apparently part of a room divider, four feet long, with gilded carving on both sides. On one face there is a pot of incense and lotus flowers, the curling smoke wrapping around some lucky bats in flight. On the other face there are delicate reeds with many-bladed leaves, and a poem in Chinese, carved in gilded wooden characters, that reads: "When Autumn leaves fall/Lovers meet."

By the Autumn of 1904, however, Hor Poa may have been wondering about the wisdom of his move.

Mock Duck is back in town. He had been living in San Francisco, where he had gone after the murder of Ah Fee and the little Italian boy two years before. It seems that all the potential witnesses in that case had received mysterious letters mentioning hot pepper being thrown into the eyes, among other unpleasant possibilities, and the case collapsed without reaching a verdict. But now, in March of 1904, he's strutting around on Pell Street, covered in diamonds, shooting at an On Leonger one day (he missed), and loudly proclaiming that Tom Lee must die on the next. With Wong Get in China, Mock Duck is firmly in control of the Hip Sing, his sinister image bolstered by his long, lethal-looking fingernails, which signal that he is too grand to do the dirty work he assigns to others. He has also gained a reputation as a gambler so fearless that he will bet his entire fortune on something as trivial as the number of seeds in an orange. Ah, youth. When will it learn that one can't gamble with wily old goats and win? Mock Duck is cut down on Pell Street by On Leong bullets in November. Lucky for him, he wears chain mail under his shirt.

And so it goes. A street battle on Pell Street. A mysterious fire which kills two On Leong officers. A man chased two blocks and shot three times across from Great-Grandfather's store, who is later revealed to be Tom Lee's cousin. Of course Mock Duck is suspected, but the Superintendent of the Parkhurst Society insists that he was helping him root out vice in Chinatown at the time.

Captain Kear of the Sixth Precinct has to be seen to be doing something, however, even though he may still be in Tom Lee's pocket. So, "searching" for gamblers in Hip Sing territory, his men break down the doors of a poetry society, deep in the discussion of the classics and painting, and follow up by raiding the Chu Family Association headquarters on Doyers Street. "I suppose you're Chu Tobacco, but if you go up there I'll make you Chu Hay!" they howl as they smash the inlaid tables used for tea ceremonies and the sinister chests of mah-jongg tiles.

But if the On Leong can use Captain Kear, the Hip Sing wields the dual weapons of the ever-gullible Parkhurst Society and New York Police Commissioner William McAdoo. On April 25, 1905, a day when Captain Kear is out of town, McAdoo summons police officers and detectives from everywhere but Chinatown to join a strange secret procession through the streets of New York. Fourteen closed carriages, led by one sputtering automobile, trace a circuitous path from Central Park West, north through Harlem, and then zigzagging downtown, like a convoy of battleships trying to elude submarines. It is only when the parade nears Mott Street that most of its participants understand where they are headed.

"Say, Dan," says one cop on the corner of Pell to another from the Sixth Precinct, "Ain't that the funniest looking Dago wedding you ever saw?" At that the carriages break ranks and each rushes to a different door, whereupon policemen armed with axes and crowbars sail out to do battle. Not surprisingly, the targets are pretty much all on On Leong turf—fully ten different buildings in one block of Mott, plus two on Pell and one on Doyers. So doors are splintered and crowds of men are driven out into the street from supposed gambling dens, many of which appear to be nothing more than clan dormitories. A number of primitive tour buses "loaded down with men and women—mostly the latter in their Easter finery—" are caught in the commotion, but after an initial scare the ladies settle back to enjoy the unfolding circus. They certainly have gotten more than they paid for.

No one is ever sure exactly how many were arrested that Sunday evening. Estimates range from 168 to over 300. Frank Moss, the righteous Christian and former Hip Sing lawyer, who is now a magistrate at the Tombs, is overwhelmed by the influx of detainees, having "lost his lunch once for all, and his patience a dozen times." Paperwork is misplaced. Prisoners who had been released on bail the night before seem now to be represented by hired impostors, and three men apparently slip away forever during the confusion. The chaos is so extreme that at one point court clerks can only throw up their hands and laugh.

Finally the men are herded into some kind of order, as one Hip Singer, standing like an avenging angel, silently identifies alleged On Leong gamblers as they are made to file before him. That is, until someone whispers to him that an orange notice has just been posted on the Chinatown bulletin board at the corner of Doyers and Pell, with an offer of $6,000 to anyone who will silence him permanently. The proceedings implode. All charges are dismissed. Frank Moss declares it to be "the worst farce he ever saw."

Three days later, both Tom Lee and Mock Duck are picked up and taken to Commissioner McAdoo's office. After being scolded for forty minutes, they emerge together, "smiling and serene, as is the wont of Chinamen when they are in trouble."

But the scolding seems not to have had the desired effect. On May 30, Tom Lee incites his police allies to stage an even larger raid against Hip Sing gambling rooms. Hip Singers leap out of windows and swarm down fire escapes as fifty uniformed officers descend on Pell and Doyers Streets. Some Chinese fight back, and soon it is the police who are seen rushing into the street in panic. Dozens are arrested and crammed into the little Sixth Precinct house on Elizabeth

Street, along with all the illegal booty seized—$29. Meanwhile, Tom Lee is found by a reporter at the elegant home he shares with his German wife, miles away up on Riverside Drive. Asked to comment on the day's events, he puffs on his cigar and says languidly, "Fine day for Decoration Day. Fine day to plant flowers on graves." If it wasn't full-scale war before, it is now.

Sunday, August 6, 1905. The Chinese Opera House is packed, as it is most Sunday nights since the ban on Sabbath performances was lifted. As usual, much of the audience consists of On Leongers, eating, chatting, and occasionally grunting their approval of what is happening onstage. It's very possible that my great-grandfather is there, since the family home is right next door at Number 3 Doyers. Anyway, the performance has progressed uneventfully for several hours when, just after ten o'clock, someone tosses a string of firecrackers onto the stage. At first it seems as though it is only part of the action, but then members of the Hip Sing Tong, who, unbeknownst to everyone, occupy both the front and the back rows, rise as one and start firing point-blank with their enormous revolvers into the now screaming crowd trapped between them. With their escape routes blocked, the On Leong has no choice but to stand and fight back, and a battle royal ensues. Revolvers flare, knives flash, and the blue smoke of gunpowder rolls out into the street.

The tumult is so great that Doyers soon fills with excited slummers and Chinese running back and forth. The shots are even audible way up at the Sixth Precinct house on Elizabeth, two blocks away, causing the station to empty out as officers drop whatever they are doing and rush down to the little theater. Policemen fight their way inside, clubbing left and right in an attempt to still the enraged mob, but the Tongs carry on with their carnage as if the cops aren't there. It is only when a general alarm goes out and officers from station houses all over the Lower East Side converge on the tiny lane that the crowd disperses—some through the tunnels that are accessible from the theater, some over rooftops, dragging their wounded behind them. All they have left behind is a mess of broken chairs, hats, shoes, and four bleeding On Leong men, three of whom will be dead by morning.

Chinatown is effectively shut down as police overrun the neighborhood, bludgeoning whoever they meet, and arresting anyone who looks even vaguely suspicious. Mock Duck is found on Pell and dragged off to the Elizabeth Street Station on a tip that he is behind the gunfight. He stands, smiling, as his lawyer sputters that the Hip Sing Leader was with him all evening. The judge listens impassively, and then jails him on $1,000 bond.

Tom Lee is quick to respond. Before the week is out, five On Leongers break into the shop of a suspected Hip Sing laundryman on East 11th Street. Four hold him down on his ironing board as the fifth slices away with a razor-sharp cleaver, cutting off his nose; he is working on the rest of his body when interrupted by the chance entry of a policeman. Before he dies the next morning the laundryman is able to identify two of the three men captured by the officer. The third, a cousin of Tom Lee, is released due to lack of evidence. The following Sunday, four Hip Sing allies from the Chinese Freemasons are shot right in their own building at 18 Pell.

Probably because they have been getting caught in the crossfire, Commissioner McAdoo temporarily bans the big tourist buses from the neighborhood's narrow streets, but it doesn't really matter because whites are avoiding Chinatown in droves anyway. The Chinese themselves are afraid to leave their rooms, and those with children look at pockmarked walls and remember that poor dead Italian boy. My grandfather turned nine just after the massacre in the theater next door to his apartment.

And then the final sacrilege. Amid the din of gongs and firecrackers marking the height of the celebrations ushering in the Year of the Horse and the 32nd year of Emperor Kuang Hsü, four more On Leongers are ambushed on Pell Street in a hail of gunfire. Two are dead, including that cousin of Tom Lee suspected in the torture death of the Hip Sing laundryman. In this battle, however, he was armed merely with pockets full of lucky quarters sealed in red envelopes that he had been handing out to children. New Year's is supposed to be the time for settling debts and forgiving differences. Something has got to give.

D espite the Tong violence, Chinatown's residents have long enjoyed a reputation for being the most peaceable people in New York

City. Chinese derelicts are never seen because the Benevolent Associations take care of their own. There has never even been a Chinese arrested for public drunkenness in their entire history in the metropolis, and there won't be for another thirty-five years. They are scrupulously clean, unerringly polite, and even though they are forbidden to vote, Chinese are still actively seeking to be seen as good citizens. Next year, in 1907 the new Chinese Chamber of Commerce will even voluntarily submit a list to Washington showing the value of various goods commonly imported by their members, so that the Government can collect the correct tariffs. In Chinatown are civic organizations like the Chinese Equal Rights League and the Women's Reform Society. In the wake of the Boxer Rebellion, Guy Maine demonstrated Chinese/American patriotism by training a class of Chinese military cadets. He and Joseph Singleton are also the heads of the New York branch of the Chinese Empire Reform Association, respectfully urging social modernization back home. In 1904, they even sponsored a visit by a dynamic political visionary from China—a doctor by the name of Sun Yat Sen, who quietly stopped in at the back rooms of laundries and restaurants and spread his message of democratic reform in the homeland.

Chinese students have long been studying at such major universities as Yale and Columbia. Miss Kang Tung Bac studies at Radcliffe, and Mrs. Huie Kin chaperones the Chinese Students' Club, while her half-Chinese daughter has recently graduated from an American medical college. Chinatown even saw a fund drive to aid Russian Jews, victims of their own pogrom in 1903.

"We hoped you would, by knowing us, learn to like us . . ." pleaded the Six Companies nearly forty years ago. Yet for decades, American Chinese have suffered the indignities of whites pelting them with mud, mocking their speech, shattering the windows of their laundries while they calmly sweep up the glass and carry on. By now, most Chinese have been through too much to let the Tongs destroy the fragile face they have worked so hard to build.

So community leaders manage to appeal to higher powers—Judge Warren W. Foster for the City of New York, the Chinese Consul and the Ambassador in Washington for His Imperial Majesty, and Guy Maine for Jesus Christ—who on January 30, 1906, chair a peace conference, attended by some fifty members of the Hip Sing and On Leong, including my great-grandfather.

"No Chinaman shall carry a revolver or other deadly weapon on his person or in the public thoroughfares . . . No tribute or tax shall be levied by either society . . . The officers and members of the On Leong Tong and the Hip Sing Tong agree not to engage in gambling in any form . . . The officers and members of the On Leong Tong and Hip Sing Tong, or their regularly accredited representatives of the Chinese Government, meet and solemnly obligate themselves to do all in their power to promote peace and prosperity among the Chinese, and to aid each other in every way to compel all Chinamen to work together for the same end . . . ," run some of the ten provisions agreed to in the final document, which also calls for $1,000 to be pledged by each Tong to enforce the new code. Great-Grandfather is one of three officers who sign for the On Leong. He was described by the *New York Times* as a "well-known Chinatown merchant." I only hope he was chosen primarily for his respectability, and not for any warlike qualities. Reportedly, he wears Chinese clothes to the signing in honor of the gravity of the occasion.

Behind the scenes, it is agreed that Mock Duck and Wong Get are both to be forced out of the Hip Sing, which will now have full control over Pell Street. Doyers Street will be neutral ground, but Mott Street, the best slice of the pie, remains an On Leong fief. Once again, it looks as though Tom Lee has come out ahead. Great banquets and celebrations follow on both sides—but the On Leong's dinner at the Port Arthur is bigger.

As for Mock Duck, life is rough. He makes a half-hearted stab at forming a new Tong with Wong Get in February of 1906, but it doesn't really go anywhere, and he is constantly harassed by the authorities. Within a week of the new treaty, he is arrested on that old 1902 murder charge, for which, for some reason, he has never been successfully tried. He ends up not being tried this time either, but one year later his beloved six-year-old adopted daughter is taken from him and placed in an orphanage. It is said that she was found asleep at her father's feet while he lay semiconscious in an opium haze. With his frantic appeals to get her back falling on deaf ears, Mock realizes he is beaten. Later that year, he forsakes New York for San Francisco.

Meanwhile, on August 16, 1906, Hor Poa, who after the treaty-signing has obligingly moved his family to an apartment in the back of his Mott Street store, celebrates the birth of another son. He is my Third Great-Uncle, Hor Ting Sun.

This is also the time when Hor Poa decides to bring over my First Great-Uncle, Hor Mei Wong. Things have changed since they last saw each other in 1902. The Chinese Inspectors have become more vigilant, with Chinese entering as students now required both to prove that their studies could not have been pursued just as well in China and to promise to return home as soon as their course is finished. The definition of "merchant" is tightened once again, and laborers can now be arrested and deported if they are found without their residence certificates actually on their persons.

In October of 1902 New York's Chinese Inspectors travel to Boston to help supervise a raid of that city's entire Chinatown. They do it on a Sunday, when the little quarter is at its most crowded, first blocking off all means of escape and then moving in, ostensibly to arrest any Chinese found to be not carrying their residence papers. But hundreds—nearly the entire Chinatown population—are rounded up in a brutal rout of swinging nightsticks and kicking boots, with no warrant and no regard for whether they have their papers or not. So many are thrown onto a police paddy wagon that it overturns, seriously injuring several people, who are then denied medical attention. At the Boston Federal Building prisoners, numbering at least two hundred and fifty, are crammed into two rooms so small there is only room to stand—which they do, hot, tired, hungry, and in pain for up to eighteen hours. There are also no bathroom breaks, and the stench of urine and feces becomes so bad that the presiding judge moves the hearings to another part of the building, where half are soon released without charge. After all is said and done, five are found to be in the country illegally and deported. To their credit, the white citizens of Boston are outraged. Back in China, indignation is so great that a nationwide boycott of American goods is organized. The Government in Washington is baffled by this reaction.

Then, in 1903, all border crossings from Canada are closed to Chinese only, with the exceptions of four tiny towns. Now all the America-bound Chinese traffic from Vancouver must be squeezed through Sumas, Washington; Portal, North Dakota; Richford, Vermont; or

Malone, New York—with Chinese travelers trying to cross at any other point subject to immediate arrest. A Chinese trying to *leave* the U.S. through Buffalo was threatened with deportation for not only using an illegal port but having no residence certificate. As he had no intention of returning to the United States anyway, he just got a refund for the Canadian-Pacific ticket he had already purchased and allowed the American Government to deport him back home at its own expense.

At each of the designated crossing points, a large detention center is built; the one at Richford is in an old school, the one in Malone in a barn, newly sheathed with iron. Both buildings are equipped with kitchens, bathrooms, and sleeping accommodations for the expected glut of prisoners. The jail in Richford can accommodate 125, the one in Malone 200. Both are soon full to bursting.

Prisoners in Richford and Malone often stay there for months, creating an odd situation for the locals trying to feed them. Wing Wo Chung & Co. of 34 Pell Street even opens a branch store in Malone, specifically to victual their jailed countrymen, who disdain American cooking even in captivity. As for the detainees, they while away the time by scratching poetry into the walls and constructing delicate paper kites, which they sell to the village children through their barred windows. Those kites clutter people's attics for years afterwards. As for the poems, none survive today, but they must have been similar to those being written simultaneously on the walls of the Chinese detention center at Angel Island, San Francisco:

The West Wind ruffles my thin gauze clothing
On the hill sits a tall building with a room of wooden planks.
I wish I could travel on a cloud far away and be with my wife and
*   son.*
When the moonlight shines on me alone, the night seems even longer.
There is no flower beneath my pillow,
And my dreams are not sweet.

For what reason must I sit in jail?
It is only because my country is weak and my family poor.
My parents wait at the door but there is no news.
My wife and child wrap themselves in quilt, sighing with loneliness

Even if my petition is approved and I can enter the country,
When can I return to the Mountains of Tang with a full load?
From ancient times, those who venture out usually become worthless.
How many people ever return from battles?

There are tens of thousands of poems composed on these walls.
They are all cries of complaint and sadness.
The day I am rid of this prison and attain success,
I must remember that this chapter once existed.
In my daily needs, I must be frugal.
Needless extravagance leads youth to ruin.
All my compatriots should please be mindful.
Once you have some small gains, return home early.

In 1907, nineteen-year-old Hor Mei Wong is imprisoned for one month in Malone at Hor Poa's expense, which comes to all of 30 cents per day. It seems that Chinese Inspector Sisson in New York is suspicious of this supposed son, because when Great-Grandfather is interrogated in the matter, the dates he supplied for all his previous visits to China didn't match up exactly with those he gave in his 1902 deposition concerning the paper son, "Hor Yee." On the strength of this grave evidence, Hor Mei Wong is ordered deported by the next Canadian-Pacific steamer.

I suppose most people were surprised that it took as long as a year and a half for the Tong truce to begin to deteriorate, but Tom Lee just can't resist tormenting his old adversaries. The speculation is that he is behind the police raid of Hip Sing headquarters at 12 Bowery in July 1907, during which there is much smashing of furniture and terrorizing of occupants. After the police finally depart, a large amount of cash and jewels are mysteriously discovered to be missing. With that loss, as well as the lost gambling income, this particular Tong is nearly broke.

But although the handicapped Hip Sing is not strong enough to take revenge upon the lion in his lair, it mounts vicious assaults on his far-flung tributaries. Several On Leongers are killed in a gun battle in Philadelphia, and in August Worry Charles, the head of the Hip Sing in Boston—the same Worry Charles once so favored by Chinese Inspector

J. Thomas Scharf and Magistrate Frank Moss—sends to New York for fighters who will be unknown to the local police and are therefore hard to trace. They open fire on a large crowd of unsuspecting men relaxing in the center of their Chinatown after a hard day's work. At least a score are hit. Four die.

The shooting only pauses momentarily in November of 1908, when the news comes that the poor beleaguered Emperor Kuang Hsü has passed away, to be followed one day later by the old Dragon Lady herself, the Empress Dowager Tz'u Hsi. Chinatown is rife with rumors that the aunt murdered the nephew, or that both were assassinated by a rebellious general. But whatever the truth may be, Tz'u Hsi seals the fate of the moribund Empire in her last official act. Mere hours before her death, she installs Prince Pu Yi as Monarch of the Middle Kingdom. The new Emperor is two years old.

At any rate, Chinese troubles, whether abroad or in New York, result only in a sharpening of the distant disgust most Americans feel towards "Mongolians" anyway. But when the body of a young white Christian missionary girl is found stuffed into a trunk in the back room of a Chinese restaurant near Times Square, the City goes ballistic. The vituperative backlash dwarfs even the reaction to the Boxer Rebellion seven years before.

Actually, this murder has very little, if anything, to do with the Tongs, but the Authorities don't split hairs. Young Miss Elsie Sigel, whose parents run the Christian mission at 10 Mott, has had the misfortune to fall in love with a Chinese from Bayard Street—dumping her previous Chinese paramour in the process. He strangles her in a jealous rage in June of 1909, and after packing her body in a trunk with the hazy idea of sending it to Europe, he flees the city.

The New York press feeds hungrily on this outrage, whipping the public into a hysterical frenzy. Laundries are raided by concerned citizens suspecting that there might be white women trapped inside, while Asians of all nationalities are arrested as far away as Indiana because they match a vague description of the alleged killer. Business falls off disastrously in Chinatown—a reported 70 percent—as whites refuse to expose their womenfolk to its perils. The waiters at the Chinese Tuxedo Restaurant are so desperate for cash that they sue the owner to recover the investments they made in the establishment when it opened. Land-lords report that many Chinese can't meet their rents and are moving out of the quarter. These property owners worry that they might have to start renting to Italians, who would pay only about 40 percent of the rate usually charged to the Chinese.

Newly installed Captain Mike Galvin of the Sixth Precinct glee-fully uses the Elsie Sigel murder as an excuse to destroy Chinatown altogether. He first closes down the headquarters of both the On Leong and the Hip Sing Tongs, after which he stages giant raids on their gam-bling houses, posting guards to make sure they don't reopen in a few hours as they have always done in the past. Any white woman living in the neighborhood who can't produce a valid marriage certificate is assumed to be a prostitute and summarily forced to move. White men—either policemen or thugs with fake badges, it's not entirely clear—brazenly plunder private homes and stores, while their owners meekly submit, having no Authority to turn to for redress. Some blame the Chi-nese Consul for not getting involved, and on July 31 the Vice-Consul is murdered by a disgruntled cook. Meanwhile, the Police Department issues orders preventing any Chinese from leaving the city without a permit, while those from out of town are harassed to the point that they don't come in. "With the strict enforcement of the law," the police exult, "Chinatown will have passed into history in another six months or a year." The only thing that will pass into history is Galvin's career at the Sixth Precinct, as it is not long before he is transferred out of the area.

It is the murder of another woman that actually brings warfare back to the streets of Chinatown, although now it is not so much Tong Motivated as clan motivated. A Prominent Gentleman has lost face—and he wants it back.

On Leong member Chin Len had married a beautiful twenty-one-year-old named Bow Kum, or Sweet Flower, after a Christian mission rescued her from an San Francisco official of a Family Association who had paid $3,000 for her services four years before. This was, and is still, an ancient and powerful Association with branches all over the world, formed by an ancient and eternal allegiance sworn between several dif-ferent clans. Nevertheless, Chin brought her to New York, and by most accounts supported her, loved her, and seemed happy. It seems that the

Family Association official didn't mind the absence of Sweet Flower's company so much as he did the loss of his investment—and of face—and he avidly sought to recover both.

There were probably well over sixty-five Family, Village, and Trade Associations in New York, busily looking after the welfare of their members and jealously guarding the prestige of their names. The honor of their Chief Gentlemen was of supreme importance, and any slight must be redressed. If the problem was with another Benevolent Society, then usually a formal apology or the proffering of some gift would be sufficient. But in this instance, the Gentleman felt that his honor, as well as a substantial amount of money, had been stolen from him by a powerful Tong. If Chin was a member of the On Leong, then the On Leong must pay.

But the On Leong spurned this Family Association's request with a disdainful *mo hong,* or "You belong to no Tong," which of course meant that they deserved no response—an arrogant insult, only intensifying the bad feelings. So on August 15, 1909, while Chin was at an On Leong meeting in their temporary headquarters across Mott Street, someone stole through the alley between Number 17 and Number 19, through the dark courtyard and up to the second floor of the rear building where Bow Kum lay sleeping. The lovely Sweet Flower, who had never done anything to offend anyone other than being born female, was killed with three ruthless thrusts through the heart. Her body was slashed, her fingers cut off. The murder weapon, an eight-inch stiletto, was left impaled in the floor. The two gas jets were left flaring so that her husband could experience the full impact of the horror when he came home.

It just gets worse and worse, for the Family Association has enlisted the Hip Sing chapter in New York to avenge their grievance with the On Leong. For their part, the Hip Sing is happy to do so, especially after On Leong testimony results in the execution of several Hip Sing gunmen involved in the Boston Chinatown massacre. So the shooting continues, with the trademark .44-calibre Colt revolvers so favored by both Tongs. Sometimes there are daily killings, sometimes a month or more goes by. Some deaths are retributions for violence, some for things as trivial as defacing an On Leong notice on the community bulletin board. Two victims are well over seventy years old. At any rate, no member of the Hip Sing can venture onto Mott Street without putting his life in serious danger, just as no On Leonger can walk on Pell in safety. For now, whenever Great-Grandfather or any of his fellows want to visit the Opera House, they must use the arcade connecting Mott and Doyers.

It is at the Opera House, at Christmastime 1909, that the most bizarre incident in this never-ending war unfolds. Actors are about as low as you can get on the Chinese social scale, and therefore are pretty much ignored whenever they are offstage. Ah Hong, however, seems to be an exception. He is a loyal On Leong man, as well as being a leading actor and assistant manager of the Opera House, which has somehow always managed to stay open despite morality crusades and Tong battles. Hong is quite the comedian, it seems, and as the theater is largely On Leong territory, he doesn't mince words when speaking of the Hip Sing. He will cheerfully break character, ad lib, and do anything to skewer his target *du jour,* much to the delight of his own Tong and the consternation of his rivals'. The Reverend Huie Kin, who has taken over at the Morning Star Mission, warns Ah Hong that he is treading on thin ice, but laughter and applause are intoxicating, and besides, who would want to harm someone as unimportant as an actor?

In New York, all the Chinese Opera House performers, which by 1909 even include some women acrobats, live together in a crowded tenement at 10 Chatham Square just behind the theater and connected to it by a tunnel. But when on one December day a death notice is posted on the door, Ah Hong's predicament is brought jarringly home to him. His fellow actors are justifiably alarmed, but still he persists, although he does obtain police protection, with officers escorting him back and forth to work and even standing guard in front of the stage where Hong continues to deliver his dangerous barbs. Reportedly, however, he has made plans to flee the city, and on December 29, with police officers stationed at the door to his tenement, he quietly packs in his room. Late that night, his downstairs neighbor (a Bowery chanteuse by the name of "Hoochy Coochy Mary") hears a shot. She goes upstairs and finds Ah Hong dead, with a bullet through the eye. His assailants had apparently been lowered from the roof to a window outside his room.

The next day the theater closes down for the first time in its his-

tory. When it reopens, two months later, it will offer a pathetic mixed
bill consisting of snatches of Chinese opera sandwiched by chorus girls,
moving-picture shows, and a "Professor" demonstrating the wonders of
electricity. Electric it may be, but the Chinese Opera House has lost its
magic forever.

There are truces and there are treaties, but in the first eighteen
months after Sweet Flower's murder, over fifty people are killed (plus a
horse caught in the crossfire) and scores are injured, among whom are
tourists, bystanders, and even the middle-aged female employee of a
Chinese laundryman unlucky enough to be at work when the Tong
paid a call.

The Truce of 1911 seems as though it might hold. On January 3,
both Tongs give grand banquets for each other, drink toast after toast of
sweet plum wine, and then, with great ceremony, cut off their queues—
over two hundred at once—in anticipation of the great things going on
in China. The long awaited revolution against the moth-eaten Manchu
Dynasty has finally broken out and is rolling easily across the vast
Empire. Great cities and whole army units turn their faces towards revolution, led by a courtly, slender forty-five-year-old man who speaks
impeccable English—Dr. Sun Yat Sen.

Dr. Sun, raised in Honolulu as the son of a rich merchant, has
been traveling the world for more than fifteen years now, spreading
his message and raising money to finance the rebellion he knew was
inevitable. At first he supposedly wanted merely to reform the
Empire, making Kuang Hsü a constitutional monarch and installing a
democratic parliament like the one in England. The Emperor probably would have welcomed that, as anything would have been better
than living as the personal whipping boy of the Dowager Empress.
But old Tz'u Hsi, unsurprisingly, would have nothing to do with Dr.
Sun and his asinine ideas, and after her ruthless suppression of the
Hundred Days' Reform in 1898, she placed a price on Sun's head of a
reported $100,000. Since that amount of money would make any
common assassin fabulously wealthy in China, it is actually remarkable that he survived.

Once he was nearly caught in Canton, forced to flee over fences and rooftops until suddenly yanked inside a house and hidden by a sympathizer who had witnessed his predicament. From the windows of that house a few days later, Dr. Sun secretly watched the beheading of a number of his closest associates. In London he was actually kidnapped and held by the Imperial Legation, and only the intervention of the Marquis of Salisbury prevented him from being returned to China and certain death.

Since 1896 Sun Yat Sen has been making quiet visits to New York, including the one where he supposedly had to hide in a loft on Canal Street to evade Tz'u Hsi's spies. But now that the revolution is underway, Dr. Sun can be a little more bold, openly soliciting large sums from bankers and merchants and sometimes even making public speeches. In April of this year of 1911, after a large bazaar on Doyers Street where even Chinese women staff booths to raise money for famine relief in war-torn China, he makes a surprise appearance at the old Chinese Opera House (a space which by now has finally given up the ghost and is occupied by Tom Noonan's Rescue Mission) to give a rousing speech and rally optimism in a neighborhood that has been as beleaguered as any Toi-shan village squirming under the thumb of the Empress Dowager's minions.

In October he is rumored to be back, and Chinatown is in a whirl of celebration. Chinese Boy Scouts march up and down Mott Street with wooden rifles, celebratory posters are displayed at On Leong headquarters, and some two thousand people cram themselves into the Opera House/Rescue Mission in hopes of hearing him speak. "Dr. Sun will not be here this afternoon," says Jue Chok Man, one of the rebel leader's lieutenants. "He is not far from here, but I am not permitted to say where he is. I can only say that he is not in New York at present. Long live Dr. Sun and the Republic!" Thunderous cheers break out and money pours in, while up at the Hotel Arlington on West 25th Street, a mysterious Asian gentleman sits secluded in his suite. No one is quite sure who he is, but he seems to be someone of some importance, periodically sending his secretary to order pots of tea brewed to very exacting specifications. After three weeks in residence, this enigmatic gentleman slips quietly away, reportedly to England. Meanwhile, the price on Sun Yat Sen's head has supposedly been doubled to $200,000.

The Empire finally expires from old age, and on January 1, 1912,

Dr. Sun is declared the first President of the Chinese Republic. Meanwhile, back in Peking, five-year-old former Emperor Pu Yi continues to live in the Forbidden City, and will do so until he becomes an adult. It will be some time before the Royal Eunuchs will tell His Ex-Imperial Majesty exactly what has happened.

But as Chinatown celebrates, both the Hip Sing and the On Leong suffer one setback after another. Barely three weeks after the Tong truce, federal agents raid two locations of an importing firm on Seventh Avenue owned by one Lee Quong Jung, a.k.a. Diamond Charley, a.k.a. Charley Boston—who, as a "cousin" of Tom Lee, is an important officer of the On Leong Tong. In his late forties, Diamond Charley Boston is a predictably dapper man, affable and polite, with big diamond rings on his fingers and a diamond horseshoe pinned to his coat. His stores, open for at least ten years, profess to sell "fine, imported teas," and are strangely fitted out with stout counters behind thick, iron bars running to the ceiling. White patrons of all descriptions are seen coming and going all day and night, and Authorities suspect that it is something other than tea leaves being passed through those iron bars. The Feds find letters from police bigwigs and politicos in other cities, like J. M. Morin, Director of Public Safety in Pittsburgh, who writes to thank Charley for the gift of tea and the kimono "for Mrs. Morin and myself." Police suspect they have stumbled on a national distributing center for an opium ring huge enough to keep city police departments in its pay.

Oddly, the only current legal restrictions on opium use in this country are about its use as an ingredient in certain medicines, and that measure was only passed in 1906. Opium has been sold openly in New York for decades, from Wong Gee, one of the founders of the predecessor to the On Leong Tong, who was casually identified in the 1880 census as a "dealer in opium," to a lawsuit brought in court in 1888 against the wealthy Chu Fong for selling "fraudulent" opium to a distributor. (It turned out to be barrels of flour.) What the Feds are after Charley Boston for is that he imported the narcotic without paying the Customs duty. He is quickly arrested and sent to jail for eighteen months.

But the rumor is that either the Hip Sing or the aggrieved Family Association had tipped off the police to Charley Boston, so less than two weeks after his arrest, fifty federal agents sweep down on Hip Sing territory in another flashy drug raid. All they find are a "two cans of regularly labeled and stamped [and therefore legal] opium, a few pipes, and . . . small change in bad coins." The Feds arrest several people in connection with the counterfeit change—which has a total face value of $2.50—but decide to release them before they get to the D.A.'s office, because even they realize how ridiculous they will look.

Then in October the Hip Sing suffers another blow. A strange notice appears in the New York papers. "$1,000 REWARD for information as to whereabouts of Lee Hing (Chinese)," it reads. Apparently, Lee had been the treasurer for the Hip Sing and had absconded with their operating budget of $6,000. Why they advertise for him in English-language papers is anyone's guess.

At any rate, there are tensions in the air. And then on January 5, 1912, almost exactly a year after the great Tong truce, Lung Yu, the President of the Hip Sing Tong, is shot dead in a Pell Street gambling hall concealed behind a store. As the police enter to find the dead President Lung in the dimly lit room, littered with overturned tables and light bulbs shot out in the gunfight, they are startled to be confronted by an old friend sitting in a corner. "Very bad business," sighs Mock Duck, as he sips a cup of tea and placidly surveys the carnage.

The war is on again.

So the merchants and laundrymen will cut off their queues and dodge the bullets as they try to go about their daily business. They walk their birds, sip their tea, and read their newspapers—the weekly *Chinese Chronicle* or the semi-weekly *Chinese Reform News*, depending on their politics. The Reverend Huie Kin preaches at the First Chinese Presbyterian Church on East 31st Street, while Dr. Huang Coong Chen teaches Confucianism at 9 Mott. Miss Mary Banta ignores the worries of her friends as she trudges the streets, as she has since 1904 when she took over for Miss Helen Clark at the Chinese Mission. Miss Banta is especially fond of children, who call her *sing sang paw*, or Teacher Lady, and she will patiently sit for hours, gently teaching them English by holding up objects and repeating their names. She taught my grandfather, and my great-uncles, and my great-aunt. She would go on to work with the next generation, the next, and still the next after that.

There are banquets and picnics and of course work, lots of hard, hard work. For despite all the trouble, the purpose of the Chinese in being in New York still is to make enough money to leave. These are a people who have been living with authoritarian oppression for millennia, and the ability to deal with it is in their genes. In Chinatown they continue to display their remarkable ability to ignore the Tong or the Police or anything else that gets in their way.

This Chinese single-mindedness and ability to plod right ahead despite daunting obstacles is revealed rather dramatically in the story of a group of six "Celestials" sailing to New York from Hong Kong via England. They were, of course, in third class, but they didn't complain or take notice of the open-mouthed hostility exhibited by some of the other European immigrants in the ship. They also didn't panic when, several days into the voyage, the vessel suffered an accident and started to sink. Although most of the third-class passengers were left to mill around far below decks by a crew too preoccupied by the task of evacuating the richer clientele, the six Chinese somehow found their way up to the top deck where the boats were. When male passengers were prevented from climbing into the lifeboats because of the women-and-children-first rule, the six Chinese calmly stood to the side in the darkness. Some other men panicked and tried to fight their way into the boats, but the six Chinese, taking note of those moments when officers weren't watching too closely, quietly slipped into them one by one. Several climbed into one boat early and hid beneath the seats, but it seems as though at least one of them was discovered and forced at gunpoint to climb back on deck. His place was taken by another man, the owner of the shipping line. Once safely away, the remaining Chinese suddenly popped up in the darkness, much to the astonishment of the other passengers around them.

The last two Chinese on this ship didn't make it into a lifeboat, but one of them tied himself to a door ripped from its hinges, and floated free as the vessel finally sank. When a lifeboat drew near, the officer in charge saw him unconscious in the water but said, "What's the use [in saving him]? He's dead, likely, and if he isn't there's others better worth saving than a Jap!"—making the usual mistake of confusing Chinese and Japanese. This officer actually started to row away, but thought better of his actions and came back to pull the Japanese aboard. After being revived, the small, cold, and wet man looked around, saw a sailor exhausted from rowing, and promptly bustled over to take over for him. "By Jove!" exclaimed the slack-jawed officer, "I'm ashamed of what I said about the little blighter. I'd save the likes o'him six times over if I got the chance!"

The date was April 15, 1912. The ship—*Titanic*. Of the 387 male passengers in third class, 75 survived. Of the six Chinese in third class, five survived. They didn't fight, or complain, or take what wasn't theirs— the crew of *Titanic* had been so anxious to evacuate the ship that they sent many of the lifeboats away barely half-full of women and children (while often still keeping the men out). The Chinese just went ahead and did what they needed to do.

When these five got to New York, they took up residence in China- town while methodically filing lawsuits against the White Star Line for their lost luggage. They're right there on the claims list, just ahead of the Countess of Rothes. One Japanese survivor (who had thrown himself into a lifeboat just as it was being lowered) also arrived safely in New York—and was promptly deported.

This wasn't the only sea voyage of significance in 1912. In June, Hor Poa, his Number Three Wife, and his three sons (Fourth Great- Uncle, Hor Ting Fong had been born in 1909) left the squabbling Tongs behind and sailed one last time on the *Empress of Russia*, bound from Vancouver for China. Hor Poa was getting old by now, but both my great-grandparents knew that it was high time to find my grandfather a wife. After all, he was almost 15 years old.

7

THE
CHIEF
GENTLEMAN

The oldest New York-born Chinese man would be twenty-seven in 1912. He may have fathered children himself by now, although the chances of him having found a Chinese wife in New York City are very slim. There are only fifty-six "pure" Chinese families in Chinatown this year. They have produced perhaps 150 children between them, who have grown up walking around puddles of blood on the sidewalk and keeping their eyes cast demurely downward so as not to see what they shouldn't see. These children have long grown accustomed to listening for the sound of gunfire and keeping away from the windows, but, like their parents, they just mind their own business and soldier on. During the height of the violence, Hor Poa even moved his family from the apartment at 39 Mott down the street to somewhat safer lodgings at Number 13. Even the casual passerby will note that since they are often in the line of fire, buildings like 39 Mott, across from the foot of Pell, are full of bullet holes.

The First Generation has also grown up to be wary of the white Authorities. They remember the raids, the swinging nightsticks, the arbitrary, wholesale arrests of people suspected of being illegal immigrants. They know that while they themselves may have been born with

American citizenship, a slip on their part could get their parents deported. If their uncles, or fathers, or neighbors are, in fact, "paper sons," the children know that those men may be called by certain names in private, but they are always strictly meticulous in remembering to use the "paper" name when addressing them on the street. Even the smallest children, if traveling outside the country, are subjected to the same grueling interrogations given to their elders, all of which take place in the Chinese Inspector's branch office directly over Hor Poa's store. My Great-Uncle Sun is not yet six years old when the family departs for China in 1912. A stenographer records his encounter with officialdom, which takes place in English.

> Q. *What is your name?*
> A. *Hor Ting Sun.*
> Q. *How old are you?*
> A. *I don't know.*
> Q. *I show you that picture and ask who it is? (Referring to photograph of applicant)*
> A. *My picture.*
> Q. *Who is this man? (Referring to Hor Poa)*
> A. *My papa.*
> Q. *Who is this lady? (Referring to Mrs. Hor Poa)*
> A. *My mama.*
> Q. *Whose picture is that? (Referring to photograph of Hor Ting Pun)*
> A. *My brother, Hor Ting Pun.*
> Q. *Whose picture is that? (Referring to photograph of Hor Ting Fong)*
> A. *My brother, Hor Ting Fong.*
> Q. *Do you know where you were born?*
> A. *No.*
> Q. *What do you do?*
> A. *I go to school!*
> Q. *Where is your school?*
> A. *On Mott Street.*
> Q. *Can you write your name?*
> A. *In Chinese.*

And then Great-Uncle Sun happily writes his name in clear, well-formed Chinese characters. I wonder how many of the Inspectors were fully bilingual, or could even have written their own names when they were in kindergarten?

All the school-age children go to a special Chinese School in the afternoons at the CCBA building at 16 Mott Street. Professor C. H. Chu is the teacher, and was a cofounder when it was formed in 1908 under a special charter from the Imperial Government. The fathers want their children to know the correct way to read and write Chinese, for many still hope that the family will return to China someday and that the sons will grow up to be great officials in Government and bring honor to the family name. But even without that ambition, every good Chinese man wants his sons—and in New York, sometimes his daughters also—to start learning to write that ancient language early, for they know that to achieve even newspaper-level literacy could take up to ten years. Then too, fine handwriting is more prized among the Chinese than perhaps anyone else in the world. It is a language written not with a pen but with a brush, and the best examples of this writing are considered art of the highest order. Classical Chinese paintings are not considered complete until their successive owners have added their own poetry of praise, written directly on the picture in their distinctive, exquisite script.

Actually, a Chinese childhood is almost all school. When old enough to leave their mothers, the children toddle off with their fathers down to the Kindergarten, now run by Mrs. Huie Kin of the Morning Star Mission, where they are taught simple Sunday School songs and told moralistic fables based on the Bible. The first couple of years of grade school are at the old P.S. 108, just above Bayard Street on Mott. Third through eighth grades are at P.S. 23 on the corner of Bayard and Mulberry, a school built in 1891 to serve the Italian community. But since about 1900 there have been an increasing number of Chinese children there, children who are scrupulously well behaved because they are required by elders, concerned about family face, never to give their teachers any problems and to get excellent grades.

The boys had been given names by their parents which meant things like Strong, or Hero, while the girls were called Dainty or Beautiful. But once in an American classroom they are all given somewhat awkward English "school names" like Mildred or Quincy, Eunice or Chester. Grandfather's school name is George, which he will use with white people all his life. Great-Uncle Fong's is Harold, which he will strive to forget as soon as he is allowed to. Great-Uncle Sun (a name which might mean "New") doesn't take a school name at all, but is always known as Sunny, which perfectly fits his cheery disposition. Still, like all the rest of the Chinese kids, they are teased mercilessly over their Chinese names, the verbal abuse only intensifying for children with surnames like Hor. The girls have their lucky jade jewelry or gold earrings stolen by Italian girls on the playground. And for boys wearing queues, the torture wrought by hostile young minds can only be imagined. After school, the Italian kids swarm out onto Mulberry Street to play hopscotch and stickball. The Chinese kids always go straight home.

Still, the teachers seem to like their bright Chinese students. Grandfather would always brag that whenever his teachers couldn't get an answer out of the white kids they'd call on him, while Great-Uncle Fong was particularly fond of Miss Wolf, whom he had in fourth grade. She would take the class on trips outside of Chinatown to places like Central Park to see the Punch and Judy shows or visit the animals in the zoo. By the time he is ten years old, he has undoubtedly seen far more of New York City than his mother.

Closer to home, however, P.S. 23 is about as far as a Chinese child in New York can venture into Little Italy without getting beat up or having stones thrown at him, and even then, children are always escorted to and from school by their fathers. Of course there are plenty of Italian kids who live right in Chinatown, and as long as they're on Mott Street the two nationalities suffer each other's presence. But any Chinese child who ventures up Mulberry or Baxter or even, God forbid, to the other side of Canal Street does so at his own peril. "Oh, there wasn't any trouble," one man demurs. "They never did anything to us at all—except maybe beat us up and throw rocks." Of course Chinese kids, especially the girls, are pretty content to stay close to home and mind their parents' warnings. "I don't know what would have happened to me north of Canal Street," one lady who went to school with Great-Uncle Fong told me recently. "But then, why would I go there?" Canal Street is all of two blocks away from the epicenter of Chinatown.

One block to the east is another place the children can't go. The Bowery languishes in the shadow and the dust of the Third Avenue El. It is bad enough that the spirit of the place has made inroads into Chinatown with places like "Nigger Mike's" on Pell Street and the Chatham Club on Doyers, housed in a rickety old wooden building bristling with dormers and angles. But the Bowery itself is full of flophouses, filthy bars, and tawdry "hoochy-coochy" dance halls, not to mention a plethora of moving-picture houses, always a draw for low company. Number 29 is "one of the oldest and most notorious saloons in the city," frequented by "the lowest type of women." Number 9 Bowery is described as "Tom Lee's old panhandler's dump," while the New England Hotel on the corner of Bayard is another institution owned by the "Mayor of Chinatown," with women for hire waiting in a sleazy barroom. Other saloons like Steve Brodie's and McGurk's "Suicide Hall" have dark back rooms or private quarters upstairs for the confidential pursuit of personal pleasures. But not only do the children not go near these places, even the toughest Tong hatchet men give white drunks and their hangouts a wide berth.

To the south, on the other side of Chatham Square, is part of the Jewish section, with Division Street occupied mainly by Jewish tailors and hatters. The Chinese word for this particular boulevard is *Mai Mo Gai*, or "Selling-Hat Street," and when men want an American suit or a hat, they will venture into to a place like Moe Levy's, which they call Moe Lee-*vooy* in their Cantonese singsong. Chinese children can go into this neighborhood, where they are treated a bit better. Some of them even have Jewish friends, just about the only non-Chinese friends that their parents will tolerate.

Still, being a Chinese child does have its distinct advantages, especially during this period when they are so few. After all, for the boys at least, we are talking of a life that starts out with a huge party where people cover them with money—and it only gets better. For instance, there are the Five Festivals, like the Autumn Moon Festival, where the bakeries are kept busy for weeks preparing the special moon cakes, dense and sweet, and stamped with a lucky message on their surface. There is the Dragon Festival on the fifth day of the fifth lunar month, with the wonderful dragon parade and delicious food. At the Festival of Lights, beautiful lanterns are hung and lit in front of everyone's window, and Chinatown looks more enchanted than ever. At the Cold Festival particularly tasty dumplings are made, and all the celebrations end with the burning of incense and of gold and silver paper money, for the Ancestors must be included in all the fun.

But child heaven is really reached on New Year's. Then the boys are dressed up in gorgeous silk clothes, the most expensive money can buy, in peacock colors that would delight any youngster's eye. The sleeves of their *shams* are so long that they hang down to the knees, and they have special contrasting vests, and round, bright red silk caps to go on their heads. The fathers, also dressed in their best, proudly take their sons calling, the boys receiving sweet cakes and lucky red envelopes every place they visit. The envelopes always contain at least two pieces of silver money, for just one piece is what you would get at a funeral and that would be bad luck. Along the way there are fabulous sights to see, and especially to hear, for at each store long strings of firecrackers, sometimes several stories high, are set alight, creating machine-gun explosions that ripple up the faces of buildings. There are more firecrackers thrown in the streets, and rockets hissing skyward, and really loud bombs exploding in the air, until the sidewalk is just a sea of the shards of red paper left over from the wrappings, and the air is acrid with the smell of gunpowder. The older boys revel in the fire-cracker siege, and craftily toss a couple in the direction of the crowds of white tourists, also known as foreigners, who jump and yelp most gratifyingly. Everywhere there is the color red, the color to encourage prosperity—red lanterns, red streamers, red banners, and still more smiling men stuffing red envelopes in your hands, and melon cakes (stamped with red messages) in your mouth. And then, amid a cacophony of gongs and an even more intense shower of (red) firecrackers, the Lion appears, his long, twisting body trailing out behind that huge brilliantly-colored head, both frightening and fantastic with its rolling eyes, his flowing mane, and his snapping jaws ready to consume money offered by store owners eager to have the beast come and frighten those evil spirits away for another year. The older boys have been training to make the Lion dance, working their way up from drum-beaters to tail-wigglers to the honored place inside the head, jumping and leaping and showing off. Maybe the father lets the small son approach the rearing, snorting creature and reach up a hand, trembling with terror mixed with delight, to feed that gaping mouth a red envelope filled with coins. A lunge, a snap, and the money is gone, while the little boy squeals in pure pleasure.

Meanwhile the girls are at home, helping their mothers prepare the special treats for the expected visitors, the sweet buns, the sugared melon seeds, the delectable candied orange slices and the sliced stalks of sugar cane. Last night they finished scrubbing the entire apartment so that it sparkles, and fought with their brothers over who would have the honor of smearing the Kitchen God's mouth with honey before they burned him in the stove. Today they have special clothes also, their frog-buttoned *chong shams* swirling with intricate embroidered designs, and big bows in their hair. Even though it is still winter the windows are wide open, and when the strings of firecrackers hung by the shopkeeper downstairs suddenly fires off up the wall, the girls and their mothers know that it is time to greet the Lion as he prances and struts downstairs. Of course, they don't go into the street, but they have prepared heads of lettuce, stuck all over with red envelopes, which they lower down on long lengths of string so that the lucky Lion can swallow them down whole (or at least so that the man standing next to it can drop them into his satchel) thus bringing good fortune on the household. This it does in more ways than one, since the various Lions are sponsored by benevolent associations who use the money to help members in need.

And then, in the afternoon, the entire family and guests gather for a sumptuous banquet, running into the tens of courses, with sweet suckling pig, roast chickens, and lucky shellfish steamed with seaweed. It might be held at home, but most people go to huge affairs hosted by their family or village associations, and the Hor family undoubtedly attends the great On Leong feast held at the Port Arthur Restaurant. On this joyous occasion a closed carriage is obtained so that Gon She can attend, and she sits proudly with her younger children at the women's table, while Hor Ting Pun joins his father and the men. Tom Lee, his revered secretary Gin Gum, and probably Hor Poa himself happily make the rounds of the restaurant. At each table they are expected to drink a toast to the diners' health, which is returned with raised glasses and a

loud acclamation, toast after toast of sweet rice wine. After such a dinner, Hor Poa needs to ride the half block home in Gon She's carriage, for
walking has become strangely difficult.

Gon She and the other Chinese wives really treasure these
rare outings, but usually the children are the dutiful eyes, ears, and
ambassadors for their mothers, who, of course, typically can only
watch the world from their windows. They run errands, carry messages
to their fathers, and eagerly relate the neighborhood gossip later, as
they sit at home and help with the piecework left by the man from the
garment factory. His instructions they patiently translate into Chinese.
The girls would help to maintain the Ancestors' Altar, with tablets venerating three generations back, and several times a year the mothers
might be released again to go to Cypress Hills and tend the graves of
anyone whose bones are waiting to be sent back to China. Grace Lee,
the daughter of Lee B. Lok ("The white people always called us the
'Lok Girls' because they didn't realize my father's family name was
Lee") shares a dilemma with many of her friends in that her mother
has bound feet. These ladies can barely get around their apartments,
let alone the world outside, and their daughters learn to help in the
daily wrapping and rewrapping of their mothers' feet, while silently
thanking whatever gods they believe in that they have been spared this
awful fate.

Even now there are at the very most only about a hundred Chinese
girls of marriageable age in Chinatown, out of a total New York City
Chinese population of 4,614, which is down 25 percent from ten years
ago—the Exclusion Law has done its work. But however conservative
some of these daughters may still be, especially in comparison to their
Italian and Jewish classmates, this first generation of Chinese-American
girls is vastly different from their mothers. For one thing, they are getting a real education.

There was, of course, Miss Kang Tung Bac who was at Radcliffe
in 1903, but in a city where it is still a little unusual for immigrant
girls of any nationality to go to high school, a substantial proportion of
the Chinese girls are there, with two at teachers' college. Lee B. Lok,

the manager of Quong Yuen Shing, intends to educate all six of his daughters. "Why educate your girls?" his more old-fashioned friends say. "They're just going to be someone else's daughters someday." That would be true in China, but Mr. Lee knows that in New York the possibilities are endless. As for his son, he goes to the Cheshire Academy in Connecticut.

Of the boys, most expect to go on to public high schools like DeWitt Clinton or Stuyvesant High, where many distinguish themselves on the basketball and baseball teams, much to the surprise of their fathers, who were raised with the idea that a Gentleman did not exert himself for any reason. There are also about forty currently studying at Columbia University in 1912, and three have just received their Ph.D.'s in Philosophy. One of those graduating this year will go on to law school and become the first Chinese admitted to the federal bar. "I shall not specialize in work among my countrymen," says Hua-Chuen Mei to a reporter, "though doubtless I shall be able to help them, since the poor Chinese frequently fall into the hands of shyster lawyers."

Like their sisters, these young men are perfectly bilingual, the boys often interpreting for their fathers when they help out in their stores after school. This is a generation that will look to move up and out—that is, if the city around them will let them. They wear sharp suits and straw hats, and many pick up the latest Bowery slang, although they are careful not to use it at home.

Not all the fathers are happy about this. One man absolutely forbids his children to go to the public library on East Broadway until he is finally convinced that it is free. But even then he isn't sure it's a good idea. After all, how can you make money in a library?

Quong Yu Chong actually tries to have his twelve-year-old son arrested on a charge of "incorrigibility," marching him into the Elizabeth Street Police Station and complaining to the white desk sergeant that his boy is being un-Chinese. Not only does he associate too much with Americans but, horror of horrors, he has become a Boy Scout. For his part the son, who wears a natty outfit that he bought himself, says he can't stand the smell of fish in his father's store any longer and he wants to run away and get a job. There is no record on what action the police sergeant takes.

But many of the older well-to-do Chinese fathers feel that the only proper education for a young gentleman is one obtained in China, and Lingnam University, also known as the Canton Christian College, is just about the most popular destination. So it is here, after finishing the first year at DeWitt Clinton High School, that Grandfather is deposited to prepare himself to meet adulthood.

In Canton, my Grandfather Hor Ting Pun spends a year at the College, polishing his Chinese calligraphy skills, and learning about the Bible and modern literature. The advent of Republicanism in China has meant that there is a new spirit there as well, with queues having disappeared as if by magic, and a new railroad connecting Hong Kong and Canton. This spirit extends to women, as well as men, with girls beginning to appear in schools and foot-binding declared illegal for the first time in a thousand years.

But all the time he is there, his parents and brothers are at the family compound in Hor Lup Chui. Now it is Sun's and Fong's turn to experience the yucky sensation of walking around outside barefoot, while their parents prepare for a wedding, bound by tradition seemingly as old as time. This is all much to the chagrin of Number Two Wife Yau She, whose son Hor Mei Fun left for New York just last year. He is not married, and therefore some younger half-brother from a Number Three Wife should properly defer to him by marrying after he does. But Hor Poa just ignores her scalding looks, and Yau She seethes with jealousy over her younger rival's progeny.

Gon She and Hor Poa had probably contracted with a family in a neighboring village for Grandfather's marriage to their child on their visit back in 1902, when Grandfather was only five. Their choice was a daughter of Chin Dung Gee and his wife Lee She, a graceful, shy little girl named Yuet Kim. Thus two of my maternal great-grandparents and a grandmother come into the picture.

My grandfather is not pleased at the prospect. True to tradition, he has not actually met his bride-to-be. But not only is she a year older than he, all these country people are such hicks, with their pigs and chickens and old-fashioned ideas. Most of them have never even seen an automobile or ridden on a train, let alone switched on an electric light or flushed a toilet. Besides, Grandfather is already a budding Big Shot back on Mott Street, and is apparently in love with a girl he left behind, someone whom I suspect was not even Chinese. In his mind there was no way that his parents were going to shackle him to some bumpkin who probably shares her bedroom with the family cow. But here his mother Gon She demonstrates where a woman's power lies in this rigidly codified society. She coolly informs her Number One Son that he either marries the girl they have chosen or they return to New York without him. After all, they have other sons.

Matriarchal authority is an immovable force, and Grandfather's resistance crumbles to dust.

It is a blow-out wedding, loaded down with every trapping that Hor Poa can afford, plus a few more, for family face greatly depends on putting on a good show. The Chin family has similar concerns, so they deck out their daughter in the most splendid red silks and hire the grandest sedan chair with the smartest-looking bearers to carry her across the fields to Hor Lup Chui. There are so many firecrackers and gongs and horns going off upon her entry into the village that it sounds as if a small war has erupted, and birds for a mile around take to the skies in alarm. Everyone in the village is fêted at the three-day banquet that follows, and the countryside is depleted of its suckling pigs, ducks, quail, and standing stocks of sweet plum wine. The locals eat and eat until they think they've gone to heaven. It is a very satisfactory party indeed. Thus, Grandfather's formal marriage name becomes Hor Gong Ng, an appellation that hereafter will only appear on ancestral tablets and other such musty testimonials.

As for the seventeen-year-old girl who steps out of the sedan chair to meet her sullen groom, let's just say that there are many men who would have been happy to have been in Grandfather's shoes. For Chin She is beautiful—no—the only word to describe her is *lovely*. She has the high forehead that is viewed as the mark of intelligence, along with arched pencil-thin eyebrows and perfectly sculpted cheekbones. But most importantly of all, Chin She has the bearing of a princess.

I only have one picture of my grandmother. It is a formal studio photograph, taken of the family to commemorate the birth of her First

Son, my Uncle Everett in 1919. Here she is about twenty-three, sitting to the side next to her two daughters, while my grandfather holds up his baby boy like a trophy won at a horse race. But Chin She is who my eye is drawn to. She is staring straight at the camera with a slight smile playing on her lips, possessed of a tranquility that only adds to her beauty. Unlike her mother-in-law Gon She, who in her wedding picture is all dolled up in a rather garish red gown slashed by stripes of what are probably gold embroidery, Chin She is dressed in the simplest of silk *chong shams,* with a very high Mandarin collar that just brushes her cheek. Around her neck is a jade pendant, gold rings are on her fingers, and her wrists are thick with jade, ivory, and gold from her trousseau. But you have to look hard to see these ornaments, because what transfixes you is that exquisite face, that graceful figure, the Mona Lisa smile. She looks kind, my young Grandmother, and a little fragile as well. She has the appearance of someone who has had to put up with a lot, but still manages to hold her head up and look straight ahead.

The wedding could only take place after another event, nearly as momentous, had taken place. For in the spring of the Second Year of the Republic, a.k.a. 1913, Gon She, who is still only thirty-three herself, gives birth to another girl, Yee Bik. So the Hor family returns on the *Empress of Russia* in November of that year with two extra daughters. The Chinese Immigration Stations in Malone and Richford had been closed in 1910, so now New York-bound Chinese passengers are sealed into their trains in Vancouver and sent straight across the continent to Halifax, Nova Scotia, where they are put in ships bound for Ellis Island. Chin She, the wife of an American citizen, is admitted without any trouble, but she will never be permitted to become a citizen herself. Hor Yee Bik, who will spend all but the first eight months of her life in New York, is probably viewed with some suspicion, and she will not even be eligible to be naturalized until she is thirty years old. Both could be deported at any time, and if that happens there is nothing their American families can do about it.

It is a new Chinatown they return to at the end of November, 1913. In celebration of the fall of the Manchus, the past January 1 had been the first time that Chinatown had officially celebrated the Occidental New Year, replacing the traditional Lunar New Year's celebration. Gone were the lion dancers and the firecrackers, the lanterns and the divining sticks. Instead of the customary banners, American and new Republican Chinese flags fluttered in the breeze. "American celebration, all American!" called out one merchant happily, adding dismissively. "They are looking forward to die!" as he looked in the direction of the few old men who seemed to be the only ones still wearing queues. Chinatown will eventually revert to celebrating the traditional holiday, but the spirit of change is strong in the air.

Chuck Connors has also died this year, of pneumonia, at the age of sixty-five. He had been slowing down for a couple of years, worn out by drink and high living. But the final insult came when a hanger-on known as "Mike the Dago" suddenly declared himself "The Young Chuck Connors." He even formed a Young Chuck Connors Association and hosted a ball in imitation of his namesake. Old Chuck just let the young punk have his glory, retiring more and more to his room, where he finally passed away. Chinatown's best-loved blowhard, the source for its most titillating myths, is laid to rest after a funeral at the Transfiguration Catholic Church. Forty people attend. It is followed two weeks later by the demise of the infamous Chatham Club, the colorful Doyers Street dive and Tammany Hall hangout that Chuck helped to make famous.

As for Transfiguration, it is in the fourth year of running its Chinese Mission, the last major church in New York to do so. Even so, the ministry is not conducted in the church itself, but around the corner on Park Street. The congregation of the Transfiguration Catholic Church is still almost entirely Italian, and it will be a long time before there are more than a tiny handful of Chinese Catholics in Chinatown.

Meanwhile, the St. Bart's Chinese Guild has moved to 10 Chatham Square, and the Reverend Huie Kin has celebrated the forty-fifth anniversary of his Chinese Presbyterian outreach, which for the last five years has manifested itself in his church on East 31st Street, the only organized Chinese church east of the Mississippi. It is a direct outgrowth of the long-gone Sarah Goodrich's work at the old Five Points House of Rescue in the years following the Civil War. But this is also the year that the House of Rescue's parent organization, the old Five Points House of Industry, is torn down to make way for a new courthouse. It is the last vestige of the Five Points neighborhood, that internationally notorious intersection now covered by Columbus Park and is only identifiable by tour guides with antique maps or very long memories.

The year 1913 also sees the arrival in Chinatown of the Reverend Lee To, who has been put in charge of the joint Baptist/Methodist mission. His "Trust in God Club" at 11–13 Doyers costs $100 to join, the money going largely to support Christian missionary work in China. Reverend Lee is known for his personal charity, once carrying a dying man down four flights of stairs to his own apartment so that he would not have to suffer alone. Working for him is the trusty Miss Mary Banta, still shepherding Chinatown's children and gently teaching a combination of Christianity and the English language to their mothers.

"The white people come and talk Christianity to my mother today," says one Americanized boy. "Tomorrow other people come and say their Christianity is better, and still other people tell her on the next day that their way is still better. She don't know what to believe, but it's all Jake with me. I'm an American, see?"

All this feverish Christian activity is simultaneous with (or is it the cause of?) perhaps the grandest Tong truce to date, signed in August of 1913. It caps a year and a half of spiraling violence which had started with the murder of the president of the Hip Sing and the startling reappearance of Mock Duck. Even though Mock is finally jailed six months after the killing (not for the murder, but because he was found to have gambling slips in his pocket) the war rages on; tourists as well as Tom Lee's nephew are killed, and a giant bomb is set off under the statue of the God of War and Gambling in the On Leong meeting room at 14 Mott Street. No one is injured, but glass and bricks shower the street as worshippers at Transfiguration rush outside in alarm.

Because he is still in China, Great-Grandfather is not involved in these treaty negotiations, but the On Leong celebrates by staging a huge week-long national convention at their Mott Street headquarters, with Diamond Charley Boston (newly released from prison) presiding. To flaunt the peace, they march in an ostentatious parade down Pell Street, past teeth-gritting Hip Sing warriors, and then on to an excursion boat which transports them and their guests, including prominent Tammany Hall politicians and off-duty Sixth Precinct police officers, to a picnic

and clambake reminiscent of the ones Tom Lee has been staging for the
last thirty years. That tough old bird is there, of course, in his honorary
capacity as Chairman of the Committee of Arrangements, and placidly
sits with his officers as Tammany Hall and the Sixth Precinct face off in
a softball game. Meanwhile the rank-and-file On Leong gorge themselves on an international repast which includes fried eels, ham and
eggs, steamed buns, and clam chowder. Then, topping it off with ice
cream and coffee, the On Leong men get down to serious fun—gambling. Today, the game seems to be one played with cards called *pai gao
poker*.

Later in the summer, the police raid both On Leong and Hip Sing
gambling rooms, just to show they aren't partial.

So it was quite a little family that crammed in together in one of
the tenement apartments over Quong Yuen Shing in 1913. In addition to
Hor Poa, there was Gon She, her two little boys, Sun and Fong, and the
baby girl, Bik, who would always be referred to as Bickie. Grandfather
and his bride were there, of course, and for a short time Hor Mei Fun,
who was working as a clerk at Quong Yuen Shing and who would soon
be leaving on his own trip back home to China to get married. And very
soon after Hor Mei Fun's return to New York in 1915, my Grandmother
Chin She would give birth to her first child right there on the kitchen
table—a daughter, Thelma Bo Choi, the first in the family to be given an
English name at birth.

Life was not terribly pleasant for Chin She. Her mother-in-law is
remembered as being, well, *demanding,* and a daughter-in-law was almost
by definition an object of intense criticism. Poor, lonely Chin She, taken
from her rustic village where the silence was only broken by the sounds
of cutthroat mah-jongg, and thrust into a world of automobiles and elevated trains and tiny, crowded apartments stacked one atop another like
pigeon coops. Her lot was not improved any by the fact that her first-
born was a girl. For her part, Gon She had started out her married life by
producing a boy, and she never let her daughter-in-law forget it.

Chin She's life was not made much better by her husband. Grandfather still found his wife too provincial for his fast-paced existence, for
at the age of seventeen he had already developed the suave swagger that

would distinguish him for the rest of his life. He liked sharp suits, good cigars, and a stiff drink with his buddies. Grandfather was always a real good-old-boy, a natural politician who seemed to know everyone and everyone's business. He was probably a member of the On Leong by this time, but definitely not a major player, being more interested in hanging out with his friends and gambling at *fan tan* or *pai gao*. But his easy camaraderie masked the deep disappointment he felt at not getting beyond the ninth grade. Despite his year at the Canton Christian College, he was always a little envious of his P.S. 23 classmates who he saw go on to high-school diplomas and then to university. They were stepping into jobs in the professions or business, while he was left to support a growing family on a waiter's salary, with some gambling on the side. Unfortunately, with gambling you always lose more than you win.

There is no income from Great-Grandfather's store because it is gone, having failed in 1910, about eighteen months before the family trip to China. A lot of Chinatown's tourist-oriented businesses had suffered during the Tong Wars, and 39 Mott Street's immediate proximity to ricocheting bullets probably didn't help. Still, it had been moderately profitable, doing perhaps $15,000 worth of business per year, and yielding Hor Poa an income of $500–$1,000. That wasn't too bad, but ultimately it couldn't compete with some of the Chinatown powerhouses like Quong Yuen Shing, which was doing $350,000 worth of trade annually by 1910. Great-Grandfather had tried expanding by adding a tailoring department and other innovations, but it was no use.

Of course, since he was well over sixty and seemed to have plenty of money, he may merely have retired. After all, even though he hadn't worked in a year and a half, he still managed somehow to take his entire family of five on a year-long trip to China, pay for a big wedding, and then transport seven people back to New York, an enterprise that must have cost him at least a couple of thousand dollars, or about two years' salary (excluding the money he didn't tell the Chinese Inspector about). And even then, when he got back to New York he still had $1,000 to invest in a friend's new store, and even more to buy railroad stocks, among other things. Of course, he must have had "sole right of use" money paid to him by Lee Lick Yu, who succeeded him at Number 39. There was his income from shares he owned in a whole slew of Chinatown enterprises, such as Quong Yuen Shing and the saloon at 31 Mott.

And then also he must have been on the payroll as an officer of the On Leong, although not receiving amounts remotely like that of Tom Lee and his family, who owned mansions and other real estate all over New York. Still, those things alone don't seem to be enough.

My elders always told me that Great-Grandfather had been "Mayor of Chinatown," and it must have been during this period. Of course by "Mayor" they just meant President of the CCBA, the official Government of the neighborhood, the municipal Authority of the City of New York being ignored as much as possible. The CCBA regulated just about all aspects of life in Chinatown. Every Chinese person was expected to register (and pay dues), which entitled them to protection from unfair business competition and mediation in all manner of disputes. Meticulous records were kept on all stores, restaurants, and laundries, and "sole-right-of-use" fees were monitored and collected by the organization—with a percentage going to the treasury, of course. Personal and business debts were also kept track of, with an office boy kept constantly employed just checking up on debtors' movements, to make sure no one skipped town without receiving a polite reminder of his financial obligations. The CCBA ran the Chinese School, maintained the primary Taoist temple, and would even take care of funerals, burials, and sending the bones back to China, its rates for such services depending on whether or not your dues were paid up.

Every year (every two years by the 1930s), the Association would hold elections for President, English Secretary, Chinese Secretary, and office boy, all of whom would receive respectable monthly salaries in addition to whatever other gratuities might come their way in exchange for certain favors. The President was meant to be a "reputable" gentleman of some education, often retired, who had the patience to sit through endless rounds of petty arguments and tiresome legal disputes, clan quarrels and broken promises. In fact, however, he was always a member of either the Ning Young or the Lun Sing Village Associations, which controlled the voting and were always careful to see that two of the elected officers were from one Association and two from the other. Similarly, they tried to balance On Leong and Hip Sing interests, although as the On Leong was supposed to be more "aristocratic," it's hard to believe that a crude Hip Singer could ever have been elected President. For their part, the Hip Sing had long complained that the On

Leong had the CCBA in their pocket, which wasn't hard to believe, since the benevolent association was sandwiched in between the On Leong's two buildings, their official headquarters at 14 Mott Street and Tom Lee's offices at Number 18. It seemed that in most of the nation's Chinatowns, the local CCBA was in On Leong territory, but that didn't stop them from being a major mediating force in bringing about a cease-fire in the Tong Wars. Hor Poa was both Ning Young and On Leong, as well as being respectable, retired, and available. He was a shoo-in.

Life was sweet for Hor Poa as the Chief Gentleman of Chinatown. It would have meant a great loss of face for him to have had to earn his own living, so beyond his tidy salary there were other pleasant perks of office. A President of the CCBA was always deferred to, always addressed with respect, always offered the best place at table and the choicest delicacies at the banquets that he graciously condescended to host—and there were many, with no First Son's party, poetry competition, or Tong dinner complete without his august presence. As the leading elder, he could expect his pronouncements to be acted on without question, giving him great power and earning him even more favors proffered by those wishing to sway him in some matter. A benevolent look from him could mean easy access to a laundry or restaurant license, a merchant's certificate, or other such "favor papers." Impinging competition is whisked away, difficulties with the Tongs are smoothed over, and the annoyances of city ordinances are dealt with in one way or another.

Witnesses could even be found to offer testimony to immigration officials, and long-lost "fathers" could be magically created for young men seeking either to enter this country or to "prove" that they were born in San Francisco before the earthquake conveniently destroyed their birth certificates. Indeed, a veritable parade of fathers trooped through the Chinese Inspector's office, all of whom seemed to have had a child in San Francisco whom they had sent back to China to be educated and who now sought to live in New York. None seemed to have other children. A surprising number offered testimony in absolutely identical language.

As representative of the Chinese community, the Chief Gentleman was also fêted by the New York establishment, perhaps even more than the Chinese Consul, with city officials paying their respects the way they might to a foreign ambassador or minor Head of State. Indeed, the CCBA referred to the English and Chinese Secretaries as "diplomats," and for the President it was almost like being a Ch'ing Dynasty court official, a provincial Governor on a special assignment from His Imperial Majesty. Of course there was no Imperial Majesty any longer, but it was nice to pretend.

Naturally, the Chief Gentleman had to be housed decently, so sometime during this period the family moves again, to the brand-new apartment house wrapping around the bend at 33–37 Mott Street. It was the first major Chinatown construction project since Hor Poa had helped construct Numbers 16 and 18 Mott for the CCBA and Tom Lee back in 1888, and was made possible after a big fire destroyed the stables for Naughton's Funeral Home in 1914, threatening Transfiguration Church and causing half of Chinatown to turn out in alarm. Appropriately dubbed *Sun Lau* or New Building, it was the last word in luxury, at least for Mott Street. Sun Lau was the first building in the neighborhood to have real bathrooms and central heat, not just toilets in the hall and coal stoves, and the first built to meet all the "new" zoning codes for residential housing—codes which had been passed in 1901. The rooms were large and airy, with lots of windows and bright, modern kitchens equipped with gas appliances, iceboxes, and big washtubs for doing the laundry.

So the Mayor of Chinatown had his pick of apartments, finally choosing one on the fourth floor, facing the foot of Pell Street, consisting of a kitchen/sitting room, two bedrooms, and a bath—for ten people, including my Second Aunt Constance Bo Ling, who had been born in 1917. Just like most other Chinatown families, everyone slept on planks set up on sawhorses all over the apartment, with the elders using hard laquered leather pillows, brightly painted and decorated, just like their parents and grandparents before them. By day, the beds would be dismantled to give the ladies room to do their piecework and prepare meals for their children. In 1919, my First Uncle Everett Sing Ying Hor was born on one of those sawhorse beds, the First Son of the new generation, with a midwife attending and Gon She barking orders to the crowd. Chin She could now hold her head up a little higher.

It wasn't that they were poor, my family, because they weren't. It was just that Chinese were used to living on top of each other, as they had done for countless generations in their little Toi-shan villages. Indeed, they were often uncomfortable if they weren't packed close together. Even rich people like the Lee family, or Chu Fong, or old Wah Kee lived amid the familiar cramped surroundings of Chinatown, while it was the more aggressively "Americanized" Chinese, those with American wives like Guy Maine and the Reverend Huie Kin, who lived in larger quarters uptown or in Queens.

Even rich old Tom Lee preferred to live in his old three-room flat at 18 Mott Street. Of course, he had been staying in his beautiful house on Riverside Drive, but then he was married to a German and besides, there was that small matter of all those Hip Sing assassins roaming outside his window in Chinatown. Still, with peace between the Tongs and then the death of his wife, the old warrior came back to the scene of his greatest triumphs and narrowest escapes. Dozens had been killed in the battles with the Hip Sings, but Tom Lee had come through without a scratch—even if a shot did shatter an alarm clock on a table by his pillow, and someone once tried to drop a flagpole on his head. But now he would sit, skinny and stooped, in a chair on the sidewalk in front of his building, smoking a water-pipe and watching the world go by, the bemused smile showing through his whiskers the only betrayal of the sweetness of his victory. And it was there, at 18 Mott, in the rooms Hor Poa had helped to build, that Tom Lee finally died in 1918. Charley Boston said he was eighty-six years old, although many thought he was older. Regardless, there was virtually no one left who could remember a time when the wily old fox hadn't been pulling all the strings. And soon he would be followed by one of his oldest allies, for on December 3, 1919, from the same apartment that had just witnessed the birth of his first grandson, Hor Poa would ascend the dragon to live with the Ancestors. He was sixty-nine years old.

Tuberculosis killed him. It was a terrible problem in Chinatown. Horrible overcrowding, like putting eleven people into three rooms, contributed mightily to the fact that the rate of tuberculosis in Chinatown was five times what it was in the rest of the City. The only treatment known to have any effect was exposure to fresh air and sunlight, two commodities greatly wanting on Mott Street. The *New York Times* reports this story in relation to one pressing source of concern: "The Chinese are engaged mostly in laundry or restaurant work, handling the clothes or food of white customers." Of course, Great-Grandfather did neither.

The body of Hor Poa is taken to 16 Mott Street, the same place where other On Leong bigwigs have been laid out in the last few years. On one side of the coffin are the laudatory silk banners from the family, on the other side, those from colleagues. All day long a steady stream of mourners, On Leong men, members of our Family and Village Associations, elders from the CCBA, and just plain friends file into the room to light a stick of incense and to bow three times, loudly calling out the name of their organization as they do so, thus enabling Great-Grandfather to identify who is calling. Each wears a black badge, the On Leong members' inscribed in gold with "We Mourn Our Loss. The On Leong Tong Association."

The Naughtons are in charge of the funeral arrangements, as they were for Hor Sek thirty-three years before, and today they have assembled a grand parade for the trip to the cemetery. There may not be as many carriages as for Tom Lee or his right-hand man, Gin Gum, who had had 128 at his funeral four years before, but it is certainly a long procession. And as New York City disapproves of firecrackers, there is a Chinese band riding along, banging on gongs to make sure the demons stay away, helped by the professional mourners among the crowd, wailing and weeping as Hor Poa makes his last trip through Chinatown.

The entire company winds slowly around the tiny streets, halting in front of every address significant in Hor Poa's life. At 18 Mott Street, and again at Numbers 21, and 32, and 39 the back of the hearse is opened, while Hor Poa's wife, and children, and daughter-in-law, and grandchildren dutifully line up to bow three times, clapping loudly so Great-Grandfather knows to take one last look around. Hor Mei Wong, the Number One son, (who has finally made it to the U.S.) leads the family. Grandfather, Gon She, and baby Uncle Everett fall in behind him.

And then the long ride out to the Cemetery of the Ever-Greens in Cypress Hills, Brooklyn, all the while dropping red funeral money to distract the ever-present demons, through the gates to the Chinese section, dubbed "Celestial Hill." Then more bowing, followed by the offering of food and wine and incense. The company takes the traditional piece of hard candy and a towel as they re-enter the vehicles, to "sweeten the bitterness" and "wipe away the tears." As they drive away, clutching the pennies they have been given to buy more sweets, swirling red paper money fills the air, and evil demons swoop and dive, feeding on the spoils of a departed Patriarch's passing into the vapor of memory.

8

.

HOCK SHOP

The old men with the queues and the loose-fitting blouses
are rapidly disappearing, being replaced by a new generation that is dragging Chinatown into the 20th century. The Chinese population citywide
stands at about five thousand in 1920, up from ten years previously but
still well below the 1900 level. But at least there has been peace in the
neighborhood for the last few years, as the various warring factions have
found it seemly to pause for World War I. In keeping with Chinatown's
newfound spirit of patriotism, Lee B. Lok, in conjunction with the Chinatown Chamber of Commerce, had been selling war bonds right over the
herb counter of Quong Yuen Shing, eventually raising over a million dollars. Of course, the Chinese are known for their support of civic causes.
Even the Rector of St. Bartholomew's Episcopal Church, who numbered
families like the Vanderbilts among his congregation, noted this when he
said, "There is no congregation—not even the one in this church—which
gives in proportion to its means as does the Chinese."

Grandfather was exempt from the draft because of his family, but
the small handful of eligible young Chinese men from all over the metropolitan area had eagerly signed up to show their patriotism. One of them,

Color Sergeant Sing Kee, was awarded the Distinguished Service Cross for "distinguished bravery" as well as being decorated by the French Government after he single-handedly kept communication lines open during the thick of the battle at Mont-Notre-Dame, despite being repeatedly gassed. Back in New York in 1919, a reporter asks him what on earth a "Chinaman" could do to be the first to earn such recognition. Sergeant Kee (who is originally from California and speaks perfect English) looks at him slyly and replies, "Me no savee Inglis," and then turns smartly and joins the victory parade, receiving the accolades of New Yorkers of all stations and races as he marches with his unit up Fifth Avenue.

Still, for all the peace and stability, some white people are beginning to find Chinatown rather dull. To be sure, the big, gasping tour buses are back in force, doing the circuit of curio shop to Chinese temple to chop-suey house, with a running narration of Tong Wars and degradation shouted through a megaphone. But opium was finally declared illegal, at least for recreational use, in 1914, and this year the hated Volstead Act has come into effect, ushering in more than ten years of Prohibition in the nation and essentially shutting down the Bowery dives so popular with slummers for decades past. Of course, opium and liquor are still obtainable—the Tongs have even started selling string soaked in heroin, sold by the inch and meant to be chewed—but that is mostly for the residents' use, and Chinatown and its environs no longer have that allure of shimmering vice beckoning to adventurers from uptown and other foreign climes. That is just fine with the residents of the old neighborhood, who are getting sick and tired of being stereotyped as opium fiends and Tong hatchet men. When a movie crew is found to be shooting a typically sinister white-slavery potboiler on Doyers Street in 1923, the locals respond by pelting the actors with eggs and rotten vegetables.

Speaking of the Tongs, they are becoming positively domesticated. The Hip Sing has just hosted a week-long national conference of its membership at its headquarters at 13 Pell Street, followed by a grand eighty-eight-course banquet at the Chinese Delmonico's. The police, fearing trouble, turned out in force, but not a peep was to be heard.

And, not to be outdone, the On Leong has spent a reported $117,000 to build their beautiful new headquarters at 41 Mott. It is festooned with balconies and is a lucky eight stories tall, counting the pagoda garret, one of the most dramatic buildings on Mott Street. When it is dedicated in 1921, thousands of On Leongers from all over the country throng Chinatown, which is draped with strings of colored lights for the eleven-day celebration. Over five hundred people, serenaded by both Chinese and Italian bands, attend banquets and speeches in the headquarters' beautiful new meeting hall on the top floor. Mayor John F. Hylan (a Tammany Hall hack remembered as "a man of minimal ability") is the guest of honor, and even the Hip Sing send over a congratulatory bouquet and banner in a gesture of good will.

As for my family, the death of Hor Poa leaves them somewhat in limbo. Great-Grandfather has left the bulk of his estate to his sons in China. Unfortunately, the elder son, Hor Mei Wong, doesn't survive his father very long, apparently succumbing to tuberculosis right there on Mott Street before he can ever get back home. But Hor Mei Fun inherits the big house in the middle of the family compound and all the money, making him, according to village elders, "very wealthy." Reportedly, he even starts his own bank when he moves back to China for good in the later 1920s, although by american standards that doesn't necessarily make him a tycoon. At any rate, Hor Mei Wong's wife and children get the house on one side of the family compound, and Hor Mei Chao, the son of Hor Poa's long-dead younger brother, gets the house on the other side. Thus, the family Hor is snug and secure in their little ancestral village, enjoying the life of provincial gentry, and for the moment, pass out of the story.

But the pressure on Grandfather only increases. Every two years there has been a baby, and by 1923, our household at 33–37 Mott consists of Great-Grandmother Gon She, 43; Grandfather, 26; Grandmother Chin She, 27; Third Great-Uncle Hor Ting Sun, 17; Fourth Great-Uncle Hor Ting Fong, 14; Great-Aunt Hor Yee Bik, 10; First Aunt Thelma Bo Choi, 8; Second Aunt Constance Bo Ling, 6; First Uncle Everett Sing Ying, 4; Third Aunt Frances Bo Ping, 2; plus my Father, Herbert Sing Nuen, born that year on the second day of June. Twelve people. Three rooms. One income from Grandfather's job as a waiter; and, to complicate matters, Second Aunt Constance has been left totally deaf from a bout of scarlet fever at the age of two, which means that soon she will need to go to a special school. To help out, Great-Uncle

Sun drops out of Stuyvesant High in his senior year and gets a job as a waiter, but his older brother, my grandfather, is only furious with him for quitting school.

Hor Ting Pun makes anywhere from $100 to $150 per month in his waiter's job, probably at the lavish Oriental Restaurant on Pell Street, which is owned by Hor family "cousins." While respectable for the early 1920s, his salary has to stretch awfully far, and besides he feels that he is too intelligent to be trapped in some grunt job. A restaurant worker's day grinds on from opening to closing, about fourteen hours a day, although there is time for a break during slow periods. Small restaurants, like the little basement noodle shops favored by most Chinese, might be run by three partners—two cooks and a manager/waiter. The percentage of their share of the profits is according to the size of their initial investment. If business is good, a part-time waiter, maybe a college student, can be hired at $2 or $3 a day on weekends, which is always the busiest time. With tips, a part-timer can earn up to $10 a day.

But no matter how you look at it, it is still tedious, back-breaking work, and a little demeaning for a son of the former Chief Gentleman of Chinatown, who was a respected elder and an officer of the mighty On Leong. Grandfather himself is a member in good standing of the Sam Yip Family Association as well as of the Chinese Citizens' Alliance at 6 Mott. And even though he didn't go beyond the first year at DeWitt Clinton High School, he speaks and writes beautiful Chinese, better than many of his American-born friends. This is not only because of his year at the Canton Christian College, but because he has a quick ear and easily picks up the various Toi-shan dialects he hears on Mott Street. Unfortunately, as for most Chinese in the 1920s, his career options are limited to three things: restaurants, shopkeeping, or laundries. Grandfather needs something a little more swank.

One place where his lineage really makes a difference is in the On Leong, and there is always a little money to be made with them by running lottery results, taking bets, operating a little gambling room here and there. The gambling scene in Chinatown is beginning to change in the 1920s, as the old *fan tan* and *pai gao* players are being joined by younger men playing five- and seven-card poker, as well as craps and blackjack. Off-duty Chinese waiters in their sharp suits and fedora hats are now showing up in force at the horse races at Aqueduct, Jamaica, Belmont Park on Long Island and Empire City in Yonkers, while others take the bets of store clerks and launderers who can't get to the track. And whatever or wherever the game, my grandfather is there.

He isn't reckless like some. The owner of the Port Arthur lost his shirt (and his restaurant) in a gambling room on Pell Street at around this time. While he fled from his creditors to Seattle, the Port Arthur's new owners, some more of those distant Hor family "cousins," happily took over and instituted mah-jongg and blackjack on the top floor, where Grandfather soon became a fixture.

Or he'd haunt one of the smoke-filled rooms behind a barbershop or a store, where the house took a 5-percent cut but also supplied lunch and dinner. The back room behind Tuck High at 19 Mott was popular because it had two exits, so if the police came to call, there would be a quick avenue of escape. Of course, that wasn't usually too much of a worry, as any smart gambling proprietor kept an On Leong diplomat on his payroll, so that relations with the Men in Blue could be kept smooth and cordial. When a raid was necessary for political reasons, decoy "gamblers" would be hired at $2 a head, who would then allow themselves to get arrested. Everyone knew that the decoys wouldn't ultimately be charged with anything, and the "house" would always pay their fines, as well as sending over a boxed lunch and playing cards to while away their night in jail.

Wherever he played, Grandfather developed a reputation as a smart gambler. He was great with numbers, a good judge of horses, and could tell when a fellow poker-player was bluffing—usually. Puffing away on a big cigar, he played conservatively, winning often but not being devastated when he lost. He and his friends, like Jimmy Tai Pon (or Jimmy Typond) and the corpulent Lee J. Waye, who had been called "Shavey" Lee since childhood because of his shaved head, would hang out late into the night in one of Mott Street's all-night restaurants, imbibing from a pot of "tea that burns"—a teapot full of bootleg Scotch—while going over *Racing Forms* and lottery odds. It was sometime during this period that his friends started calling Grandfather by a new nickname: "Hock Shop." It was based on his Chinese name, Pun, pronounced "Pawn," hence pawn shop, hence . . . Okay, it's a stretch, but for Grandfather it suited.

The three-room apartment wasn't quite as claustrophobic as it sounds, because, like every building in Chinatown, 33–37 Mott was merely a vertical Chinese village. All the doors were always open, and everyone moved freely from apartment to apartment. The women could have a social life without leaving the building, while the children actually had dozens of mothers and fathers, as they were raised to strictly defer to any elder person, whom they would invariably address as "Auntie" or "Uncle." And there certainly was no shortage of elders in their little world.

There was the lady downstairs on the third floor who had bound feet. One of my father's earliest memories is a grotesque vision of those feet, unbound, propped up on a chair—two fists of flesh, with seemingly one toe each. Her husband owned a grocery store on Mott Street and a farm in Boonton, New Jersey, where he grew Chinese vegetables. Sometimes he would take the children out there in his car, where they would sleep on mats on the floor and roam the unfamiliar surroundings. It often seemed as though half of Chinatown was taking the air at his farm.

Then there was Mr. Chin, who made beautiful kites in the shapes of fish, dragons, or caterpillars which could stretch up to twelve feet in length. The paste he would make himself, boiling rice into a sticky mush and then pounding it fine. The struts came from bamboo packing cases carrying goods imported from China. The eyes, scales, and whiskers would be delicately painted by hand. Mr. Chin would take the children down to Columbus Park, or more often up to the roof, where his creations could sail over Mott Street like some brilliantly-colored good-luck omen beaming on the lives below. When they strayed over Mulberry Street, however, the Italian kids would try to bring the kites down with rocks and lassos, savagely ripping apart any that they caught. Mr. Chin would just sigh and go down to make another one.

Miss Mary Banta was such a frequent visitor to 33–37 that she might as well have lived there. She would come by and try to teach

English to Chin She and Gon She, who apparently never made any headway. The children she would check for lice or illness, sweeping them off to the doctor at the slightest sign of a sniffle. Sometimes her Church of All Nations would sponsor steamboat excursions up to Bear Mountain—just for Chinese—and the family, or at least the children, would clamber aboard with a big bucket of chicken gizzards and deep-fried chicken feet as tasty snacks. And for two weeks every summer, the church would host the Chinese at a seaside resort they owned in Bradley Beach, New Jersey.

There were also other kids living at 33–37, like "Little Pig" and "Pee Wee"—all Chinese children had these affectionate "milk names," although my elders would resolutely never tell me theirs—and they would amuse themselves on the streets, on the roofs, in the alleys. Just as for the adults, one of a Chinese child's chief forms of recreation was eating, and when out of sight of their parents there was much to choose from, like the roasted sweet potatoes from the Italian street vendor who worked Mott Street, at a penny apiece, or two cents for the big ones, with an aroma so delicious you could smell them coming a block away. Or there were the men selling roasted corn on the cob, or knishes, or steamed snails, or lemon tea. Then, when fortified by such nourishment, the kids would run over to Columbus Park to play volleyball or softball, often ending up in a turf battle with some Italian boys, who would snarl at them to "go back to your own neighborhood." Only when the boundaries were finally established could the game proceed.

There were occasions when the entire family would venture outside together, although it had to be something very important for Gon She and Chin She, being conservative ladies, to brave the harsh glare of a public street. Uncle Everett can still recall a visit to a First Son's party in 1924 when he was only five, but then, as a First Son himself, he would be an honored guest. As for his mother and grandmother, he remembers them stepping gingerly onto the sidewalk, dressed to the nines in clothes he had never seen before, gorgeous silks and dainty shoes, with their hair done up in elaborate coifs held in place by big hair pins like knitting needles. Once they were safely out onto the street a taxi pulled up, the party climbed in, the taxi drove to a building on the opposite curb, and the party climbed out. Even at this late date strict propriety must be maintained, and well into the 1930s boys would sit on the stoop and play a game called "count the women." There were so few, and they came out so infrequently, that the boys soon knew all of them by sight.

Other more liberal families would take a Sunday meal out together, usually not at one of the big eating palaces but at some more humble noodle house serving good Cantonese food. In the middle 1920s, the Nom Wah (Southern China) Tea Parlor opened at 13–15 Doyers, filling up the whole end of what had once been the Arcade that went through to Mott. The police had ordered the Arcade, as well as all the tunnels running underneath, sealed off in an attempt to curb Tong shenanigans.

Nom Wah serves only *yum cha,* or tea food, which is what they called dim sum back then. I know that Grandfather used to hang out there with his friends, and Nom Wah, still in business in the late 1990s, is another place where I have always seen familiar ghosts. There are still the old, worn red booths, and the row of tall gas-fired hot-water urns supported on their little curvy legs. On one wall are framed views of British-colonial Shanghai, which might be photographs, might be needlework, the covering glass being just a little too dusty to tell. There are shelves of beautiful painted-tin tea canisters, reaching all the way to the ceiling. Colorful chinaware household gods beam down from behind glass cases piled high with homemade almond cookies. And a single waiter still carries around big trays of tea food for you to select from, such as steamed roast-pork dumplings known as *char siu bao; siu mai,* or little balls of steamed ground pork and fish; the square fried turnip cakes called *lo bok gao;* little shrimp *ha gao;* and all sorts of other things that I've never quite figured out. There is no bill, so when the meal is over the owner just comes over and counts up the empty dishes, each size and shape denoting a different price.

There are other sources of entertainment for Hock Shop and his friends in the 1920s, such as the new Chinese Theater, on the Bowery above Bayard Street in the old Thalia, which had once been famous as the first theater in New York to be lit by gas. The bill is largely the same as in the old place on Doyers, with long classical fables and history plays. The seats are also the same—wooden benches, "backless and uncomfortable."

The prices have gone up, however—from $2 for early arrivals to a low of 50 cents if you get there after ten. Still it might be worth it to go and see the first Chinese-American actress, a woman by the name of Ng Ah.

There is also dancing at the Oriental Restaurant. Obviously, Grandfather himself wouldn't socialize there if that's where he was waiting on tables, but some young Chinese can occasionally be seen among the uptown crowd dancing to the "syncopating jazz orchestra," even though there is a warning sign over the piano reading, "No Charleston." Bootleg Tea That Burns flows like water, as the young men of Chinatown learn to roar with the Twenties.

The shooting starts up again in 1924. There had been tension on the street for a couple of years, especially after the National President of the Hip Sing was gunned down on Pell Street in 1922, but that turned out to be the result of a personal vendetta and not an On Leong hit. Still, every time there has been a rumor of impending violence somebody with influence—Guy Maine or the Reverend Lee To (then the President of the CCBA) or the Chinese Consul-General—has rushed in and managed to keep the adversaries calm. This time, however, the trouble starts as purely an internal On Leong conflict: fourteen Tong officers are expelled in a scandal involving power rivalries and the mysterious disappearance of $40,000 from the Tong's national treasury. As an act of retribution, these fourteen offer their services to the Hip Sing—and the time bomb explodes.

Starting on October 8, there is a killing or a gun battle almost every day in a conflict that spreads across the country. One of the first is between plainclothes detectives and suspected Hip Sing soldiers right on Pell Street; the bullets slam into the front of 33–37 Mott, leaving pockmarks in the vestibule that will mark it as an "unlucky" building for years to come. Uncle Everett can remember being warned away from the windows and policemen saturating the neighborhood—one every twenty-five feet, if the New York Times is to be believed. There are wholesale raids on stores and tenements, including 33–37 itself, where policemen smash down doors looking for illegal weapons. They find very few.

There are people stabbed, and strangled, and shot, in addition to those apparently ordered to commit suicide by one Tong or the other. The murder of one suspected Hip Sing "spy" takes place at the rear of 39 Mott in plain view of On Leong headquarters—and the Hor family apartment. Hundreds of Chinese flee the city for the relative safety of Newark, and Chinatown is so devoid of traffic that most businesses close down altogether. Only the Port Arthur and a couple of other big restaurants manage to stay open, but the few diners are mostly off-duty policemen or rubberneckers, hoping to see a murder. Before the Newark refugees can return home, there will be a massive Immigration raid in that city where over seven hundred people are herded into Newark City Hall like cattle. Of course, the vast majority are eventually released.

Truces are almost agreed to and treaties almost signed until yet another shooting ruins the deals. In desperation, the Reverend Lee To gathers the warring parties together on the third floor of the Port Arthur and embarks on an impassioned speech to bring the two sides together. "Oh sit down, Lee To, sit down!" the two sides grumble, as he preaches his message of Christian forgiveness. As if in response, he suddenly collapses from a stroke and dies the next morning. A sorrowful Jewish neighbor pays the supreme compliment to the Chinese Christian leader when he says, "He was a real Jew." The day Lee To is buried, Thanksgiving Day, the shooting breaks out again. Before it is all over, at least eighty have been killed or wounded.

Meanwhile, Chin She is showing signs of strain herself. The many children, the shootings, the mother-in-law are all taking their toll, and in the late Spring of 1925 the children are all suddenly removed from school one day to go and see their mother in Beekman Hospital. Aunt Constance, who has come down from the Association for the Improved Instruction of Deaf-Mutes on Lexington Avenue, where she lives, is told that there is something wrong with her mother's heart. Chin She does manage to return home to 33–37 Mott, but only to die, suddenly, from a heart attack. It is June 19, 1925, and she is twenty-nine years old. Chin She, my young grandmother, is buried the next day.

That October, Grandfather is obliged to join the On Leong at a huge peace banquet at the Chinese Delmonico's on Pell Street while his mother looks after his children and siblings. Eight months later, almost exactly one year after Chin She's death, Gon She has a stroke and dies also. She is forty-six. Now my twenty-nine-year-old Grandfather must feed all those mouths alone.

On July 1, 1924, a year before Chin She's death, Congress imposed a new restriction on the Exclusion Act, barring the immigration of any more Chinese wives, even if they are married to American citizens. So, if Grandfather had wanted a traditional Chinese stepmother for his children, he certainly couldn't have gotten one from China. Instead, it is a new kind of Chinese lady who comes to the rescue. Mrs. Matilda Halle, whose Chinese name is so hidden in the past that no one is quite sure what it was, is a tiny, fashionable woman who wears smart hats and silk stockings, speaks perfect English, and—most wondrously—drives a car. A pillar of the Baptist Church, she has the reputation in Chinatown of being highly educated and sophisticated, causing other Chinese ladies to look up to her for guidance in a white society that is often still rather intimidating to them.

Mrs. Halle, who will always be referred to as Auntie, has a somewhat mysterious connection to our family. It was back in 1910 when she first appeared in Chinatown, obviously a young lady of good breeding—but with a baby of uncertain origin. Apparently she had been disowned by her wealthy family in San Francisco, and had brought the baby all the way across the country in a desperate search for the father. No one knows if she ever found him. At any rate, my great-grandfather took her in and found a home for her child, a single mother being in an almost impossible position in that enclosed and gossipy society. He then found the lady a legitimate husband, a "cousin" named Hor Tun Fook who had Anglicized his name to T. F. Halle.

Mr. Halle, who will always be referred to as Uncle, was a rather fuddy-duddy young man, a fifth-generation Christian, caught up in missionary work at the Baptist Temple in downtown Brooklyn; he probably wouldn't have bothered to find himself a wife unless commanded to marry by Hor Poa, who was perhaps the senior-most elder in his Family Association. That is fine by Auntie, however, as Uncle will provide her a good home and the only kind of respectability available to a woman. The baby is heard of no more, but as for Auntie, she owes a solemn life-debt to Hor Poa's family for his kindness towards her. The Chinese do not say "thank you" so much as expressing their gratitude through some deed. In this case, a very large deed is necessary.

Therefore, on the death of Gon She in June of 1926, Auntie Halle sweeps down on 33–37 Mott Street in her shiny new Essex sedan and takes my father and all four of his siblings to live with her in her house in Brooklyn, while Great-Aunt Bik is sent to boarding school. My father is at this time barely three years old. His memories of Chinatown, nebulous at best, will gradually grow dimmer and more fuzzy, until finally he isn't sure if those images are remembered or just dreamt. Thus he takes the first step on his long march away from the ancestral neighborhood. He will not often look back.

Hock Shop and the Great-Uncles continue to live at 33–37 Mott, but perhaps in a different apartment, because after the death there of Chin She (Gon She died in a hospital) the one on the fourth floor is certainly unlucky. But then the number four is unlucky anyway. Grandfather becomes the headwaiter at the gaudy Palais d'Or Chinese Restaurant on West 48th Street, and soon hires both his brothers Sunny and Fong, even though Fong has dropped out of school as soon as his mother died, much to the chagrin of his older brother.

Hock Shop still sends money to support my father and his older siblings in comfortable exile in Brooklyn, but he doesn't see them very often. Instead he is at the track, shooting craps, running lottery tickets and lording over seven-card poker game (which they call *pai gao* poker) in smoky basements, that ever-present pot of Tea that Burns at his elbow. More and more he can be seen swaggering around with his On Leong buddies, hanging out in some noodle shop, passing the time over cigarettes and gossip.

Those Sunday School steamboat excursions continue every summer, just as they have since the 1880s, providing one of the few settings where On Leong and Hip Sing members can relax together on neutral territory. So it is on one such trip that Hock Shop joins his Hip Sing friend Edmund Wong and his pretty Caucasian wife, Betty, for a relaxing day on the river.

Edmund and Betty have been together for several years now, their somewhat gooey romance expressed in letters from Edmund, which I will find in an uncle's attic some seventy years after they were written. The early ones are apparently composed by a professional scribe:

You know dearest, I have not seen you for a week almost, and it seems more than a year to me. As the true saying is: 'When love waits, minutes are hours . . .'

But as Edmund Wong grows more confident with his young sweetheart, he throws grammar and spelling to the wind and writes the letters himself while out of town on his frequent trips, apparently on Hip Sing business:

I hope you well take good care of you and don't in love with some one, kid, only me. I hope I well make good, kid. Don't worry about me. I am always your Darling, with love and Kiss your Honey, Edmund XXXXXXXXX.

These letters reveal more than just details of the couple's love life, however. For instance, in several, Edmund worries about his *feng shui*, or the effect the physical environment has on his personal fortunes:

I am full sick and Very Bad Luck. I don't know why I can't make a Penny this week. I think I am Bad Luck for broken dishes on you apartment New Year's night. Will you Please moves out that Room? There is Bad Luck for you too and I don't think I well sand you a money this week . . . I don't know what to do. I think I well go some place for my luck.

He also reveals some of the day-to-day troubles within the Hip Sing Tong:

R—'s Father was lock up last night because he try run way with Hip Sing money. You know what is R—think? She think I take the Cop up there and have her Father lock up. But I never mean that because

. . . no one can tark [talk] to Cop. About 3 o'clock in the Morning when the Cop ask me to go up the hotel and I go up with him, we get him. Ha. Ha.

And a series of letters to Betty from Edmund Wong's brother speak of the problems of a beloved First Son trying to juggle age-old filial obligations with the fast life of a Mott Street hot shot in the Roaring Twenties:

Those letters in Chinese that [our mother] sent to Edmund a few months ago—Kindly tell me the reason why was he didn't answer. Betty, I wish I can tell you how much has been, and today is still his mother suffering. Just because of Edmund. She doesn't care how much money he's sending back, but it's him that she really want. Would you blame her for wanting to see her son?

Edmund's brother then goes on to butter up Betty so she will convince Edmund to finally make a visit back home.

I told [our mother] the truth, how good you are and how helpful you have been to Ed. She impressed, and felt comforted. But she ask that if you can only send him back to see her just for once, then she will owe all there is to you, says she, in front of me. If Edmund or you only know how weak she is. I am sure he or you will cry your head out.

But then buttering up his sister-in-law has more than one purpose. Edmund's brother closes (as he usually does) by hitting Betty up for a $20 loan.

Today, however, the sun is shining, the band is playing and Edmund and Betty are out to forget their troubles on the Sunday School steamboat outing up the Hudson River with their good friend Hock Shop. Betty has brought along her sister, a pretty little German-Irish flapper named Frances Wolff who has her auburn hair in a smart bob and an engagingly shy smile.

For Frances, outings like this are a real thrill, because she gets to wear pretty clothes and be flirted with by all these, well, *dangerous* Chinese men. Her late father, God rest his soul, had always raised her to believe that if any white girl went to Chinatown she ran the risk of disappearing down a concealed trap door or being secretly doped up on opium in order to be dragged off and sold into a vile life of White Slavery. But since Betty has Edmund it's, well, just too *exciting*. And now here on the boat is this dashing, slightly wicked-looking Chinese man leaning against the rail and eyeing her in a not exactly unpleasant manner. She eyes him back. He offers her a stick of gum. Hock Shop and Frances are married in 1927, but are wise enough to leave no letters behind for me to find.

The prejudice is not as bad as it had been, but a Chinese man with a young white girl still arouses a lot of hostile reactions among the uptown landlords the young couple go to in search of an apartment. Occasionally, the doors to their rooms are smashed in by narcotics agents, certain that Grandfather has seduced this Caucasian female by means of opium. Eventually they have to move in with Edmund and Betty Wong way up in the Bronx, partly because there is safety in numbers. As for the new Mrs. Hor, there are the snide remarks and leering looks from the milkman and the iceman when they learn her name. Frances soon becomes as retiring and home-bound as the most old-fashioned Chinese matron.

Grandfather and his brothers are sick and tired of waiting on tables, with insensitive patrons shouting at them in pidgin English, the added volume supposedly making them more understandable. The black customers are much nicer, perhaps because Chinese restaurants are almost the only decent restaurants where they are welcome during this period. But the final straw comes on New Year's Eve in 1928 when Great-Uncle Sun is arrested on the complaint of a man partying on the holiday. He claims that Sunny tried to pick a fight with him after he refused to pay an exorbitant $10 bill for an order of ham and eggs and chop suey (such was the fare at the glamorous Palais D'Or). Of course, such a meal should only have cost 75 cents or a dollar, so a sour-faced Uncle Sun is fined the amount of the disputed check in what the Court thinks is poetic justice. But what he can't tell the judge (although anyone could guess) is that the $10 was not for a couple of plates of lousy food but for the copious amounts of Tea That Burns ordered by the drunken party crowd on that Prohibition-era New Year's Eve—unless, of course, they ordered "Cold Tea"—bootleg beer in a teapot—instead. So Sun and Fong have had enough, and when opportunity calls, they bail out of the restaurant business. Their new career description: vaudevillians on the Orpheum Circuit.

It is another "cousin," Hor Chee Chong, also known as Harry Haw, also known as the Honorable Wu, who hires the two for his splashy vaudeville extravaganza. It has gone by several names over the years; The Honorable Wu Revue; The Honorable Wu and his Chinese Showboat; The Chinese Nights Revue; or my favorite, The Chinese Whoopee Revue. Harry Haw is a dapper bachelor, born in San Francisco, and probably the biggest Chinese star on the vaudeville circuit, where, surprisingly, there are several others. Long Tak Sam is a magician whose two daughters dance and play the violin. Toy and Wing are a husband-and-wife song-and-dance team, and then, of course, there is the band leader known as Ho Li Wun and his orchestra. But the most famous Chinese performer in any medium has to be American-born film star Anna May Wong. Silent-movie fans across the country know her as the exotic, wicked vixen who usually gets her come-uppance in the last reel. When Talkies come in, the studios make her speak in a phony "Oriental" accent in order to make her sound sufficiently sinister.

Harry Haw has been treading the boards with his sister Florence for about ten years now, doing impressions of big celebrities like Eddie Cantor, while his twenty-five chorus girls and boys back him up performing the Charleston, the Black Bottom, and elaborate tap routines. There is a handsome couple, Harry Lowe and Miss Kee Kee, sweeping romantically around the stage to the "Merry Widow Waltz," "Prince Wong" sings and plays the Hawaiian guitar, and Helen Wong leads six girls in dancing the "Floradora Sextette," in addition to singing a medley of current hit songs. But mostly the kids that Harry Haw hires are amateurs whom he has to train. So somehow Sun and Fong get assigned to a place tap-dancing in the chorus and doing an act composed of twirling plates on sticks. They are billed, appropriately, as "Sun and Fong Hawe, The Two Chinese Brothers." Well, it's a living.

Traveling in a headline act on the Orpheum Circuit is a pretty darned glamorous experience. The company has a private railroad car and stays in big hotels, where my Great-Uncles practice their act while standing on the bed so as to reduce the number of broken plates. They visit San Francisco and New Orleans, Boston and Atlanta, and even play the Palace Theater in New York, the glittering dream of every vaudeville "artiste." Sometimes they cross into Canada in order to play Vancouver or Montreal, but each time they do, on their return there are all those tiresome Immigration interviews to go through, even for American citizens like Harry Haw and the Chinese Brothers. Lucky for Harry, since the Immigration authorities lost his birth certificate several years ago, he can make up any age he wants, and he seems to actually be getting *younger* with time, which is not a bad deal. Sun and Fong sometimes get left behind on these little Canadian bookings because the paperwork is just too daunting, but in 1929 they get included in the best gig yet—a six-month trip to Paris. It sure beats waiting on tables.

Chinatown in 1930 is spreading out. About 7,500 Chinese live in New York City, the men outnumbering the women eight to one. The City has just widened Canal Street and the Bowery, which on one hand creates new commercial space for Chinatown businesses to expand into, but on the other hand makes a kind of a moat, surrounding the neighborhood on three sides with broad boulevards and elevated trains. Still, the transplanted Toi-shan village has nearly filled that space, with Chinese investors buying and improving many of the tired old buildings, and for the first time, Chinese businesses are crossing Bayard Street and putting up their signs in the short block of Mott Street before Canal. Bayard itself is known as "Chin Street" for the massive headquarters of the Chin Family Association at Number 62, which opened in 1927.

The ubiquitous Chinese bachelors are aging, living out their solitary lives crowded into the Chin dormitory, or the one provided by the Wus, or the Wongs, or the Moys, or the Gees or whatever their particular Family Association may be out of the sixty-five or so in Chinatown today. According to local doctors, a lot of these men have syphilis, contracted from the prostitutes they visit in the absence of any other feminine company. This means that, in this era before antibiotics, they face a year of weekly IV infusions with a solution of arsenic, which sometimes results in blood poisoning or neurological damage. Many of the bachelors seek help at their local herbal counter, but this is one condition that the old medicine won't help.

By now the bachelors have entirely shed their queues—well, all except one old man on Bayard Street, and he doesn't get out much. But in warm weather they often put on their old frog-buttoned tunics and their light straw slippers, because Chinese clothes are so much more comfortable than those tight American suits, especially in the city heat. These men also still hoard their savings—50, 60, 80 percent of what they earn, which they carefully squirrel away in secret hiding places under the floorboards or in the walls. When a rickety old boardinghouse building on Doyers Street goes up in flames later in this decade, firemen find can after can of melted coins amid the smoldering ruins. As for the resident bachelors themselves, many perish, including those who desperately try to inch their way along the clothes lines strung between the dormitory and the building on Mott Street where my cousin lives. The lines break, of course, and my cousin, who is only a small child, watches in horror as the men fall six stories to their deaths. The Benevolent Society takes care of the survivors so that the City won't be troubled.

The few older women are starting to get out more. A couple of years from now when Grace Lee takes her mother, bound feet and all, to Radio City Music Hall, it will be the first time that the old lady has been outside of the three blocks of Chinatown—not to mention the first time she has seen a Rockette. Of course, she has only lived in Chinatown for some thirty years. She likes what she sees, however, and soon starts joining groups of other Chinatown matrons in shopping expeditions to Wanamaker's Department Store on Broadway at Ninth Street. It's not because they like Wanamaker's so much, but the store is only a couple of steps away from the Third Avenue El, and with bound feet every step is very important.

Another older Mrs. Lee, this one living with her family at 21 Mott, complains to her husband that she wants to get out too. So he builds her a wooden stall on the corner of Mott and Park Streets, where she happily installs herself as a purveyor of pickled onions on a stick. Two cents, no waiting. At least here she is free to watch the street and get her gossip firsthand.

There is one more business that in the last ten years has given Chinatown ladies more money and power than they have ever even dreamed about—bootlegging. Every restaurant needs a certain amount of rice or plum wine for cooking, and as women did in the old villages back home they have been doing on Mott Street, fermenting wine in little batches in their kitchens, for local restaurant consumption only. It's just that now, with Prohibition, this skill is rather more highly in demand. The Chinatown ladies have been in this country long enough to know that they can get paid handsomely for their trouble.

The teenagers are getting out a little more as well. They hang out at the local movie theaters like the Venice or the Florence where a movie and a vaudeville act is 50 cents after twelve noon. The boys like to go to Coney Island, since a quarter will cover the day's expenses—round-trip subway fare plus 15 cents for a Coke and a hot dog. They change under the Boardwalk, and those who forget to bring towels use old newspapers to dry themselves, leaving newsprint all over their bodies. During the later 1930s, some of these kids will spend their summer in the Catskills, performing at Jewish resorts with the Honorable Wu Revue in the last, gasping days of Vaudeville.

Of course most of Chinatown's boys, and sometimes now even the girls, help out in their fathers' businesses, but more and more are getting hired in jobs uptown—the girls are hired as clerks in hotels, while the young men are all the rage as houseboys in fashionable houses and apartments. Even my Uncle Everett will be hired as a houseboy later in the 1930s, by a chic lady artist living at the Hotel des Artistes, just off Central Park West. When he's not answering her door or her telephone, she has him pose in exotic costumes for her to paint. She sells the pictures for big bucks. He takes the subway back to Brooklyn.

As for Chinatown's children, they have the run of the place as they always have, a pleasure that my father will not experience. Auntie does bring the five Hor children in once a week after church, for *yum cha* at the Nom Wah Tea Parlor on Doyers Street, but they rarely see Chinatown otherwise. Not that my father grows up without Chinese children to play with, because Auntie will come all the way in from Brooklyn to pick up another motherless Chinese boy on Mott Street to take him back to Brooklyn to play with little Herbert. But as these two sit together, a little uncomfortably, in Auntie's rather starchy living room, my father is discovering that he has less and less in common with the world of his own father and grandfather. And he likes it that way.

Chinatown has become very political since the advent of the Chinese Republic. There have been rallies and fundraisers and no end of partisan opinions expressed on the community's public bulletin boards, one at the corner of Doyers and Pell, and the other at the corner of Pell and Mott. In front of the latter sits an old man with his feet on a charcoal brazier, selling copies of Chinatown's lively newspapers. The eight-page *Chinese Nationalist Daily* is known for its support both of the Democrats and the Kuomintang, although they aren't as strident as the *Chung Shan Daily News*, which is basically just a propaganda organ of Chiang Kai-shek. *The Chinese Republic News* is the voice of the Chinese Freemasons, the three-hundred-year-old politically-minded Tong originally devoted to the overthrow of the Manchus. The emerging Chinese Communists weigh in with the *China Vanguard*, which has just appeared for the first time in New York this year. And finally there is the *Chinese Journal*, which taunts the other papers by stating on its masthead, "We are absolutely independent in our finances and in our editorial opinion, and we do not submit to direction by any party or clique!" Farther down in English it also reads [*sic*]:

> PublishedDailyExceptSunday&CertainHolidaysorDayFollowing-
> SuchHolidaysByTheChineseJournalInc.

Their printing plant is right on Chatham Square, on the second floor, and people riding the El can look straight into their composing room and see the typesetters racing up and down, grabbing type from an enormous jumble of unmarked boxes to set the day's news.

Mott Street's restaurants and curio shops are thriving, since the advent of the Depression has meant that uptown swells need a cheap place to entertain their girlfriends. So they can pay 50 cents for dinner at Lee's, or the Oriental, or the Port Arthur, which is now equipped with a huge Victrola. From there they can go next door to the "Chinese Temple and Museum" at 5 Mott, where the smartly dressed young woman puts down her fan magazine long enough to try and make the visitor believe that the Buddha statue was actually discovered in the very first Buddhist Monastery, and the flanking lions are really from the Ming Tombs. There is a pagoda and some supposedly Ming Dynasty paintings depicting the "punishments of man," and overhead hangs the great Lion that the "Temple and Museum" parades through the streets at New Year's, collecting money for his upkeep.

After this they can slip into the Chinese Emporium on the ground floor of the Port Arthur building and buy a souvenir like some cheap, porcelain "antique" (the tourists never know), or perhaps one of these back-scratchers known in Chinese as *bot kow yun,* or "need-not-depend-on-others"—arguably the greatest invention of the entire Chinese Empire. If the man really wants to impress his girlfriend, he can take her to the *Ching Chong,* or Genuine Prosperity jewelry store at Number 37 and buy her some love token in jade or ivory or gold.

Tourists can never visit Mott Street without peeking in at the Post Office, an eight-by-ten-foot space squeezed into the front of China-town's principal "Joss House" at Number 13. Ng Kuo Sou is the Post-master, the only Chinese Postmaster in New York. He also doubles as the Joss House's "chief priest." In this role he will gladly accept a small compensation for lighting some incense or casting a few divining sticks in front of the Goddess of Mercy's statue on the visitors' behalf. He will then quote some wisdom from Confucius and let them admire the monkey statues representing "See no evil," "Hear no evil," and "Speak no evil." On the way out, visitors are permitted to pay an additional fee to tap the "sacred" drum for good luck.

But here also, one wall is covered with row upon row of tomb-stone tablets, supposedly representing every Chinese buried at Cypress Hills. Perhaps it has the tablet of Guy Maine, who died last year after nearly fifty selfless years of "gaining [his countrymen's] con-fidence first . . . with a homeopathic dose of religion after each assis-tance rendered."

"When Death touched and closed the eyes and lips of Guy Maine," a colleague from the St. Bart's Chinese Guild wrote, "He robbed earth of a great soul and enriched the glorious company of the saints with a new comrade of the Gleam. Guy Maine was a son of China, a disciple of Jesus, and a lover of man . . ." With his death, the old St. Bart's Chinese Guild closes forever.

Also, if all of the tablets are there on the wall, then my whole family, Hor Poa, his brother, wife, and daughter-in-law, should be represented. The actual bodies, of course, are returned to China ten years after burial by the person's Family Association or the CCBA, that is, unless someone takes them back first. Hor Poa returned his brother's body, and Hor Mei Fun took back his father's when that young man returned to China for good a few years back. There the gentlemen wait in a tomb built outside the village wall, while the two ladies remain, largely ignored, in their desolate plots in Brooklyn. After their scheduled ten years are up, the company hired by the CCBA or the On Leong will dig them up and scrape their bones clean. The information written on slips of paper and sealed inside bottles in the caskets will let the packers know who the bones belong to, and how to address the box for shipment back to China. So this is how my Grandmother and Great-Grandmother finally return to Hor Lup Chui. It is a place where they have absolutely no friends. No one will leave roast chickens at their graves.

But even attitudes toward death are changing. With the demise or retirement of Joseph Naughton, who had been Chinatown's undertaker for some fifty years, a son of the Leung family, who calls himself Bert V. Eutemay, has recently defied all predictions of bad luck through association with the spirits of the dead by becoming the first Chinese mortician, not only in New York but in the nation. He opens his funeral home on the corner of Worth and Mulberry Streets, right next to the Pioneer Club, that white men's gay bar that no one wants to talk about. One of Eutemay's first customers is none other than the old friend of the On Leong, Diamond Charley Boston, who dies in 1930. Since no one can be found to intone Taoist rites, the Reverend Huie Kin's Presbyterian prayers will have to do.

Eutemay will soon be followed by Benny Kimlau, who sets up shop at the other end of the tiny block in the space formerly occupied by an Italian bank. He saves money by sleeping in the former vault.

These two have further broken with tradition by doing business on the previously all-Italian Mulberry Street, right across from Columbus Park. The two businessmen assuage any bad feelings by hiring Italians as drivers, as well as supplementing the traditional Chinese orchestras with mournful Italian brass bands in the processions (Charley Boston had two of each). It's a way to keep the peace, and besides, Chinese instrumentalists are getting harder to find anyway.

Great-Aunt Bik is another person who has been breaking with tradition, as the sixteen-year-old has been at boarding school in Carmel, New York, ever since her mother died in 1926. She will become the best-educated and perhaps the most independent of the four siblings, thus avoiding the fate of her childhood friends; they are at the public high school, where teachers will make a Chinese girl stand in front of the class to illustrate her "Mongolian" characteristics with a pointer—straight hair and a "nonexistent nose," or where another teacher sighs that it's "a pity that a foreign girl had to be chosen," when a Chinese is elected president of her class. This teacher may be referring to my father's eldest sister, Thelma, at Girl's High School in Brooklyn. When she is elected to lead her student government in 1932, the fact that she is Chinese makes the event newsworthy enough to get it reported in papers as far away as London.

When Bickie comes back to Mott Street after her graduation in 1931, she has been free from the watchful eyes and restrictive life of Chinatown for nearly five years, and it shows. She hangs out with her girlfriends and flirts with the boys, and before long she marries the cutest, one Walter Hom. Settling down with him at 33–37, she then proceeds to have a baby in 1932, my cousin Walter, Jr., whose "milk name" is Sookie. Cousin Sookie will be a full-grown man before he discovers that Sookie means "sour taste," a reference to the fact that he was always throwing up as a baby. Charming. Gon She is probably spinning in her grave.

Meanwhile, Grandfather has finally quit the restaurant business for good, but the going isn't easy for a Chinese man named Hor in Depression-era New York. He gets a job as a census-taker in 1930, and when that is over he applies for a position as a Government interpreter at Ellis Island. The Feds put him through an elaborate interview process, where they test his literacy by handing him cards with complicated printed instructions for actions which he then has to perform. In a letter to the Commissioner-General of Immigration in Washington, the New York Assistant Commissioner praises his appearance, his intelligence, and his language skills. But in closing he states, "We have also heard rumors that the applicant is connected with one of the Tongs. It is not believed that his employment at this port would be desirable."

Nearly sixty-five years later, in my last conversation with Hock Shop's wife Frances, I gingerly bring up the subject of that letter, which I had just found. "Oh, they knew about *that* did they?" chuckles the tiny woman, who is now well over ninety and totally blind. "Well, he didn't *shoot* anybody, you know. They shot at *him,* but he never shot anybody back. That wasn't his job."

His "job" is to manage gambling interests and other nonviolent Tong activities. There are times when he reportedly has to "lie low," hiding out in Brooklyn with Auntie and his children, but that is because the Italian Mafia is after him, not the Tong. The Mafia want a piece of his growing gambling action. Apparently, they are able to reach some sort of "understanding."

Then there is the day when his brother-in-law, Edmund Wong, who happens to be a member of the Hip Sing, sheepishly admits that he has been ordered by his Tong to beat up my Grandfather over an incident where Hock Shop was caught with his pants down, figuratively speaking. He had discovered where one of the Hip Sing-controlled Chinatown lotteries chose their winning combinations, and secretly rented the apartment upstairs. Drilling a hole through the floor, he spied the winning combinations through a tiny lens, and then rushed out and played to win—not in amounts so large that it would draw suspicion upon him, but enough to live on pretty comfortably. Unfortunately, the lottery operators discovered his little ruse one day and complained to the Hip Sing, which is where Edmund Wong comes in. So the two go off together and come back the next day, claiming the deed has been done. Hock Shop looks suitably chastised, but in fact they have just spent the night carousing in some speakeasy uptown.

Still, there has been some more serious Tong violence lately. The On Leong now controls all of Mott Street and one-third of Pell, while the Hip Sing has the rest of Pell and all of Doyers, and both Tongs are suffering from loss of revenue due to the Depression. Thus, the competition has grown more fierce and there are shootings all through the summer of 1930. Some who were children then tell me of seeing a friend's father shot dead in a doorway. Another man is chased down the street with a hatchet, only to reappear the next day with a huge bandage on his head. And then there is the barber who has been enlisted as a hit man by one Tong or another. He waits for his adversary to come and have his hair cut and then stabs him with the scissors. The target is not killed, but he is *really* mad.

All entreaties for peace, even from the Chinese ambassador in Washington are ignored, until finally the police threaten a mass deportation and an agreement is signed. Within a year the white press learns that the head of the Hip Sing since 1929, Mock Si Wing, is in fact none other than everyone's old friend Mock Duck, who had been thought long dead. The general public's amazement is short-lived, however, as Mock is shot, once again, in February of 1932. He survives (of course) but after that both Tongs agree that warfare is just too expensive, and things calm down.

Since he still is trying for something "legit," Hock Shop goes to work for his friends Shavey Lee and Jimmy Typond, the two pre-eminent "fixers" in Chinatown. Shavey, big and fat, like a happy Buddha, and Jimmy, who had married a beautiful Eurasian showgirl from that Chinese Whoopee Revue trip to Paris, would act as liaisons between non-English-speaking launderers and waiters and the confusing world of New York's bureaucracy. Need a laundry license? Need to negotiate a lease? Need help in figuring out taxes, understanding restaurant codes, buying a building? Shavey and Jimmy will fix it for you—for a fee. They can fix anything with their "see-the-landlord" service, and eventually develop a thriving commercial insurance business out of their little office at 40 Mott Street. However, the life-insurance policies they try to get Hock Shop to sell for them fall flat at first. "Why do you want to sell me life insurance?" his neighbors ask suspiciously, "Do you want me to die?" The twenty-year endowment policies they introduce later are much more successful. The bank-shy Chinese just use them as savings accounts.

The two also open a restaurant on Mulberry called Shavey Lee's Tung Sai, Where the East Meets the West. Since it is the first Chinese restaurant in Italian territory, some Mott Street wags refer to it as "spaghetti à la Chinese," but in fact it is the white power crowd from the courthouses and federal offices a block a way that Shavey wants to attract. They come over in droves, drawn partly by the location, partly by the bonhomie, partly by Jimmy's captivating wife Lonnie, who dresses in tight *chong sams* that show off her gorgeous legs. Shavey loves being around the big shots, and will hold court with judges and politicians, even Mayor Fiorello LaGuardia, over Scotch and plates of butterfly shrimp at the long bar in the front of the restaurant.

He also appreciates a pretty girl, and when a pair of stunning Chinese models come in for a drink one evening, he gallantly squires them to a meal. Unfortunately, chivalry turns to dismay when he sees them eat and eat and show no signs of stopping. "I never saw a couple of skinny dames eat so much!" he hisses to Jimmy Typond. The two of them blow cigar smoke into the ladies' faces to try to curb their appetites—and the bill.

Shavey Lee becomes so well known that the New York press starts seeking him out for statements as a spokesman for the Chinese community—that is, when he isn't the one seeking them out instead. It isn't long before he is being commonly referred to as the Mayor of Chinatown," a role which he takes up with relish. He becomes omnipresent, with his huge cigar, huger belly, and classic "Noo Yawk" accent. At every Chinese New Year celebration, every patriotic rally, every visit from some celebrity of screen or state house, Shavey Lee is there, slapping backs and cutting deals. He is the judge of the Baby Parade, the judge of the Miss Chinatown pageant, and year after year he dons a red suit to become a jolly Chinese Santa Claus for the local children he loves so much.

When Chinese are refused admittance to the professional bowling leagues, he, along with Jimmy Typond and Hock Shop, forms the Chinese Bowling Club. Whether or not they ever bowl a game is up for debate, but the Bowling Club does host big dinner dances at the Essex House Hotel every year, at which they ceremoniously "reelect" the beaming Mayor to yet another term. One year his friends run an "opposition" candidate as a joke, but the jolly incumbent is so hurt that they immediately regret their little prank. The Bowling Club also sponsors a softball team, a girl's basketball team, and the Chinatown Midgets, which is a Police Athletic League boys' basketball team that you have to be under five foot three to join. The Midgets triumphantly thwart the snickers of the rest of New York when they win the citywide championship in the early 1940s. It is a victory that people will still be talking about fifty years later.

The bowling club evolves into the Chinese Community Club in the mid-1930s, and Shavey Lee, Hock Shop, and their friends like to hang out at the Sugar Bowl restaurant, where they strategize over gossip and coffee. But for more nocturnal diversions, they also sponsor a famous floating poker game for members of the inner sanctum who can afford the stakes. "Friendly games for serious money" are held in hotel rooms all over the city, with the Chinese Community Club taking a percentage of the winnings. But they aren't unusual in that. Most Benevolent Societies are financed through ruthless play at poker or mah-jongg.

Meanwhile, the CCBA, which used to have a monopoly on the same kind of "favor papers" that Shavey and Jimmy provide, begins to get a little panicky at their perceived loss of control over Chinatown. Of course, it didn't help when the "daughter" living with a former Chief Gentleman was revealed to actually be his mistress and the beneficiary of lavish gifts at CCBA expense. Thus he became known as the *hua-tan* President, *hua-tan* being somewhat quaintly defined as "actress in flapper roles." Another president grandiosely adds the title of Chinese Consul to his business card. And then there was the English Secretary who didn't speak English. At any rate, rumor has it that votes for officers are being bought for as much as $50 each—with winners having to pay off the vote-buying expenses of the losers. The financial setback is only temporary, as the cut from the fees imposed on CCBA members more than compensates.

According to the new by-laws of 1932, "Each laundry or restaurant keeping its location must pay the Association two dollars per annum . . . Each store or restaurant must pay the Association monthly dues according to its volume of business . . . Laundries must pay four dollars per year for a one-man laundry, and eight dollars per year for a two-man laundry . . ." In addition, there is a charge for every business transaction ($5), the removal of a business ($10.50), and even a $3 "port duty" for any Chinese leaving New York for any reason. This is all on top of the $3 that every single Chinese resident of New York is supposed to pay directly to the CCBA as dues. The charges don't sound like much by themselves, but when one considers that there are over 3,500 Chinese laundries, a thousand Chinese restaurants, and some eight thousand Chinese residents in New York City, it all adds up—and all fees are split between the treasury and the officers. No wonder a former president was able to return to China "very rich." Coincidentally, $10,000 was found to be missing from the treasury after his departure.

A major blow comes to the CCBA with the revolt of the laundry-men. There has been a growing anti-Chinese-laundry campaign orga-nized by white laundry owners of mostly large steam laundries in New York City, featuring among other things a poster showing an evil-looking Chinese spitting on a white man's shirts. In 1933, a City ordinance is proposed which would require all independent laundries to pay a $25 annual license fee, in addition to a $1,000 security bond—a crippling sum for any small Chinese laundryman hobbled by the Depression. This can only mean mass bankruptcy, leaving a clear field for the larger white-owned businesses to move in.

The CCBA doesn't do much of anything in response, beyond imposing an additional charge of their own, a $3 "anti-placard" fee which will no one believes will actually go towards protecting Chinese laundry interests at City Hall. So late in April 1933, six hundred laun-drymen meeting in the basement of Transfiguration Church unani-mously vote to form a new and totally independent union. Several weeks later, officers from the Chinese Hand Laundry Alliance success-fully convince the New York City Public Welfare Committee to scale back the new fees to a manageable $10 for a license and $100 for the security bond. By the end of May, the Laundry Alliance has two thou-sand members and a simple motto: "The Laundry Alliance is for the laundrymen." Their chairman, Louis Wing, is even appointed to the board of the City Laundry Code Commission. At his first meeting, a white lawyer asks if he can address Mr. Wing as "Charlie Chinaman." "You can call me anything you like," comes the reply. "But I am afraid you are not a gentleman." Eventually the Chinese Laundry Alliance will even unite with the white laundry owners to push for better overall conditions.

Unfortunately, it takes another war to unite the CCBA, the Laun-dry Alliance, the Tongs, and everyone else in Chinatown. But this time, the enemies are not hatchet men or Immigration inspectors. They are, instead, the Communists and the Japanese.

Chinatown had always been a fervent supporter of Dr. Sun Yat Sen, with thousands attending rallies supporting his causes right up until his death in 1925. Now they are equally enthusiastic supporters of his successor, Generalissimo Chiang Kai-shek, who unfortunately finds himself besieged on all sides. After Sun's death, China descended into a period of barely-controlled anarchy, with independent warlords seizing huge chunks of territory for themselves and a Communist Party fomenting trouble all over. By 1931, Mao Tse-tung, who also considered himself a successor to Sun Yat Sen's ideals, had proclaimed his "Chinese Soviet Republic" in Hunan and Shensi provinces and is now engaged in a fierce civil war with Chiang and his Nationalist or Kuomintang Government. To the north Chiang is further harried by the Japanese, who are busily occupying all of Manchuria, setting up the deposed Chinese Emperor Pu Yi as a puppet head of state while they continue their expansion. Chinese in both China and New York are still smarting after their humiliating rout in the 1894–95 Sino-Japanese War, and this recent action is just like pouring salt in a wound. So, following Dr. Sun's lead, General Chiang turns to overseas Chinese for funds to pay for his anticipated victories. In America he finds a very sympathetic audience.

Starting in late 1931 every organization in Chinatown, from the Tongs, to the Chinese Bowling Club, to the CCBA, to the Trust in God Church, to the littlest Family Association competes to raise money for the war effort. Shavey Lee seems to be at every one of the big parades held on Mott Street, with Benevolent Society lions gobbling down cash for the Kuomintang. In 1932 a brand-new troupe of women Lion Dancers closes down Mott Street as they raise war-fund money in "the first public demonstration of Chinese women this city has ever seen." At the same time, actresses from the Chinese theater, known as "fancies," raise cash for the Cause by using their powers of pursuasion with their rich men-friends on a more one-to-one basis.

Meanwhile there is a mass protest of Chinese students from Columbia University against the Japanese, and on the anniversary of the founding of the Republic later that year, two thousand Chinese New Yorkers march on City Hall to demonstrate that they are also loyal Americans. In 1933, the Kuomintang stages a massive five-day convention in New York City, with over ten thousand members living in the United States attending.

And when General Chang Fa-hwei, a great Kuomintang hero also known as "The Iron General," schedules a propaganda visit to New York in 1934, Hock Shop's brother-in-law, Edmund Wong, decides to stage a spectacular welcome.

Edmund has taught himself to fly. In fact, he is one of America's only Chinese aviators, and with his friend, Fong Tru-shek, he has even bought his own plane—with money saved from his waiter job and whatever it is he does for the Hip Sing Tong. It is the fulfillment of a dream he has had since childhood, when he was known in his home village as the boy who would catch wild birds so he could release them and watch them fly. He was also known as a boy with an irrepressible nature, so despite the fact that he only has about fifty hours of flying time to his credit, Edmund concocts a plan to welcome the Iron General with his own little show in the sky over the ocean liner carrying the illustrious gentleman and his wife as it steams into New York harbor. Unfortunately, the inexperience of the young hot shot means that the air show will not go off as planned.

With Fong Tru-shek flying their plane and Edmund piloting a rented one, the two are looping, diving, and otherwise happily showing off in the air as the ship steams into view. But suddenly, Edmund, who has been flying beneath his friend, pulls up without warning. The tail of his tiny monoplane is sliced off by the other plane's propeller, and Edmund's fragile craft spins out of control, crashing nose-first onto the roof of a Brooklyn tenement. No one inside the building is badly injured, although when the elderly tenant of the top-floor apartment looks up and sees Edmund Wong's body protruding through her ceiling, she staggers out into the hall and faints dead away, tumbling down a flight of stairs.

But as for the young pilot, he is dead, his neck broken. Fong Tru-shek, meanwhile, crash-lands in a ballfield in Queens and is immediately hauled off to the local police station to be interrogated. It is only after three hours of hard questioning that Edmund's friend politely requests a doctor. Apparently his arm is broken in three places and his shoulder dislocated.

Almost immediately the rumors start flying all over Chinatown. Some people are saying that Edmund had had a premonition in a dream; others say that it was his wife, Betty. Both sides agree, however, that before he took off, Edmund had told Betty that he wanted an iron coffin in case the worst should happen. It is an expensive request, but it does not prove to be a problem, because donations for the funeral are already pouring in, with the Iron General, Chang Fa-hwei, personally providing a gleaming steel casket—a "warrior's casket"—at the incredible price of $750. Young Edmund Wong is being loudly hailed as Chinatown's first hero in the war against the Japanese.

This is all small comfort for Betty, however. "They were a couple of grand kids," a friend of theirs tells a reporter, "They never had eyes for nobody except each other from the time they met." That it is still true is shown by the fact that the wife sits all night at the morgue, waiting for the autopsy to be finished on her husband. Benny Kimlau, the Chinese mortician who will conduct the funeral, gently urges her to go home, but Betty refuses to leave without her Edmund. So she sits and grieves, rocking back and forth as she stares silently at the floor "too weary of weeping to weep." At the same time across town, a columnist for the *Daily News* prepares his commentary for the morning paper.

"Somehow, the Chinese do not seem to make very good airplane pilots," he writes, almost gleefully. "I have often wondered why that is, since they are small people, highly intelligent and mentally alert. But they are always getting into some scrape or other when they fool around planes, and the air school at Roosevelt Field used to get the jitters every time a Chinese would come along and sign up for a course." The columnist, Paul Gallico, then goes on to explain that a "true Chinaman is utterly fearless" because his naturally fatalistic nature leads him to calmly accept death as something over which he has no control. "Now Fate is all very well and good," he snickers, "But the point remains that [airplanes] will not fly without wings, as poor Wong discovered when he turned around and discovered that Sheck's prop had chewed off his tail surfaces." Gallico makes a lot of other painfully flippant remarks over the death of Edmund Wong, all illustrated with cartoon caricatures of pig-tailed Mandarins passively looking death in the face. The paper is on the newsstands for Betty to see when she finally drags herself home from the morgue. Later she will miscarry Edmund's child.

Chinatown pulls out all the stops for the funeral of their new war hero. Laudatory banners are strung across Pell Street, the scene of a mournful procession consisting of a band, four flower cars, and over thirty limousines carrying representatives of the most prominent Chinese political, family, and social organizations on the East Coast. Even the officers of the On Leong Tong ride stiffly in the back of a car to honor the dead Hip Sing soldier, for Edmund Wong has become such a sainted figure that all Tong rivalries must be put aside, at least on this occasion. The shining, steel coffin is carried, not in a hearse, but on the shoulders of pall-bearers for all to see, as is befitting a knight fallen gloriously in battle. Betty, supported by her sister (my step-grandmother Frances) stumbles along behind, swathed in black veils, while Chang Fa-hwei, the Iron General himself, emerges from his limousine to give a rousing speech. He urges the young men of Chinatown to emulate Edmund Wong by learning to fly and joining Chiang Kai-shek's fledgling air force to rid the Chinese motherland of her enemies. Mortician Benny Kimlau's teenaged son, Ralph, takes the Iron General's words to heart, and from that day on, he is determined to one day fly in battle against the evil Communists and the Japanese invaders. The adults heartily approve—partially because no one expects the Chinese war to last long enough to give the sixteen-year-old the opportunity to fight.

Despite all the brave speeches, Chiang Kai-shek's forces labor on, year after weary year, with no victory in sight. In July of 1937, the Japanese invade and occupy Peking, Shanghai, and Tianjin, while in Nanking they engage in an orgy of violence that shocks the entire world. In a period of only six to eight weeks some 300,000 of Nanking's civilian residents are slaughtered by methods of appalling cruelty. Japanese soldiers stage beheading contests, people are flayed alive, others are hanged by their tongues, and children are tortured to death with needles. In addition, an estimated 20,000 women are raped—many by their own fathers or sons at the point of Japanese bayonets—before the entire families are murdered and their bodies mutilated. And all this without a fight from Chiang Kai-shek's army, which he mysteriously deems too ill-equipped even to attempt to stop his Japanese foe.

New York's Chinatown is roused into action, however, and within two months, over $1.5 million in nickels and dimes has been donated to aid the Kuomintang. Groups like the newly-formed Chinese Women's Patriotic League, which includes Great-Aunt Bik, stage fund-raising fashion shows at the St. Moritz Hotel, or march through Chinatown with enormous Nationalist flags stretched out flat, into which people toss money from upper-story windows. Chinese Boy Scouts and college students canvass Times Square for donations, and even the annual Baby Parade becomes a fundraiser. Bickie enters Cousin Sookie in one of them, and Shavey Lee awards him first prize.

Meanwhile, all of China seems wracked by war from both the inside and the outside, and Chinatown families start hearing dire tales of starvation and murder from home. In the little village of Hor Lup Chui, the bank started by Hor Mei Fun has failed, and my China relatives have exhausted the legacy left behind by Great-Grandfather Hor Poa. To avert starvation, the formerly "very wealthy" family is reduced to tearing down the central house in the compound built with Hor Poa's hard-earned fortune. They sell the pieces for scrap.

I t is during this time that Betty Wong first hears from her late husband's mother, Soo Hoo She, who writes through an interpreter from her Toi-shan village. It took over a year for her relations to break the news of Edmund's death to the old lady, but now Betty is getting a crash course on what is expected of a daughter-in-law in a traditional Chinese family.

After my cousins revealed the tragic death of Edmund, which they had tried so hard to keep it away from me because they've considered my age, and thought I couldn't be able to stand the blow. At first, everything seemed black around me . . . Then your kind letter came and the big check enclosed has brought me the first smile . . . I was very pleased to know that you are so devoted to my dear son by your frequent visits to his grave . . . I pray that you will also extend my love to him on your visits.

It is plain that the entire Wong clan expects Edmund's wife to support her aged mother-in-law. To the Chinese, the filial duties of a married woman to her husband's family are so obvious they don't bear discussion. But where Betty is concerned, some not-so-subtle nudging is in order.

I am old and feeble now, and I'm afraid I won't have many years in this world. But what is left, I hope you will think kindly of me and send a trifle sum now and then to comfort us for dear Edmund's sake.

So Betty sends a little trifle, to be followed two months later by another lesson for Betty in Chinese family life.

Your letter and the check enclosed (for $15) was duly received, and am sending a few words to express my heartiest thanks and to let you know how happy I am in knowing that you take such kind consideration towards me . . . Perhaps you have received my answer to your previous letter by now, and you are told how anxious I am to adopt a little son to carry on my late son's name. This is the traditional custom here, and I hope you will try to understand and help me financially towards this serious matter for the sake of the dear memory you hold for Edmund.

Betty, who works as a waitress on Doyers Street, manages to send some more money, and soon Soo Hoo She is writing again.

Your letter and check enclosed for the sum of $100 was received with great joy in my heart . . . Words couldn't express how glad I am to hear that you acquiesce financially in adopting a little son to carry on my noble son's name. I was so afraid at first that you wouldn't understand, but now that I have your faith and responsibility, I must try my utmost to keep up my health and strength for my son and your sakes, who is thinking so much for my comfort.

The die is firmly cast. With every new letter comes an increasingly desperate appeal for cash.

> *I regret very much to tell you that things at home are not so bright as I hope for. Lately, a terrific hurricane had swept through this part and has ruined all our crops and every things that we were depending on the soil for food. And at the same time, your nephew was not able to find any kind of a job to help towards the family expenditures that you are so heavily responsible . . . With each year rolled by, my health and eyesight are growing weaker, but I want you to know that my faith in you is growing stronger . . . I wish you will be kind enough to send me a photograph of yourself for me to keep and treasure in my heart . . . I am so sorry to hear that you was not been working steadily . . .*

It is true, Betty is not working steadily. The Depression has not been kind to waitresses in Chinese restaurants, and six months go by during which time she sends no money. But Japan has not been kind to China either, and Soo Hoo She's worries increase.

> *Not long after cousin Wong Foon's return here [in September 1937] this terrible war broke out with Japan and no doubt you have read of the terrible happenings that goes on here. On account of this war, everything has gone way up beyond normal, and it surely has made life very uncomfortable for the poorer class which includes my family. The money you gave to Wong Foon to brought back to me has long been spent, and at present we are going through many hardships and in a very tight financial state. With hope in my heart, I am turning to you for sympathy and for financial helps . . . I want to remind you, also, that I am growing very old and feeble and one cannot tell when I will leave for the Great Beyond and I wish you will help and send a small sum for me to put aside for that case . . .*

Betty manages to find another $100 and puts it in the mail. As the war heats up, the letters get more desperate. Betty sends money when she can, but every Chinese New Year, she knows she will receive an urgent reminder from some Wong relative to play the dutiful daughter-in-law and send a check to Edmund's mother back in China. By 1941, Soo Hoo She apparently can't afford a decent interpreter any longer, and sends one more plea for help. The fractured English doesn't allow for beating around the bush.

> *My home not receive your letter and your money so long; as well as well nigh one year (was twelve month). I want money for buy rice and any Goods. Remember me every day and night. Well nigh dead possible! Hope you soon remit money to China for me. Recourse your money save my life and my home all life! Not dead by want rice . . . Now China in War. Any goods quite good dear! To trust you in U.S.A. reading newspaper by China now know begin and end! Last year and now time, hope you remit money for me! But alas! In vain! Remember me very sorry! I written few line deliver for you. Now almost by end. Bless you in abroad good health! And good luck! But take care you remit money for me! Save I and your nephew life in China. Do answer my end! I will so happy!—From your Mother-in-Law (ill, too), May 27, 1941.*

It is November before Betty can send another $100. She never hears from Soo Hoo She again.

Betty is not the only person in Chinatown receiving despairing letters, and everywhere, it seems, overseas Chinese are digging deep into their little hidden hoards of gold to send money orders back home. Hock Shop and all his friends believe that the only way to bring stability to China is to support Chiang Kai-shek, and between 1936 and 1938 the CCBA collects $1 million from New York's Chinese for the Kuomintang. By July of 1938, 78,000 Chinese across the nation have sent an additional $25 million.

And when it is announced that the still-neutral American Government plans to allow the sale of scrap steel from the newly defunct Sixth and Second Avenue elevated train lines to the Japanese, an ear-splitting howl rises in protest from Chinatown. Why send steel to the Japanese, who will just make it into fighter planes with which to attack us? And why doesn't anyone else see this danger? The generals in the War Department in Washington just chuckle to themselves. Everybody knows that with their little slanted eyes no Orientals could ever see well enough to fly a fighter plane.

On December 7, 1941, the War Department reassesses that assumption.

My father Herbert is at home in Brooklyn when he hears the news. He is eighteen in 1941, and has lived here in genteel poverty with his brother, his sisters, and of course Auntie, since that day in 1926 when she gathered them into her Essex sedan and brought them way out to her neat little house in Cypress Hills. There are trees in the yard, and right down the street is a dairy farm where they can go to get their milk every day. Although they can see the fence surrounding the Cypress Hills Cemetery, apparently none of the children realizes that their mother and grandmother are buried there.

Auntie's fussy husband, known only as "Uncle," lives in the house, too, but in name only. When he's not at his job as a corporate interpreter or minding the Chinese curio shop he owns around the corner, he stays in his room, appearing at the dinner table only on Sundays, after the entire crew has come home from long services at the Baptist Temple in downtown Brooklyn. There Uncle is known as a fiery preacher and leads the Chinese mission. I have been told that he also perfected a machine to make fortune cookies, that Chinese delicacy having been invented by a Japanese-American businessman around World War I. Hitherto, whenever the odd little confections have appeared at all, they have been in the form of flat cookies, rolled into a tube with a message inside. They're still fairly rare, but recently they have begun to assume the soon-to-be-familiar winged shape. Uncle may have had something to do with it, but I have never seen any evidence (like money) to prove it.

If it is true, he couldn't have made too much money on his invention, because the Depression hit Auntie and Uncle fairly hard. The first thing to go was the Essex sedan, and then the comfortable house was exchanged for an apartment a block away, and then a cheaper apartment, and then one even cheaper. But wherever they have lived, Auntie has always kept her refined manners and her fervent Baptist faith. She also still has her stylish wardrobe, some nice Chinese porcelain, and a piano, always a piano, even if it means hauling it up the outside of the latest fifth-floor walk-up apartment she has moved the family into. On the rare occasions that Cousin Sookie and his younger brother Carl come out for visits, they feel strangely intimidated. Auntie Halle and their cousins seem so elegant and sophisticated. And as humble as Auntie may find her current surroundings, they seem vastly luxurious to these boys who have been raised in old-law cold-water flats on Mott Street. "They had separate bedrooms where you could close the door," Sookie recalls, "And real bathrooms, right there in the apartment, so you didn't have to go out in the hall. They even had the toilet and bathtub in the same room together. We had never seen anything like that before."

Another thing that seems strange is that Auntie has always insisted that her "children" speak nothing but English. "You are Americans, and that's what Americans speak!" she would say, sending my ten-year-old father to a speech class to lose the heavy Brooklyn accent he had acquired. He emerges sounding like Edward R. Murrow.

But all this is only because she wants life to be easy for these little ones that she wishes were hers. Auntie has never had any more children of her own—indeed, she may never have even consummated her marriage with Uncle—so she pours her heart out on these five who she feels she has rescued from the very brink of degradation. But it is my father who is the baby, and that makes him the hands-down favorite.

"He always got the new shoes," Uncle Everett says sixty years later with a lingering twinge of irritation, "and the best cuts of meat. And he got to go to camp, and got the scholarship to Columbia." It's true, my father grows up getting pretty much what he wants, making him very poised and very sure of himself, while also being very handsome, with a beautiful singing voice and stellar report cards. But he is still Chinese, still named Hor, and this is America, circa 1940. The comments about his name he has learned not to hear. The mothers of the white girls he dates will take him aside to politely suggest that maybe such a relationship isn't "appropriate," and he will withdraw, because he knows that it is true.

About once a month, Hock Shop will roar up to the house, trailing cigar smoke and racing forms out of his big, sleek automobile. He loves flashy cars, and is especially fond of his 1938 LaSalle convertible, taking the kids for rides, racing through the narrow streets at breakneck speed with his youngest son gripping the dashboard with whitened knuckles. He has always provided money for their upkeep, even though Auntie sometimes has to send Uncle Everett to find him and get some cash, but he is a distant presence at best.

Of course, he doesn't really have much time for such domestic concerns, for by this time Hock Shop has developed quite a reputation as Chinatown's pre-eminent bookie, and is in the process of opening his famous flower shop on Park Street. This is partly to service the Chinese funeral parlors around the corner, but mostly to serve as a base for his bookmaking operation. This is Hock Shop's contribution to the War Effort.

His new shop is next to a space used to store gambling equipment with which to resupply the smoky basement rooms after those raids where the police destroy the old tables and *fan tan* cups. When the proprietor reopens in a day or two, he goes to 106 Park Street to buy new accoutrements.

So, to keep up the spirit of the tiny lane, Hock Shop has carved the already small space next door at 104 Park into two minuscule rooms. In front is the showroom, displaying examples of the gaudy funeral wreaths that Chinese like to buy. He actually does do a good business with the Mulberry Street funeral parlors, and is known for his beautiful calligraphy, which he uses on the accompanying mourning banners. But it is in the back room that the real money is made. There can be found Great-Uncle Fong, sitting at a little table with a telephone, a ledger, and big stacks of cash. Calls come in with wagers on horse races taking place all over the country, which my Great-Uncle carefully notes down in Chinese, so that the police won't have any evidence that they can readily use. They never take bets on anything but horse races; the allure of betting on other sporting events is lost on most older Chinese, for whom football and baseball are still perplexing mysteries. When too many people bet on one horse, the surplus is "thrown off" to an Italian bookie on Mulberry Street to offset any potential losses.

So older Chinese men, working as Hock Shop's runners, visit laundries and restaurants citywide, taking down bets and either delivering them in person to the flower shop or phoning them in. To handle all the volume, Hock Shop has installed "secret" telephones all over Chinatown in semipublic places like apartment stairwells or restaurant storerooms. When a phone rings, the runner on duty will note down the bets in a code that is not only written in Chinese but reads as a take-out order for food, so even if the police get the slips translated they will not do them much good. Not that the police are really much of a problem, because Hock Shop is always careful to pay the cop on the beat $25 a month to leave him alone. He also gives a percentage of the take to the Council of the On Leong, which guarantees that there won't be any undue problems from sources higher up.

As the winning races are broadcast over the radio, the payments start going out. However sometimes at local tracks such as Aqueduct or Belmont the only way to get the results is through an agent in the stands. Since no telephones are permitted anywhere within the grounds, he will go to the fence and make hand signs to a confederate standing outside, who will then rush to a pay phone and call the race in. Hock Shop's runners can expect a handsome tip when they deliver the winnings on a successful bet. But then, Chinese gamblers are traditionally expected to share their bounty as "good-luck money," and hangers-on are always to be found around a successful gambler in hopes that a little will come their way. Of course, even for the winners, their money has a way of finding its way back into the bookie's pockets. Hock Shop, the biggest winner of all, doles out his "good-luck money" in the form of Christmas presents—the more you lose, the more you get. Hock Shop is a very popular man indeed.

I think my father is a little embarrassed by Hock Shop and his swaggering friends, but since he sees him so infrequently he is free to pursue his fantasies of life in the country-club set. He works hard, and at sixteen enters Columbia University to earn a degree in chemical engineering, a popular choice for Chinese boys in 1939. Every day he pays his nickel and takes the ninety-minute subway ride; this involves a trip to Queens, where he can make a transfer without having to pay an additional fare. After Pearl Harbor, sometimes he wears a little Chinese flag on his lapel, so that people on the trains can tell he's not Japanese and won't give him trouble. On Sundays he still dutifully trudges down to services at the Baptist Temple, perhaps followed by a family lunch of *yum cha* at the Nom Wah Tea Parlor, and then a rather suffocating evening sitting around the radio with Auntie and his sisters. But back at school, he joins the fencing team, the sport of European aristocrats, eventually rising to the post of captain. His father goes to see him in exactly one match, which he plays against New York University. Luckily, it is the one where Father delivers the winning point in the saber competition, clinching Columbia's victory. Hock Shop congratulates him, but then doesn't seem to know what else to say.

The first draft-registration drives come in 1940, more than a year before Pearl Harbor. World War I hero Sing Kee is in charge of recruiting in Chinatown and the line of Chinese men waiting to see him and sign up at P.S. 23 stretches all the way down Mulberry Street. But Father has signed up for officer-cadet training in the Army Air Corps. Not only does this allow him to finish college without being drafted, it is the first in a long series of career moves up America's white-shoe corporate ladder. After his graduation in January of 1943, when he is nineteen years old, Father is sent first to Yale, then to the Army Air Corps Academy in Denver to complete his training. He is well on his way to making Hock Shop, Chinatown, and a little apartment on the fringe of Brooklyn nothing more than a fuzzy memory.

Of course, the whole nation devotes itself body and soul to the War, but if anything people in Chinatown take it more personally than most non-Chinese. After all, for those not born in the United States, China is their only country, as the American Government still refuses to allow them to become citizens. Chiang Kai-shek's twenty-five-year-old son, Lieutenant Chiang Wego, is joyously received by Chinatown residents as *their* hero; they rush out into the street after his speech at the Chinese school in the former P.S. 108 to burn an effigy of Wang Ching-wei, the puppet leader installed by Japan. The cops douse the flames, but the paper figure is hastily snatched away to be burned in the alley behind the school, out of the reach of New York City's unsympathetic police force.

And in 1943, when the Generalissimo's wife, the dazzling Soong Mei-ling, appears with a beaming Shavey Lee on a Mott Street choking with American and Chinese flags, fifty thousand people wearing buttons emblazoned with her likeness pack the little sidewalks to steal a glimpse. "Didya' see her?" a little girl shouts to her brother, "Pretty!"

That little girl isn't the only one who thinks so. The New York press devotes an inordinate amount of space to describing what the lady is wearing ("Over her gray and white flowered silk print dress she wore a broadtail coat, and, as in her former ensemble, a matching muff. Pinned on the left shoulder of the coat sparkled her prized jeweled wings of the Chinese Air Force . . .") But Mme. Chiang is much more than a fashion statement, and she goes on to electrify audiences of dignitaries and ordinary Chinese at speeches that she delivers in flawless English around the City. "I wish to tell you," she says, "Although we have suffered, we have been able to carry on because we knew that the American people were with us. We knew of her sympathy and her goodwill and her friendliness . . . All along we realized that justice would prevail and that the people of America knew what was at stake. This high-mindedness, this integrity, this feeling that we should suffer with others and together work and strive for a common cause constitute the meeting ground for your people and mine."

A clearly discomfited Mayor LaGuardia fumbles to find an appropriate response when Mme. Chiang appears at City Hall. "We need not, and perhaps it is better that we do not review the history of the past. Few of the great nations are entirely guiltless, but . . . rest assured, Mme. Chiang, that when you return you may bring the assurance to your country that the American people are determined to stand by China until the very end . . ."

President Roosevelt seems a little chagrined also. After Mme. Chiang visits the White House and addresses Congress, he and others begin to consider some facts, such as the fact that the 78,000 Chinese in the country make up only 0.05 percent of the population, and of those, 52 percent were born in the U.S. Out of this negligible number 13,000, or 17 percent, are in the American armed forces, one of the highest percentages for any ethnic group, with a great many Chinese women—like Great-Aunt Bik—joining the auxiliary corps as well.

In addition, some 15,000 native China-born sailors are on American and British merchant ships. Yet even though they are giving vital assistance to the Allied war effort, these men are at first denied shore leave when in U.S. ports because of the sixty-year-old Exclusion Law. Similarly, when an American consulate in China is evacuated, two Chinese wives of American citizens are deported as soon as the families arrive in the U.S. But since they have American fathers, the children, at least, are allowed to remain.

Obviously something has to change, and on December 17, 1943, the Exclusion Laws are finally repealed. Chinese can now enjoy the right to be naturalized, along with all the other prerogatives extended to legal aliens, and the first legal naturalization takes place four months later. Also, for the first time since 1882, the old immigration restrictions are dropped in exchange for a simple quota. So a whopping 105 Chinese people can now legally immigrate to the United States every year.

It's a small step, but an important one. When 12,000 exultant Chinese stage their grand parade up Fifth Avenue on September 19, 1945, their floats and banners and smiling faces celebrate a victory over more than just the Japanese Empire. For them, it has been a sixty-one-year-long war. But at last they have won the opportunity to become Americans.

9
·
CHINATOWN-
BY-THE-SEA

December 26, 1945. A 1939 Chrysler barrels out of the Holland Tunnel into a baffling tangle of skyscrapers and traffic. The young woman in the passenger seat, who resembles no one so much as the late Jean Harlow, stares in bewilderment at the strange traffic signs looming overhead. Back home in Okmulgee, Oklahoma there is a "downtown," but what on earth is an "*up*town?" She has no time to ponder this puzzle, however, as the baby in her lap begins to stir, and the Chrysler races down Canal Street toward the Manhattan Bridge and Brooklyn. Thus my mother is on the verge of her first brush with Chinatown.

Auntie is all smiles when the new Mrs. Hor arrives at the family apartment, but it hasn't always been this way. When my father first wrote to tell her that he would be marrying a Caucasian girl—a *blonde* Caucasian girl—that was bad enough. But when he added that he was going to become an Episcopalian in the process, that was tantamount to disaster, for Episcopalians, as every good Baptist knows, are a bare half-step away from Satan himself. "I am sorry you are leaving the Church," Auntie wrote back, "And I'll bet she's nothing more than a gold digger!"

My father had met the pretty young Jane Ann McConnell at a church dance in Denver, where he was in cadet training and where she had just moved with her family. To her this handsome Chinese man seemed particularly dashing and romantic, with his officer's uniform and his Big City poise. As for him, all he has to say is, "She had great legs." The courtship lasted six months. If anything, her family was less enthusiastic about the impending wedding than Auntie had been.

"Jane Ann, your mother will be turning over in her grave!" Great-Aunt Mabel declared from the old place in Okmulgee. "Remember, *you* are a *blueblood!*" As for my mother's father, suffice it to say that neither he nor any other family member from either side attended the ceremony. After all, it was April of 1944, and this was a rather new concept to them. But my parents both expected Father to be shipped out to the South Pacific any day, so time was of the essence. It turned out that he remained stateside.

The only reason my father left the Army Air Corps with the rank of First Lieutenant as opposed to Captain was because of an incident with a half-track Army vehicle he happened to be in charge of one day. He had always heard that such vehicles were designed to float, so he drove his into a lake to see if this one would. It didn't. That was in Texas, where he was stationed, and it was the closest thing to action that Father saw for the duration of the War. That is, except for the birth of my brother David, right there at the Texas base on November 12, 1945.

That Army hospital was staffed by stern, no-nonsense nurses not much used to Asians. "Gee, he looks Oriental," one of them said to my mother on seeing my infant brother for the first time.

"His father is Chinese," came the response. Then the nurse, without missing a beat, asked my blond, blue-eyed mother,

"Oh. Are you Chinese too?"

At first it had been difficult for my very fair "blueblood" mother to get used to her new name, but now she is growing accustomed to the double takes, snickers, and outright rude remarks from store clerks and delivery men. I once asked her if anyone ever gave them trouble during that time because they thought that Father was Japanese. "Of course not!" she said firmly. "Your father is Chinese!" But then after a pause she muttered, "Well, there was one very *stupid* man. . . ."

And now the young family has come back East to live with Auntie while Father looks for a job. Basically Auntie locks my mother into the kitchen for six months and teaches her to cook good, wholesome Cantonese food because, blonde or no blonde, Auntie is going to make sure that her baby Herbert eats right.

Her first view of Chinatown is a fog of Uncles, the flower shop, and the Port Arthur, which is the first place she sees my father eating deep-fried duck feet, a particular favorite of his. When Mother meets Hock Shop for the first time, she is a little unsure of herself. She has never met a bookie before. But Hock Shop is polite and courtly, although nothing much more. As for his new grandson, he's proud enough, but then he's never quite known how to act with babies. Besides, he and Frances are about to have a baby of their own, their first and only child, my second Uncle Richard. Soon, Hock Shop and his little family will forsake Manhattan for an impressive house in Forest Hills with a shiny new Buick in the garage. That Buick will often be seen on Park Street while its owner figures the odds over Tea-that-Burns, late into the night.

Shavey Lee is all boisterous charm, however, when my parents stop in to see Great-Uncle Fong, who tends bar at his restaurant. Fong's and Sun's vaudeville career hadn't lasted long. Too many broken plates, I suppose. So now they both tend bar in upscale Chinese restaurants, which suits their temperaments just fine. Fong has an easy, genial nature that is popular with the customers, both here and at the flower shop. He also has just gotten married, to a stunning former Chinese WAC named Ruth, whose favorite activities include accompanying her husband to the track and playing solitaire. Where gambling is concerned, however, Grandfather considers Fong to be a "crybaby"—one who worries over every little loss instead of playing to win in the long term. Fong and Ruth will never move into an impressive house anywhere, no matter how much they figure the odds.

My parents run into Great-Aunt Bik on the street, which delays them considerably in their rounds, since Bickie seems to know absolutely everyone she sees. Any conversation with my great-aunt is constantly being interrupted as she laughs and carries on with friends who have some juicy new piece of gossip that they just *have* to share. I think that by this time, Bickie has chosen her third husband in a process the Mott Street Aunties call "pursuing her hormones." This is the man I will know as Uncle Duck, who is gentle and sweet but a little mysterious, speaking nary a word of English despite having lived in New York for decades. He doesn't speak much Cantonese, the language of choice in Chinatown, either, so he generally says nothing at all. Supposedly Uncle Duck ranks high with the Hip Sing, and I'd love to believe that he is, in fact, Mock Duck, the famous Hip Singer whom no one can kill. But that man would be pushing seventy in 1946, and while Uncle Duck is old, he's not *that* old—at least I don't think he is.

In the past, a prominent Hip Sing man's marriage to a sister and daughter of longtime On Leong members would have been a big problem, but by this time the two Tongs have settled down into the more mundane roles of mediating petty business disputes and oiling their gambling machines. For now, their rivalries will be of a more prosaic nature. So, in 1949, just before the advent of the Year of the Ox, the Hip Sing proudly opens a brand-new headquarters at 16 Pell Street, directly across from their former home of thirty-five years at Number 13. It is equipped with a temple, offices, and an impressive assembly hall. Reportedly, it costs them $60,000.

Not to be outdone, however, the Year of the Rabbit, a.k.a. 1950, sees the On Leong finishing their new building, right at the gates to Chinatown itself, the corner of Mott and Canal. Here Art Deco meets the Imperial Empire. An ultramodern structure decked out with balconies and topped with a three-tiered pagoda, bedecked with curving eaves of yellow-glazed tiles, it far outshines the Hip Sing headquarters in size and magnificence. And in case you don't notice it, at night the pagoda is lit with orange neon. The cost for this monument: $500,000. Once again, the On Leong has won a Tong war.

Great-Aunt Bik, being "just" a woman, is barred from any position of power in the Chinatown Establishment, whether in a Family Association or a Tong council. But somehow she always manages to maintain a sort of back-seat-driver role, which she skillfully uses to her advantage. My father used to say that she made brownies for On Leong meetings. Undoubtedly, they were accompanied by her two cents' worth of opinions.

Great Aunt Bickie is better known as a prominent member of the True Light Lutheran Church, which in 1948 will build a brand-new sanctuary of their own on the site of that old gay bar at the corner of Worth and Mulberry. The True Light has really become a major influence in Chinatown since its founding in 1936, not only because of its pastor, the Reverend Louis Buckheimer, but because they have been joined by Miss Mary Banta, who seems to have attached herself firmly to any Protestant evangelical organization over the past forty-five years that will allow her to keep fussing over Chinatown's children. When Cousin Sookie was in the second grade she even came, unannounced, to his classroom at P.S. 23 and dragged him down to the hospital to have his tonsils removed. She had decided on her own that they needed to be taken out, and nothing was going to stop this diminutive force of nature. She will keep going for years and years, only giving up when she finally dies at age ninety-six. By that time it will be 1971 and she will have been making her presence felt in Chinatown for sixty-seven years.

Great-Aunt Bickie is quite a force of nature herself, and at True Light she leads what is politely known as the Sewing Circle. Among their number are some of Chinatown's Power Aunties, such as Auntie Oye Chu, Auntie June Moy, Auntie Lonnie Typond, and Auntie Pearl Wong, one of New York's first female restaurateurs, the owner of that flashy Chinese eatery near Times Square. The ladies meet regularly to sew and knit up a storm—mostly little things because Bickie gets bored easily—but after each session they break out the cards or the mah-jongg tiles and gamble the night away. The stakes are small, nothing to compare with Hock Shop and Shavey Lee at one of their floating poker games, but the cards and the gossip flow as they laugh and bet and eat the homemade dumplings that magically seem to appear whenever two or three of the sewing circle are gathered together.

One of them is a young half-Chinese bride, just being introduced to Chinatown for the first time. The new Mrs. Tso tries very hard to adapt to her husband's culture, but she was raised in a totally white environment, so there are problems and missteps from the start. For instance, soon after the young couple moves into a building in the alley behind the funeral parlors, Mrs. Tso hears a screaming commotion down in the courtyard and rushes to the window. Thinking that an assault is being carried out, she throws open the sash and leans out, shouting vigorously that she is going to call the police. But for some reason her husband forcibly hauls her back inside. "What the hell do you think you are doing?" he angrily wants to know. The commotion she has heard is a group of professional mourners warming up for a funeral.

On her first Chinese New Year in Chinatown, Mrs. Tso desperately wants to make a good impression, especially as they are going to be visiting Auntie Oye, the formidable Matriarch who reigns at 33–37 Mott Street as if the all the residents were her children—or maybe her subjects. All Mrs. Tso knows about New Year's is that red is supposed to be an auspicious color, so she brings a basket of luscious red apples to Auntie Oye's party as a gift. It is an unfortunate choice.

Mrs. Tso doesn't know that the Chinese word for apple is *ping gor,* or "peace fruit," the peace referred to being the peace of the dead. Apples are for dead people, therefore unlucky, therefore . . . Mrs. Tso withers under Auntie Oye's censorious gaze as she struggles to think of a way to get rid of the damned fruit.

She keeps trying and trying, but always seems to do something wrong. On another visit to Auntie Oye's, Mrs. Tso suddenly fears that she is having a heart attack. But she isn't worried about the pain, or even getting a doctor. In fact, she isn't worried about herself at all. All Mrs. Tso can think of is that Auntie Oye would be offended if she were to die right there in her apartment, for a death in one's home is supremely unlucky. So Mrs. Tso rushes out into the street so that her imminent demise won't insult the sanctity of the venerable Auntie's home.

A short time later she is back, sheepishly explaining to a certain puzzled Matriarch that what she thought was a heart attack was in fact, only a problem with the stays in her corset. Sometimes they just *pinch* and, well . . .

By this time, Auntie Oye has learned to make allowances for her young friend. Not that Mrs. Tso's fortunes have changed. The last straw for her may be when she goes to Frank Gee's Chinatown Fair, the arcade palace that has replaced the old Emporium underneath the Port Arthur. The Fair is noted for its pinball machines, shooting gallery with real bullets, and funny little "museum" with its golden globe encircled by snarling dragons. It eventually will also be the home of another Wonder from the Orient—the famous live chicken who plays tic-tac-toe for a quarter. Mrs. Tso challenges the chicken to a game—and loses. Chickens are really stupid. She may be the only person to have ever lost to the chicken in the history of the Chinatown Fair.

There is another group of young women coming to New York about this time, but they need a different kind of guidance. For they are Chinese war brides, hundreds, perhaps thousands of them. Married to American military and diplomatic personnel, they are beneficiaries of the War Brides Act of 1946, which means that for the first time since 1924 Chinese women have the right to emigrate to the United States as the wives of citizens. By 1950 there will officially be 3,127 Chinese women in Manhattan, along with 10,560 Chinese men. It's still a ratio of three men to one woman, but it's almost three times as good as it was before the War. And now these new arrivals need English lessons and instructions on how to live in a modern American city. It is just like with the Chinese of seventy-five years ago, and once again, it is the churches that come to the rescue.

Miss Banta is in the forefront, of course, but Dr. Mabel Lee is also there, in the Baptist church on Pell Street that she had founded as a memorial to her father, the much-venerated Reverend Lee To, who died during that passionate Tong-War conference at the Port Arthur in 1924. Many Chinese have passed through the narrow doors to receive the English and (obligatory) Bible lessons offered there, and Mabel Lee is very proud of her work. So even though the Trust in God Baptist mission that her father used to work for is now on Elizabeth Street, Dr. Lee is undaunted. She defiantly calls her congregation the *First* Chinese Baptist Church.

The War Brides can even go to Transfiguration Catholic Church, which has slowly, almost agonizingly opened its doors to Chinese over the years. Their congregation is still dominated by Italians, for Little Italy has years to go before it is gobbled up by Chinatown. But now there are a number of Chinese parishioners, and more are welcome. There are even fifty Chinese boys and girls in their school, assuring a Chinese Catholic future for the oldest house of worship in Chinatown.

As for the Temples, they are almost entirely for tourists. Whatever Taoists are left in Chinatown light their incense in their Benevolent Society meeting halls or at the little shrines keeping guard over their stuffy little rooms.

All of Hock Shop's grown children marry and start drifting to the suburbs around this time, following the lead of my father, who has gotten a job with a big chemical company in Camden, New Jersey and moves his family into a little Cape Cod tract house down there. When Auntie Halle goes to visit her favorite grown-up baby boy, she always steps onto the stoop with its view of the dreary Camden skyline and row after row of crackerbox houses, inhales deeply and exclaims, "Smell that fresh country air!" Well, Auntie had always been a city girl.

My sister Judy is born in 1947 in a suburban New Jersey hospital where the staff isn't much used to Asians. "Gee, she looks Oriental," a nurse says to my mother on seeing my infant sister for the first time.

"Her father is Chinese," comes the practiced reply. And then, in a stranger-than-fiction replay of my brother, David's birth, the nurse then asks,

"Oh. Are you Chinese too?"

"I couldn't believe that actually happened to me twice," my mother would say later. "I'm still waiting to see my first blond, blue-eyed Chinese woman."

Meanwhile, my father is accepting transfers around the country as a way to move deeper into the executive suite. And then in 1950, while my Mother is pregnant with my brother Stephen (this time, no one will ask her if she is Chinese) and David is getting ready to start kindergarten, my parents both come to a conclusion: a name like Hor won't help a little boy negotiate the traumas of grade school in lily-white suburbia. That summer my mother and father go to see a judge, and with a stroke of his pen we become Halls.

"He can give himself an English name, but he can't change the color of his skin!" a disapproving First Aunt Thelma will scoff to her children. But by that time her name is Fung, and it seems that everyone in the family with children in this generation modifies their names. Even Uncle had changed Hor to Halle way back before 1910. But Aunt Thelma does have a point. My father, the Episcopalian, golf-playing, junior corporate executive with the beautiful blonde wife and exactly (in 1950) 2.3 children, may in fact be trying to change the color of his skin, at least in his own mind. It seems to be the thing that all sorts of non-Anglo-Americans are doing in the 1950s, especially in the white male corporate world, so my father wasn't so unusual. But all I know is that as we move into bigger and bigger houses and his corporate titles become more impressive, the visits to Auntie become less and less frequent, until finally she sees her favorite baby boy only at the infrequent family banquets we attend at the Port Arthur. By the time I am conscious of her, I am barely told who she is.

Even Great-Uncle Sun has changed his name, but just to the more modern spelling of "Ho." He too has gotten married during the War, to an elegant Chinese girl my mother's age, my Great-Aunt Dorothy. And now, with the birth of their first child, he is busily saving his money so that he can also retire to the suburbs and still have something in the bank. He had been helping with the family "business" in a small way, but his recent gargantuan gambling loss to a bunch of card sharks has not endeared him to that particular form of amusement. As for Great-Aunt Dor, she may have just come out of a snooty finishing school, but because she is a girl her wealthy but traditional family has left their fortune in the hands of her only brother, who ceases to acknowledge any of his half-dozen sisters as soon as they obtain husbands.

At the moment they also live in the building situated in the alley behind the Mulberry Street funeral parlor owned by Benny Kimlau. It is Benny's son, Lieutenant Benjamin Ralph Kimlau, who is the hero to whom the first Chinese-American Legion post in the Eastern U.S. has just been dedicated. That other war hero from the First World War, Sing Kee, who is now a rich businessman adept at negotiating the intricate politics of official bureaucracy, has greatly facilitated the founding of the post in which Chinatown takes so much pride.

They all remember the good-looking and playful Ralph Kimlau who worked with his father—how he would sometimes hide in one of the coffins stacked outside on the sidewalk and suddenly leap out to give his friends heart failure. He was always such a cut-up, that one. They also remember how impressed he was with the aviator, Edmund Wong, who had fallen in the skies over Brooklyn in his enthusiasm to honor China back in 1934. And how when war came to America Ralph was so quick to sign up for the Air Corps, eventually becoming a pilot with the famous Flying Circus in support of MacArthur's forces in the South Pacific. Of course when his parents learned that their only child had been lost in a fierce air battle in 1944 they, along with the rest of Chinatown, were utterly devastated. Ralph's room was thereafter left untouched, almost like a shrine. But old-timers in the neighborhood also shook their heads and whispered that the older Kimlau had brought bad luck on his family by working in the funeral business, even though the "innocent" Ng family had lost not one, but two boys during the War. Proud as they are of their native son, on New Year's the locals avoid walking by the funeral parlor so that they won't be obliged to go in and wish Benny good luck.

The Allies may have won World War II, but the fighting still continues in China. Chiang Kai-shek, the hero of Chinatown, the man whose picture hanging in almost every meeting room and office, is reverenced as was once the image of the Emperor, the embodiment of the Cause for which Lions had danced and money had rained from windows—Chiang Kai-shek is losing China. The Kuomintang is infested with corruption, meaning that Chiang's and his charismatic wife's families are living like imperial royalty while the people starve under a rate of inflation that has seen his unit of currency, the *yuan,* go from a value of four to the U.S. dollar to four *million* to the dollar in five months. The American Government has been shoveling military aid into Chiang's armed forces, confident that airplanes, tanks, and ships alone will mean a victory over a People's Liberation Army made up of peasants lacking any air force or navy at all. But after what basically amounts to a three-year rout, Mao Tse-tung triumphantly declares the founding of the People's Republic of China. It is October 1, 1949.

Meanwhile, Chiang and a million of his followers have taken refuge on the island of Taiwan. The docks of Amoy and Foochow are strewn with crates of family heirlooms abandoned by fleeing Nationalist refugees. But the Generalissimo makes it to Taiwan with the cream of the treasury of the Ch'ing Empire. From there he will continue to rattle his bejeweled saber at Mao Tse-tung for the rest of his life.

Almost immediately after the Communist victory, Chinatown residents start getting quiet requests for donations to something called the Troop Comfort campaign to benefit the Communist armies. The pro-Communist *China Daily News* makes a discreet appeal, while foreign-born Columbia University students visit stores and laundries asking for one-dollar donations. For the most part, they are scornfully turned away.

At the same time, stories start circulating about Chinese bones shipped home for burial being refused by the Communist authorities.

Stranded in Hong Kong, these bones are stacked in warehouses, or even worse, thrown away once the storage facilities are full. For traditional Chinese men or women who depend on the goodwill of the Ancestors for favors from heaven, it is their worst nightmare come true.

But no, it actually gets worse than that, because then the letters start coming—disturbing and upsetting letters from Toi-shan, to which no one is sure how to respond. They say that venerable patriarchs are being arrested for nonpayment of back taxes. Wives are being thrown into prison for not paying "rent" to the State for the farms which have just been seized by "Farmers' Cooperatives." And then there are those who are jailed for reasons that are not entirely clear. Or there are the other letters, the ones from Hong Kong. These claim that a relative on the mainland has been kidnapped by bandits and is being held for ransom. The writers all ask, beg, plead for money to pay off the fines which will release these family members from jail or save some loved one from torture and murder.

Betty Wong receives such letters from the nieces and nephews of her husband, Edmund, dead now for close to twenty years. "Something unfortunate has happened to us recently," they write in one of them, "of which we didn't want to tell you about, so as not to cause you needless anxiety . . . We hope that you will kindly send us another $200 through Mr. Dong Wing Do in Cuba, as you have done previously." As usual, Betty gives the money to Hock Shop, who makes all the clandestine arrangements.

Chinatown is caught in the middle. On the one hand, the American Government has forbidden the sending of money to Communist China (or Korea, with the advent of that war). On the other hand, the *China Daily News* prints careful instructions on how to avoid the ban, identifying which banks or businesses to use and what to write on the cash-laden envelope sealed inside the innocuous outer one. People can try to buy their families in China a little peace, a little time to breathe, which no one really believes will last long. Or they can bankroll a movement which will mean the destruction of everything they remember about home. The dilemma becomes: save the family, but destroy your own childhood.

There is some response, estimated at "running into the millions," but no one is ever sure how much cash the Communists manage to extort. Betty sends $1,000 in one eighteen-month period. All that is known is that after the first payment, a cable is received asking for more money, and then more, and more, and then when it looks like no additional payments are forthcoming, the final word: the relative has died in prison—or committed suicide—or has been executed for crimes against the State—or murdered because some greedy American cousin was too cheap to cough up a ransom. A few hear that their relatives have escaped to Hong Kong, like Betty Wong's niece and nephew, who arrive in the British colony in 1956—and continue to implore Betty for money well into the 1960s.

The CCBA chastises their members for being "gullible." They further try to retaliate by threatening to expose the immigration status of renegade paper sons, while the Government sweeps down on the *China Daily News,* arresting the editor and publisher for supporting "an international racket entailing murder, extortion, torture, and in general, commerce in human misery." The newspaper is fined and the men are sent to jail. But after the American money dries up, from Toi-shan there is only an unnerving silence.

So the survivors of Old China drift in lifeboats called Taiwan and Hong Kong; Chinatown, Singapore; Chinatown, San Francisco; Chinatown, New York; meanwhile more and more people abandon the Communist ship and swim desperately toward them. Congress may have technically repealed the Exclusion Laws in 1943, but the new annual immigration quota of 105 is absurdly small, especially when it is considered that this number covers all *ethnic* Chinese, not just those with Chinese citizenship. But now the traffic in illegal aliens has taken on a new urgency.

The U.S. Government's Chinese xenophobia keeps pace. Whereas it once insisted that Exclusion was protecting U.S. labor, the Congress best remembered for Senator Joseph R. McCarthy now says it is protecting the country from the Reds. Shrill warnings are issued about Chinese Communist infiltrators among the thousands supposedly sneaking across our borders. Chinese-American immigrant-smugglers, once considered merely "wily," now are branded traitors.

Wives, children, and other dependents of American citizens are not included in the 105 number, so it is "paper sons"—which the Government estimates to be "between 85 and 90 percent of parentage-affidavits by Chinese seeking citizenship"—that the Immigration Service is worried about. As proof of these new immigrants' evil intentions, they offer this chilling fact: many Chinese applicants for citizenship are supposed "experts in the radio and electronics fields," which all the world knows are the hallmark skills of spies. And in what could be a quote from the former Chinese Inspector, J. Thomas Scharf, the Government claims that these potential spies are being forced into involvement with illegal narcotics and prostitution. It might as well be 1882 all over again.

Of course there *are* a lot of paper sons, facilitated by what becomes known as the "slot racket"—young people buying their way into family "slots" created after a Chinese-American has returned from a trip to his homeland claiming to have fathered a (nonexistent) child. However, paper-relative immigrants are overwhelmingly people *fleeing* the Red Guards, as opposed to people working for them in New York.

Two thousand dollars is the minimum price paid to one of three national smuggling rings that will plug one of them into an available "slot"; in an attempt to thwart that traffic, in 1952 the U.S. Government stops allowing prospective immigrants to come directly to America from China. Now they must stop over in Hong Kong, where they are grilled by U.S. immigration inspectors, just like at Malone, New York, or Richford, Vermont. They are also subjected to a mandatory blood test. The Government claims that one-half of the blood types collected do not match those of the Chinese-American fathers claimed by the applicants, and agents fan out through Chinatown looking for the ringleaders.

No one in Chinatown is shocked when Sing Kee, World War I war hero, World War II draft registrar, and cofounder of the Chinatown American Legion Post, is arrested in 1956. Everyone knows that since the middle 1930s, when civil war was beginning to rip the fragile Chinese nation apart, Mr. Kee has used his Mott Street travel agency to facilitate a smuggling ring that has brought "thousands" into the country, although he is specifically accused of involvement in only five cases. Of those, four applicants were refused entry. The one who made it through has recently been arrested by Immigration authorities.

Mr. Kee will be convicted of immigration fraud and sentenced to prison for two and a half years. But while he is locked away, the nation's CCBAs convince Washington to engineer some kind of amnesty for Chinese illegal aliens, mostly men who have lived here quietly and worked hard for many years. So in 1957 it is agreed that if "old" paper sons will come forward and admit their true identity they will be immune from prosecution and deportation. It is a Government promise that they can finally sleep in peace.

Well, not exactly. What is not made clear is that they will also lose their citizenship for which they will have to reapply. Furthermore, they will be forced to reveal the identities of other paper sons, paper fathers, paper uncles—anyone who helped them gain their stolen foothold. These paper people are subject to the full weight of the law. Suddenly, Chinese are being stopped on Chinatown streets to be interrogated on demand by humorless agents of the Immigration Service. People are dragged off to detention. Blameless old bachelors, who entered the United States wearing queues when there was still an Emperor on the Peacock Throne, have real reason to fear exposure of their antique deception. Even Great-Aunt Bik, who is still not a U.S. citizen, has to prove all over again the legitimacy of her 1913 immigration at the age of eight months. Elsewhere in Chinatown boxes full of family papers, photographs, even Ancestral tablets are burned, so afraid are these aging men that the Immigration Service will find out the truth. So genuine identities, as well as links to generations stretching far back into the Empire, become nothing more than smoke that floats away on the breeze. These lonely old bachelors are now more alone than ever.

As for Sing Kee, when he returns to Mott Street his business will be just as strong as ever, if not stronger. Despite his jail time he has not lost one iota of face in the minds of his neighbors.

Not that the 1950s are one unrelenting parade of misery. The world of Chinatown keeps spinning in ever more American ways. Hock Shop gets the first television set in the neighborhood; which he somehow manages to cram into the tiny flower shop on Park Street, which is now full of people watching everything from boxing matches to Liberace. There are the block parties and Baby Parades, and even the anniversary of the founding of the Chinese Republic on the tenth of October (the "Double Ten") is celebrated with events as unlikely as the Miss Chinatown Pageant, which one year includes "the Chinese

Atomic-Red Bombshell," so-called because of that particular lady's unusual red hair.

Restaurants like China Lane, the Chinese Rathskeller, and Joy Luck, with its giant neon-rooster sign, are thronged with gagging tourists who have just swallowed the messages inside the still-unfamiliar fortune cookies—the city eventually passes an ordinance requiring the sayings to be printed on nontoxic paper—and the curio shops are beginning to be supplemented by street vendors selling everything from wind-up toys to vegetables off the tops of egg crates crowding the narrow sidewalks.

Shavey Lee has even started Chinatown's first senior citizens' club, an American counterpart to the village Ancestral Hall where the old bachelors can congregate in a friendly atmosphere to gossip and complain over a friendly game of *pai gao* and a carton or two of cigarettes. Unfortunately, Shavey passes away before he ever gets to use it himself, but his spirit is undoubtedly proud that his funeral at the True Light Lutheran Church in 1955 draws some ten thousand mourners. As the cortège makes its way up Mulberry Street and down Mott, the Italian band strikes up the old vaudeville chestnut, "Chinatown, My Chinatown." It only needs Eddie Foy and the Seven Little Foys to make the moment complete.

In the summers, Chinatown moves to the beach. Actually, New York's Chinese have been spending time at the little resort of Bradley Beach, New Jersey, ever since 1922, when the old Church of All Nations hosted each of the different ethnic groups in their congregation at their own Cliff Villa—two weeks for the Armenians, two weeks for the Poles, two weeks for the Chinese, and whoever else they had kicking around there. The Villa, actually a sprawling wooden hotel, overlooks both the Atlantic Ocean and the little lake separating the village of Bradley Beach from Ocean Grove, the community founded by the Methodist Church as a religious retreat center. Ocean Grove is as prim and pristine as the calendar picture on the preacher's wall.

Over the years Chinatown families started coming down on their own, looking for landlords willing to rent them a few rooms for the season. When the neighbors complained, the Chinese always meekly moved away to another, less conspicuous location. By the late 1930s they had become a fairly common sight on the streets of the tiny resort community, lined with trees and cute little summer cottages. Still, when

Lee B. Lok's wife, bound feet and all, was walking carefully down Newark Avenue with one of her daughters in 1941, she was flabbergasted when a lady came out on her porch and called out, "Are you looking for a house? Would you like to buy this one?" Mrs. Lee may have spent most of her married life cooped up in an apartment on Pell Street, but she was no fool. Two thousand dollars later, Lee B. Lok and family were ensconced in a summer bungalow of their very own in the village where twenty years before they would have been lucky to be able to rent some rooms over a store. Sadly, Mr. Lee would die the next year, but soon his son, daughters, cousins, and friends would be flocking to Newark Avenue and buying up the little cottages, thus creating the community which would be known as "Chinatown-by-the-Sea."

So on Memorial Day weekend the exodus begins. Hock Shop in his Buick, Dr. Liu in his Chrysler, Pee Wee Wong in whatever old jalopy he has cobbled together in front of his apartment on Mott Street join the caravan of cars trundling through the Holland Tunnel and down old Route 9 to their sunny summer enclave. It seems as if everyone is there, in little pockets just like the family compounds in their ancestral villages. The Hor family is on the fourth block, the Lees in the first, the rest elsewhere on Newark Avenue, but only Newark Avenue. Even in this relatively bucolic place, there is still safety in numbers.

The men drop the women and children off for the summer and then head back to the city, commuting down on Mondays, when the Sunday rush in Chinatown is over. Dr. Arthur Liu has an especially tight schedule. A son-in-law of Lee B. Lok's, he has been Mott Street's premier general practitioner since 1936, and is much in demand. Patient visits to his hopelessly cluttered office in the building his father-in-law built at 45 Mott cost $3, house calls (sometimes to as far away as the Bronx) $5. Sometimes he has to convince people not to rely on herbal medicines, especially when he feels that antibiotics are required, although "herbs are good for colds," he grudgingly allows. Sometimes he will climb five flights of stairs to find an abandoned old bachelor delirious with hunger, and so will go down to Lee's or the Rathskeller (they have especially good chickens) to get him a meal. Then too, he often has to deal with all sorts of problems unique to those ladies who still bear "golden lilies"—bound feet. Even "released" feet don't ever resume their natural shape, and difficulties with the leg and back muscles and the spine will plague these women for the rest of their lives. But there is one problem Dr. Liu is especially happy not to be faced with: opium addiction. The growing stability in Chinatown, largely brought about by the slowly increasing number of women and children, has worked to calm many anxieties and make the old scourge passé.

However, it is for the delivering of their babies that Chinatown most often seeks out Dr. Liu above all others. He is known as "the doctor with three sons," and the prospective mothers (and fathers) earnestly hope that Dr. Liu's good luck in such matters will rub off on them. Arthur Liu has such a good bedside manner, in fact, that he even regularly treats the white family who owns the fruit stand he stops at on the way down to Bradley Beach. One day when he was looking through their produce he noticed a cough, offered his services, and suddenly another family of loyal patients was added to his practice.

At Chinatown-by-the-Sea, Great-Aunt Bik's sewing circle is in full swing, only here people have so much time on their hands that there might be one mah-jongg and two poker games going on simultaneously. In Bradley Beach nobody locks their doors, so if one of the marathon card games runs out of beer in the middle of the night someone just might slip into your kitchen while your family is asleep and borrow a few bottles. They are always—well, nearly always—replaced the next day.

Great-Uncle Fong and Ruth are right next door to Bickie, and Auntie Pearl Wong is on the other side, with Hock Shop and Jimmy Typond close by in whatever bungalows they manage to rent for the summer. At Bradley my Step-Grandmother Frances is, if anything, more retiring than at home, her summertime world confined to the four blocks between her cottage and the beach, where her chief activity seems to be taking photographs of her little boy, Richard. As for the men, Monmouth Park Race Track is close by, so they follow a regular routine of running down there in Hock Shop's Buick, probably spending more time with the ponies than they ever do by the ocean. Later Great-Uncle Fong takes over the driving when he gets a car of his own—an Edsel, an *orange-and-white* Edsel. Once again, Fong shows that he just isn't good at figuring the odds.

Meanwhile the kids hang out over pizza and ice cream at Virgil's Lunchroom, or walk the few blocks up the Boardwalk to Asbury Park, where there are arcade games and rides, with a giant Ferris wheel thrusting right up through the roof of one of the graceful old beachside pavilions built when Asbury Park was still a fashionable resort. Another one of those pavilions also holds the nearest movie theater, from which the kids will come back late at night along the beach, clutching each other and trembling with fear after having had the living daylights scared out of them by some thriller like *Psycho* or *The Birds.*

No one notices any real prejudice from the white residents of Bradley, although they do remember the time, not too long ago, when one group had tried to swim at a beach in Maryland and had been unceremoniously thrown out. The blacks there had offered to let them swim on their beach, but the Chinese declined. "We felt a little odd there, too," one of them says later, "Sort of betwixt and between . . . We are not as thoroughly American as the Negro." But here in New Jersey the situation is somewhat reversed, because at nearby Asbury Park there is a tiny blacks-only beach—a strip barely a hundred feet long, hemmed in on both sides by whites making sure that the borders are not violated, while the Chinese bathers no one seems to mind.

On Sundays the residents of Chinatown-by-the-Sea will troop over to Ocean Grove to hear one of the fiery revival preachers shaking the rafters at the Great Auditorium, or maybe they will go to a band concert or hymn-sing when the poker gets tired. Yet the Chinese still tend not to be included in the barbecues and picnic outings hosted by their Caucasian neighbors. And although no one ever tells them that they are not welcome, the Chinese kids hang back from attending the weekly dances in the old wooden pavilion on the boardwalk. "Those were for the white kids," one of my cousins tells me, "and I suppose we were just afraid that they would make fun of us. It was just easier not to go."

Chinese kids have weekly dances of their own to attend back home in Chinatown, which has grown enormously by 1960. Now its population is around 20,000, with the male-to-female ratio standing at its lowest point ever—two to one. Some of the old places still remain, the Port Arthur, the Nom Wah Tea Parlor, Quong Yuen Shing, but the early sixties see the addition of everything from pagoda roofs on the telephone booths (a dubious inspiration of the city's tourist board) to a giant new housing complex called Chatham Green, filling up the wedge between Park Row and Worth Street, and obliterating the southernmost end of Mulberry. Robert Moses—New York City's powerful parks commissioner and head of the Mayor's Committee on Slum Clearance—had wanted to tear down all of Chinatown for a massive new development, but saner minds prevailed.

Meanwhile, even though my family is growing up under a thick varnish of country clubs and Episcopal churches, the Chinese still shows through. Father (never Dad) doesn't really know what to do with toddlers, but we, his children, all seem to know instinctively that we are expected to act like adults—or at least as much like an adult as a four-year-old can. As in more tradition-bound Chinese families, he is the undisputed head of the family, never wrong, never to be questioned, although his chief concern about us seems to be our table manners at restaurants. Our public deportment reflects on the family name, he solemnly reminds us, and he ruthlessly pounces on any regionalisms that appear in our speech, for perfect grammar and diction re also essential for a representative of our clan. Of course, when we discover an old recording of him in his speech class from when he was ten years old, we are delighted to find that he once referred to "boids in the twees," and gleefully plunk it down on the hi-fi at one of the stuffy cocktail parties that regularly takes place in our living room. To our dismay, that recording soon suffers a sudden and mysterious disappearance, never to be explained.

But honor, in our family, does in fact extend beyond table manners. My father's extreme honesty in all things seems to buck the trends of the society around us, but to be anything less would be a disgrace. We are taught to own up to our mistakes, whether in school, to a policeman, or to the Internal Revenue Service, and to submit both to Authority and to the truth. So when their high-profile business venture went sour, and the company employees started suing for back wages and going to the press, Father's two partners merely skipped the country. He, however, calmly answered the TV reporters' questions, accepted the court's judgment with great dignity, and eventually sold our house to pay the debt. I think it is a Chinese thing, but regardless, it is the quality about him I most admire.

And is it a Chinese sense of resignation or a Scottish stoicism showing when my brother David dies? It is 1959, he has a degenerative kidney disease, and nothing can be done for him in an era still on the verge of developing dialysis machines. My mother begs his doctors to take one of her kidneys, but transplant surgery is also just barely over the horizon, and my oldest brother's life finally flickers out at age thirteen. He is cremated, there is no memorial stone, and barely a reminder of him in the house outside of a faded color photograph and a couple of paintings he did in school.

My mother insists that his essence was in his soul, which is now gone and cannot be reclaimed. But somehow this episode reminds me of the death of Hor Poa's little daughter some fifty years before. The fact that David is not talked about much doesn't mean that he's not loved or missed, which he is most terribly. It's just that one doesn't look back, one doesn't talk of unpleasantness from the past. A new sister, Amy, is born almost exactly two years later, as an unspoken way to salve the wound.

I am a precocious, or should I say an obnoxious child, sorely trying my father's patience with my behavior and appearance (a certain junior-high-school pair of bell-bottoms comes to mind), all of which invariably brings a lecture about the sanctity of the family name. But concerning that name I am somewhat confused as a child. I can never quite understand why my Grandfather's name is Hor, while mine is Hall. All I know is that *hor* supposedly means something bad, so when I'm around eight years old, I suddenly spring the question on my mother. "What does *hor* mean?" I ask in my high, shrill voice.

Mother (never Mom) has a policy always to at least technically answer our questions, so she purses her lips and spits out, "*A promiscuous woman!*" in a tone that I know means that the subject is closed. The next day I loudly inform my best friend's mom what I have learned.

"I found out what our Chinese name means," I tell her confidently. "It's some kind of lady."

But my father for some reason doesn't like us to talk about our being Chinese at all, which seems like something of an absurdity to me, since all through grade school I am subject to a constant taunt of "Ching-Chong-Chinaman!" despite the fact that I don't look particularly Chinese. I am also aware of the fact that around 1960 we were prevented from moving to a new house. A neighbor woman saw my father with the real estate agent and called the realty office to complain. And even though my oldest sister is nominated for Homecoming Queen, her high-school yearbook picture still carries the caption "Judy Hall, The China Doll."

Perhaps it is because of my father's apparent denial, or because I know absolutely no Chinese kids outside of our family, or perhaps because of my own naturally contrary nature that I develop a defiant interest in all things Chinese, as well as a list of ready responses to the occasional ridiculous comment from people like my high-school algebra teacher.

"Do you know how Chinese name their children?" he asks me one day in front of the class. "They drop silverware down the stairs and it makes all those sounds!"

"Oh, you mean like 'BRUCE—EDWARD—HALL'?" I answer.

"No!" he exclaims, obviously not getting my sarcasm. "You know, *Ching! Chang! Chong!* Ha! Ha! Ha!" Of course this bozo's name is Weymouth, so I don't know what he's laughing at.

Years later, when I have plowed my father's BMW into a snowbank on a country road, I stand there fuming as a local resident approaches on foot. "Wow!" he says, looking into my face. "Say 'hello' in your native language!"

"Hello," I growl back at him. He scurries away as I continue to steam there in the cold.

We see the Family at our house for Thanksgiving, where they somehow seem a little incongruous, or at the Port Arthur for banquets, where everyone is in their element. These dinners always start at six o'clock "Chinese time," which means seven or seven thirty. When I was really little, my mother used to bring along cereal for me to eat, for as a three-year-old I wouldn't touch anything else. "These are really good Chinese Cheerios!" I chirped on one of those occasions, a remark which has been repeated for my benefit at every banquet I have attended since 1958.

"Did you bring your Chinese Cheerios?" Great-Aunt Bik calls out as we enter the room. Bickie is the most fun, always the Mistress of Ceremonies, the Majordomo who always seems happy to see you. She arranges where we sit, bosses the waiters around, and laughs louder than anybody. I think she is the one who told us Cousins all those superstitions about chopsticks—cross them and it's bad luck, leave them sticking up out of your rice and it's like a tombstone, drop one and you're expecting company—but then she might have made them up for our amusement. Sometimes she brings part of her Sewing Circle along, and we know that after we all leave, they will clear a table and play some intense mah-jongg with the waiters and with Florence, the owner and Shavey Lee's sister, gossiping and gambling far into the night. In 1962, Great-Aunt Bik will finally become a citizen of the country she has lived in since before she could walk. As soon as she gets her passport, she and Uncle Duck take off for Europe.

Hock shop—Grandfather (never Grandpa; my parents call him *Ah Ba,* for Daddy, and Bekie calls him *Pun Gor,* for "Older Brother")—sits with his big cigar and patiently tries to teach me a few Chinese words, which I promptly forget as soon as we leave. He has an air of self-assurance, a definite Big Shot, someone who can say to one of my college-bound cousins, "You should become a lawyer. And then we'll get you a judgeship." He doesn't specify who "we" is, but you know he means what he says.

The Great-Uncles, Sun and Fong are almost like Tweedledum and Tweedledee, one thin, one fat, both sweet and fun to talk to. But when I ask about their vaudeville days they get all shy. "Oh that was in the past, we didn't do much, we weren't very good," and the subject slips away. Sunny is living the life of a respectable gentleman with his wife and two pretty and ladylike daughters, Pamela and Alison, out in Great Neck, Long Island. Fong is now the bartender at the Macao, one of three restaurants on Pell Street owned by Hong Kong movie people. All three (Bo Bo's and Esther Eng's are the other two) cater to the well-heeled two-martini crowd, but Esther Eng's is the first to eliminate "combination" dinners and American food from her menus. Esther is also unusual because she is an outspoken lesbian, always seen wearing men's suits and "mannish" haircuts. Her ex-girlfriends (of whom there are several) manage her other places uptown.

Great-Aunt Dor surprises me once at our house when I suggest a game of mah-jongg. I had just bought an antique set I found in a shop, and the whole family learned to play it, the way you'd play a social game of bridge or gin rummy. So when I suggest a match to my elegant and refined Great-Aunt I am shocked when her eyes light up and she says, "Oh! What are the stakes?" When I assure her that we won't be *gambling* she loses interest. "Never mind," she says.

Great-Aunt Ruth offers occasional commentary, like when I ask her what the writing on the red slips of paper hanging high around the restaurant walls means. "Who knows?" she answers dryly, taking a deep drag off her cigarette. "I don't read that stuff." Grandfather's wife Frances stays firmly in her husband's shadow, although she somehow knows all of our birthdays, even better than our own parents. Meanwhile Uncle Duck says absolutely nothing, although you have the feeling that he understands everything he hears. It's vaguely unnerving, as though he's an impostor or a spy.

Uncle Everett and Aunt Lois I think of as a mirror of my own parents, partly because she is also not Chinese and also because she is gregarious and friendly, just like my mother. My uncle has a photographic memory when it comes to food, and will rapturously describe wonderful meals he consumed during the Coolidge Administration. He also loves to go on in gruesome detail about any one of the twelve or more courses set before us, and woe betide the unprepared visitor to one of our family dinners. When my ten-year-old cousin brings his little friend along one time, Uncle Everett is in his element.

"Do you know what *this* is, Joey?" Uncle Everett asks, holding up a morsel with his chopsticks in front of the little boy who has probably never eaten Chinese food in his life. "This is *fish maw*, have you ever heard of *fish maw?*" Joey looks uncertain, "Well *fish maw* isn't exactly the fish's *crop*, and it's not exactly the fish's *gullet*. . . ," Joey's eyes are getting wider while he, himself is getting visibly smaller, "And it's not the *stomach* or the *brains*, it's, well, the *maw*. It's behind the *head*, and you have to cut through the back of the *mouth* with a *sharp knife* and kind of *dig* . . . ," Joey is turning green and leans over and whispers to Jonathan, who whispers to his mother, who slips him some money. "But after you *cook* it it's delicious and . . . " The two slink away from the table in search of a hamburger while Uncle Everett sails on, happily oblivious as he concentrates on the white substance trembling between his chopsticks, which he finally pops into his mouth. "Wait a minute!" he exclaims, "This isn't *fish maw*. This is *chicken!* . . . Joey? . . . Joey?"

Aunt Thelma and Uncle Tim drive in from Long Island. Uncle Tim always tries to surreptitiously slip me a lucky red envelope at Chinese New Year's, but I never catch on and he has to just shove it in my pocket. His claim to fame as a commercial artist is that he helped design the Wonder Bread wrapper, while his brother, Paul Fung, was once a famous cartoonist, drawing the *Dumb Dora* strip, popular in the 1930s and 1940s until high living caught up with him and he died young. Their children are the Three "K" Cousins, Kenneth, Kevin, and Karen. With Second-Uncle Richard as our unofficial dean, we Cousins conspire to get out of drinking the obligatory almond juice at the end of the banquet, while Kevin and my brother like to stick the roast chicken heads in the spouts of the teapots and take their pictures. As we get older, all of us know that if we ever appear at a family banquet with a friend of the opposite sex, the Aunties will make us miserable. Over the years, we are rarely so foolish.

My father's sister, Frances, like his sister Thelma, is still a devout Baptist and is gentle and kind, looking a lot like her mother. Her husband, my Uncle Roy Eng, originally a Hong Kong boy, is a psychiatric social worker who has, in 1964, just helped found an agency called the Chinatown Planning Council. It has been formed to offer psychiatric help to a Chinatown population increasingly made up of refugees and others for whom the culture shock has been too much.

Uncle Roy has also just scored an important victory for his family in a feud going back many generations. No one can exactly remember why, but the two branches of the Eng family have nothing to do with each other, to the point of maintaining two different stores in Chinatown for members of the opposing camps. One Eng wouldn't be caught dead shopping in the rival Eng emporium, not that a specific Eng would be recognized there, so numerous was the clan.

Well, it seems that the "other" Eng shop fell on hard times and was finally going out of business. Uncle Roy, who had never even been inside before, wandered by as the store was selling off its stock. He posed as a disinterested customer, but was really a secret agent operating behind enemy lines. "Would you be interested in selling your sign?" he asked the owner's daughter in an innocent voice.

"What crazy person would want that old sign?" he heard the father say from the back when she went to ask. "Go ahead! Sell it to the knucklehead! What on earth could he do with it?" So Uncle Roy returned to his own family store triumphantly waving the wooden banner of the rival Engs' failed enterprise. He had captured the flag. His team had won.

Aunt Constance, who also goes by her Chinese name, Ling, is never at these dinners, because she lives in San Francisco. She had always been a little apart from the rest of the family anyway, because she went to that special deaf school on Lexington Avenue and only saw her siblings on weekends. But sometime during the War she spied a photograph in a magazine of a young Chinese tennis player in California named Henry Low. Liking what she saw, she wrote to him. He wrote back. Soon she was off to the West Coast to plan a wedding. And now I have a cousin named Russell, who up to this time I've never met.

Another person we see less and less of is Auntie, the tiny old lady who always reaches out to stroke my head, and whose exact identity I am still unsure of. I'm still wondering when, at the age of eleven, I take the phone call informing us that she has died. When my parents get back from bridge at the country club I ask again, "Who *is* she?"

Thirty years later my father will be unable to recall if he went to her funeral. "I was always her favorite," he tells me in a rare moment of self-revelation, "and for some reason during the last few years of her life I pretty much ignored her. I'm not proud of that. Someday I'll have to sit down and figure out exactly why I acted that way."

Five years after Auntie's funeral, I am also the one to take the call informing us that Uncle has died. "Uncle who?" I say. I have never heard him mentioned before.

But during the 1960s one more family member is added to our banquets from an entirely unexpected source. For after a silence of forty years or more, we have once again been confronted by a cousin from the village of Hor Lup Chui.

M y eight-year-old Cousin Emily is a beneficiary of the new immigration laws passed by Congress. By Presidential order in May of 1962, immigration restrictions have been lifted as a way to help British Hong Kong, choked as it is by Communist refugees. Some seven thousand of them come to New York, according to the Immigration Service, causing Chinatown to burst its borders and spill across Chatham Square to Division Street and East Broadway, where the new Chinese movie theater is, with tendrils of Chinese colonization snaking across Canal on Mott and Elizabeth up to Hester Street and beyond. The CCBA has moved out of their cramped old building at 16 Mott and built a spacious new one up the street, on the site of the old P.S. 108. There are two new Buddhist temples, a plethora of new Chinese storefront churches, and even Chinese priests with Chinese-only services at Transfiguration, the Catholic church where once an Irish pastor had railed against the eighth hundred or so "heathens" pressing further and further up Mott Street.

But now so many are coming that the Chinese are the fastest-growing nonwhite population in New York, and the Board of Education no longer lumps them in the "others" category on their racial surveys. The Chinese now have their own designation. "After 50 years in New York City, we have finally become a minority group," is the wry observation of the editor of the *Chinese-American Times*. Of course he has it wrong. In 1962, the Chinese have been here for more than a hundred years.

The year 1965 is when the new Immigration Act comes into effect, finally eliminating the old quota system for good and opening immigration up to refugees, skilled workers, and family members of American citizens on a first-come-first-served basis. Supposedly 20,000 can be admitted from each country (with a cap of 170,000 for the Eastern Hemisphere and 120,000 for the Western), but that doesn't include all of the wives, children and parents of U.S. citizens, who are figured outside that number. The floodgates have officially opened. It also happens that 1965 is the Year of the Serpent, a supposedly inauspicious sign. Time will tell what the Serpent does.

Cousin Emily arrives in 1966 from Hong Kong, the granddaughter of Hor Mei Wong, Hor Poa's long-dead Number One Son. After Hor Mei Wong's widow and other son (Emily's uncle) had squandered whatever family fortune there had been to squander, Emily's father had made his way to Hong Kong, where he hung out with a rough crowd of gamblers and petty thieves. I don't know when and how Grandfather hears about this long-lost cousin, but according to ancient rules of filial duty, a Chinese's responsibility extends to cousins of the fifth degree. At our banquets, we Cousins always try to figure out exactly what degree of cousin Emily is to us, but whatever it is, she is certainly family.

Great-Aunt Bik is the one who takes Emily to live in her little apartment, the same one that Great Uncle Sun had once occupied in the building in the alley behind the Mulberry Street funeral parlors. I don't know if any of the other relatives had been approached, but Great-Aunt Bik not only feels sorry for the little girl who has basically been left to raise herself on the grim streets of Hong Kong, she wants a daughter who will be around to look after her in her old age, especially since Sookie and Carl are off on the corporate fast track and have suburban families of their own. Emily is meant to be almost like a *moi ji*, as Gon She had been, not quite daughter, not quite servant. Unfortunately she will have nothing to do with such an antiquated idea.

Although at this time I only know Emily as the pretty, meek young girl in Mary Janes sitting quietly with Uncle Duck at family banquets, the rumor is that at home there is nothing but trouble. The cute little moppet is still a wild Hong Kong street urchin, and all attempts to rein her in are met with snarling fights and furtive deceptions. She starts hanging around with other tough refugee kids, and is even caught carrying a knife, hidden in her sock, to school at P.S. 23. She certainly is smart, though, and within a few short years is speaking and writing fluent English. But to Great-Aunt Bik and the Aunties of the Sewing Circle, this willful child is a baffling mystery.

Chinese children have always been a baffling mystery to school authorities in New York, but because they have been so unnaturally good, not bad. A Chinese child has rarely been known to get in trouble, rarely to talk back, and in the extremely unlikely event that one is caught scribbling on the walls of P.S. 23, the other Chinese children will band together to scrub the offending graffiti off the venerable bricks and thus preserve their community's good name. When one Chinese child is brought into Truancy Court after skipping school for a couple of days in the 1950s, his father makes this plea to the Judge, "Kindly send me to prison for a long term in place of my unknowing son. I am at fault. I have lost much face. I thank you."

"With us, parents are responsible for the way their children behave," says one of Cousin Emily's teachers, Mrs. Grace (Lee) Mok, "In all Chinese homes, children are told that they must be good or the family will suffer disgrace." But a Chinatown public-health nurse sums up the situation in one brief comment: "The police have nothing to do here."

All of this is changing by the 1960s. The Chinese women pouring into New York are delighted to find themselves in a society where it is permissible for them to go out and get jobs, although they are hampered by their lack of English. So, as with Gon She's generation, they go to work for the garment manufacturers. But instead of the Factory Man bringing piecework or unstrung beads around to each apartment, sweat-shops all over the Lower East Side are now hiring Chinese women to run the dozens of sewing machines crammed into the hot and dusty lofts, each equipped with a single toilet that may or may not function.

Also, instead of the owners always being white men, now they are frequently Chinese themselves—and not above making a dishonest dol-lar at the expense of their countrywomen. They regularly keep two sets of books—one for the authorities, and one for themselves—and there is nothing their employees can do about it. "He is the only one who speaks English, so the Americans listen to him," one woman says, "and then he makes me sign a paper saying I got $60 a week instead of $30. But what can I do? I cannot speak English."

With the mothers out of the home and the fathers working four-teen- and sixteen-hour days, Chinatown's children are left more and more on their own. Some of the new kids form gangs—not the benign gangs of Cousin Car's youth, where they would hang out in a coffee shop and be home by ten o'clock—but arrogant, defiant gangs that sometimes give the police trouble. The newspapers cite statistics show-ing the rise of Chinese youth crime, although as one Chinatown lawyer rightly points out in 1965, "After all, from zero to one is a 100 percent increase." The kids still go to school all day and Chinese school all evening. Most of them don't have time to get in trouble.

Our semiannual forays into Chinatown continue unchanged. The banquets are always followed by a shopping expedition so that my mother can stop into Mr. Leung's store on the corner of Pell and Mott, where he somehow understands her excruciatingly tortured Chinese pronunciation for things like his delectable Chinese sausages, or partic-ularly delicious roast pork, strips of which are hanging in the windows along with the fresh chickens and ducks dangling by their heads, making the tourists squirm. There are bunches of Chinese broccoli and winter melons and hairy squash to buy. And then there is the trip to the little old Mei Le Wah Coffee Shop to pick up a dozen of the best, the juiciest roast pork buns, or *char siu bao* to be found in New York, so we'll have something to munch on during the trip back home.

But just before the advent of the Year of the Ox, a.k.a. early February 1973, it is time to celebrate Great-Aunt Bik's sixtieth birthday. The sixtieth is an especially auspicious birthday in a Chinese lifetime, so I am determined to attend the party at the Port Arthur. On this occasion, I manage to borrow a car and drive down from college on my first solo motor trip to New York City. Since I know that Broadway leads down to Canal Street and Chinatown, I exit the Parkway at the first "Broadway" sign I see—which happens to be in the northern suburb of Yonkers. Two and a half hours later I burst breathlessly into the restaurant just as the fruit is being brought out. "Bruce is here!" Great-Aunt Bik shouts to the room, "Everyone sit down!" And she commands the waiters to go back into the kitchen to bring me a serving from every one of the twelve or fifteen courses from her banquet, while the Great-Uncles sit close and tell me to eat faster. Every Chinese person I have ever heard of is there, table after table of cousins, second cousins, Aunties from the Sewing Circle, and friends from the street.

Well, not everyone is there. First Aunt Thelma died in 1965, and Third Aunt Frances in 1970. I knew Aunt Frances better, and particularly miss her gentle warmth and soft smile. Uncle Roy has endowed a Bible school at a Baptist summer camp in her name.

But Second Uncle Richard says that Grandfather was devastated by the death of Thelma, his firstborn. Perhaps that is a little surprising to those around him, who know only that he gave his first five children up to be raised in relative poverty by someone not even related to him while he himself chased the ponies, and caroused with his cronies, and raced around in his flash cars. Richard also says that Grandfather is full of regrets that he wasn't a better parent, to Herbert, to Thelma, to the rest of them. He knows that some other old men may shake their heads when they look at my father and say, "Look at Nunnie [as they call him, using his Chinese name], he doesn't even speak Chinese and he has that foreign wife and those half-foreign children. And he even changed his *name*. Is he ashamed of his father?"

But now there is no time for regrets or anything else, because on the night of Great-Aunt Bik's birthday party, Hock Shop lies in a hospital in Queens, sinking fast from his cancer. My father has been out to see

him, and Grandfather tells him that he has just been visited by his own
mother in a dream. Apparently, Gon She has told her first-born son that
in three days they will be together in heaven. That is Saturday, and
Bickie's party goes on.

On Monday evening my father gets a call from Great-Aunt Bik,
telling him that his father has just died, right on schedule. That is bad
enough, but while they are discussing funeral arrangements Bickie suddenly starts gasping and choking in pain. My father is horrified to realize
that she is having a heart attack, right there on the telephone. Stranded
and helpless in Connecticut, he frantically tries to figure out how to
place a long-distance call to New York City's emergency number, 911,
120 miles away, but to no avail. He is possessed by a mounting panic as
he dials Great-Uncle Fong, who then runs as fast as he can down to
Bickie's apartment, where he finds Uncle Duck and Emily watching
television in the living room, oblivious to the drama going on around
them. A few minutes earlier they had quietly gone into the bedroom,
thinking that Bickie had fallen asleep while talking to one of her friends.
They hung up the phone and turned out the light, leaving my wonderful
Great-Aunt to get ready with Oldest-Brother for the move to either a
new place or a place as old as home. It is information that I am not yet
privileged to know.

A week later I am back in New York, only this time I don't take
any chances; I fly. It seems as if all Chinatown is at the Wah Wing Sang
Funeral Home at 26 Mulberry Street for their funerals, stretching to the
limit the resources of the owners, Maurice and Martha Yick. There is
the usual candy for the bitterness, and the towel to wipe away the tears.
A steady stream of mourners files in—mah-jongg partners, distant relatives, aged Tong members and leathery old gamblers in baggy black suits
and wrinkled ties. Martha Yick is as efficient as a grade-school teacher
marshaling her students. She deftly straps mourning bands on our arms,
then hands each of us sticks of incense to place before the open caskets,
for while these will be Christian funerals, the Ancestors don't know that
and will expect the amenities to be observed. .

Everyone bows three times before going to their seats, although
many of the Sewing Circle Aunties are overcome with grief and sob

loudly over Bickie's body. A murmer goes through the crowd after one of these displays, because such things are unheard of in the normally placid Chinese world. But this is Bickie's party, and she was anything but placid.

Uncle Duck sits silent and apparently emotionless, but his peers know that he has been wounded deeper than most of them. Sun and Fong have had to talk him out of hiring a wailing troop of professional mourners, because they believed that he couldn't afford such a luxury, although much later they learn that he has cash secreted in hiding places all over his apartment. He does manage to obtain three brass bands for Bickie's funeral procession, however, and three flower cars are needed to carry the masses of bouquets sent in tribute to Chinatown's favorite daughter. It turns out that he didn't need the professional mourners anyway, as the crowd wails loudly enough without them.

Grandfather's funeral and procession are separate from Bickie's, sending Martha Yick scrambling for every available limousine and Italian horn player on the Lower East Side. His widow Frances has insisted on a Catholic service, so an awkward eulogy is delivered in English and Cantonese by a Mandarin-Chinese-speaking priest for whom both are foreign languages. He goes to great lengths to avoid any mention of horses or the Tong, but mainly delivers bland commentary on the flowers Grandfather provided to the church. It doesn't really matter, because very few people in the room can understand what he is saying anyway.

I count over thirty cars in Grandfather's procession (Bickie's had something like sixty), bringing Chinatown to a standstill as it winds slowly in and around the tiny streets of what has now become our ancestral village. As is the custom, we stop at each place important in Hock Shop's life, but Martha Yick bows the customary three bows on our behalf, as a courtesy to the Family. With the door of the hearse wide open, she loudly claps her hands, and Grandfather's spirit gets out to look around at the ghosts of a family growing up with a country within a city.

There is Hor Poa at 18 Mott Street, where he is building a meeting hall for an old schemer who will plunge Chinatown into war for more than twenty years. Then there is Number 32 Mott, the Quong Yuen Shing store, where his artistry and craftsmanship defines Victorian New York's notions of the Mysterious East. At the Port Arthur, scene of Tong peace conferences and wedding banquets, Grandfather can watch himself as a baby being held aloft and covered with money, a sure omen for the future.

At Number 21 Mott he sees himself learning to talk, a sister passes into oblivion, and Italians use the outdoor privies rather than run the risk of sharing a toilet with him and his kind. He jumps ahead fifty years as he peeks into the tiny flower shop, with a gleaming new Buick hauled up on the sidewalk, and stacks of cash being counted out in the back room while Liberace effervesces out of the black-and-white TV.

At 33–37 Mott, *sun lau* is still a new building, and a shy Princess peeks out at him from behind a shade as his own children bubble over with laughter as they fly a giant dragon kite from the roof. The string glistens in the sunlight as Grandfather's spirit glides up to join the grimacing creature with his wild eyes and lethal-looking fangs. Together they gently ascend, to keep an appointment with Mother and Little Sister in a land where all the mountains are made of gold and there are no longer any odds left to figure.

EPILOGUE

.

Of course Chinatown continues to grow and change through the 1970s, while the old ghosts fade further into the woodwork. Cousin Emily, who begins calling herself Ruby, starts hanging out with the new street gangs, which have adopted names like Ghost Shadows and Flying Dragons. The new head of the Hip Sing, Benny Ong, who is also known as "Uncle Seven," is almost as press-friendly and prominent as old Tom Lee once was. He is rumored to have moved beyond gambling into drug smuggling, and is credited with starting up the Tong violence again—only this time around he uses the Flying Dragons to do his dirty work. Of course, the On Leong isn't exactly blameless, as they recruit the Ghost Shadows to retaliate on their behalf. Once again, there is gunfire heard in Chinatown and nonchalant young killers clutter the police-station holding rooms. It even affects us out in the suburbs. When the owner of our favorite local Chinese restaurant refuses to play with one of the Tongs, they dispatch gang members from New York who shoot his daughter to death in cold blood, right there behind the cash register. In this case, the lucky goldfish in the tank on the counter didn't help.

The last I hear of Cousin Emily/Ruby, she has become pregnant by her gang-member boyfriend and is hiding out with him somewhere in

Brooklyn. Carl and Sookie are not surprised. They still feel that it was her bad behavior that brought on their mother's heart attack.

The Port Arthur hangs on for a while, the very last of its kind. But within five years of Hock Shop's funeral it dies an ignoble death. The big Chinese grocery store that replaced the Chinatown Fair downstairs wants to expand, so the restaurant's owner, Florence Ho, is frantically running around trying to sell inlaid tables and carved teak screens to the guests at the last banquet held there. "Take this—fifty dollars!" she shouts from the balcony to a departing diner as she waves an ebony stool in the air. "Okay—five bucks! My final offer!" Most of the decorative fixtures are eventually yanked out by the men from the carting company the grocery store has hired, but luckily they too are charmed by Great-Grandfather's handiwork. Now the pieces decorate their homes in the outer boroughs and New Jersey.

There are almost none of the graceful old wooden shop interiors anymore either, with new owners ripping them out and replacing them with burnished-silver and brass finishes in an attempt to transform Mott Street into a Hong Kong-style shopping mall. Quong Yuen Shing is the lone survivor—only now bus tickets for Atlantic City gambling junkets are sold under the magnificent carved arch, and a Ticketron computer is disguised by an old packing crate on the counter where sumptuous brocades were once measured by the yard. Tuck High, founded in 1879, was finally dismantled and moved, stock and all, to the State Museum in Albany. Now it has become part of an exhibit on vanished scenes from New York City life.

Some seventy thousand people live in Chinatown in 1985, drawn by the lure of money as surely as were the original guests of the Golden Mountain. A huge new housing project called China Village has gone up along the Bowery, and now Chinatown threatens to swallow up what is left of Little Italy, with Chinese stores and apartments going all the way up to Grand Street, and expanding east and west for blocks beyond the territory that my father's generation could have safely explored as children.

In the mid 1980s my friend Wu Jen-sing comes over from Canton. He steps off the plane at Kennedy, bewildered and unsure. A familiar voice in his dialect alerts him to a contact, who takes him to a basement one-bedroom apartment where eight other young men sleep on mat-

Epilogue

tresses scattered about the floor. Within two days he has been plugged into a job shoving menus under people's doors. Within two months he has saved enough to pay for his first term at college. Within ten years he is buying his second house with cash stored in hiding places all over. When I arrive there for dinner, he and his brother are deep into a discussion on how to place a goldfish tank between the front door and the staircase so that the evil spirits won't rush up the stairs and catch them when they are sleeping. He also has become a Catholic, just to make sure all his bases are covered. His experience is not much different from that of those wobbly-legged boys stumbling off the ship in San Francisco more than a hundred and twenty-five years before.

Then there are the illegal immigrants, which the Government says are becoming more and more of a problem. Jen-sing's brother stowed away on a ship to Panama, then made his way to Mexico, and would have paid a smuggler to get him over the border into Texas if he hadn't gambled all his money away. Jen-sing just sent him more, and now he too lives in New York.

His experience was still better than that of their friend. This young man escaped from Canton by burying himself in a shipment of frozen chickens being sent to Hong Kong by train. He made it, but just barely. Several of his companions on the same train froze to death.

And yet both of these boys have had a better time of it than will the half-starved crowd discovered on the *Golden Venture,* the rusty old freighter that ran aground off a Queens beach in 1993. There the smugglers merely order the three hundred confused and exhausted passengers to leap into the surf and swim for their lives. Before the Immigration Service catches on, at least ten have drowned, while the rest are rounded up, cold and wet, to be sent off to detention. They will be incarcerated for years in a rural detention center, where they stave off the boredom by making intricate handicrafts out of scrap paper to sell. They seem to be almost like the young Hor Mei Wong, locked up in Malone or Richford in 1906. He and his fellow inmates made kites to sell through their barred windows while they waited for Deputy Chinese Inspectors to decide their fates. The *Golden Venture* detainees wanted to make kites also, but the authorities don't trust their prisoners with the strips of wood necessary in their construction. Instead, they make soaring eagles and Statues of Liberty out of toilet paper and gum wrappers.

Even in an American prison, these people honor American ideals of freedom through their art.

And in 1997 Doris Rosenquist from Flushing writes to the *New York Times* complaining about the Chinese taking over her Queens neighborhood. "Some Asians do not want to assimilate but to replace us," she gripes. "Our best neighborhoods have been taken over after former owners were paid in cash, the provenance of which is questionable." Ms. Rosenquist could have been writing in 1897 or 1867, so antiquated are her xenophobic ideas.

But then she is just echoing the views of the Republicans in Congress, who would have us believe that Chinese are here to buy our very Government out from underneath us. Once again, they say, the Yellow Peril threatens our very American way of life.

There are other Chinatowns in New York these days, one in Flushing, Queens, and an older one in Sunset Park, Brooklyn. But most of these new immigrants are from parts of China other than Canton. Now Fukienese is the language of choice on Mott Street, while the Old Toi-shan Guard hunkers down in their Benevolent Society meeting rooms under Nationalist flags and faded portraits of Chiang Kai-shek and complain about the new foreigners and their ways. Even the CCBA isn't really in charge any longer. Their Chief Gentleman receives only the second-best place at the banquets where his Fukienese counterpart is fawned over like a movie star.

Yes, there are many similarities between the old immigrants and the new, but there is one very important difference. Mao Tse-tung has cut out the new ones' heart. Re-education, the Great Leap Forward, the Cultural Revolution, famine, oppression—all of those things have helped sever the modern Chinese generation from the five thousand years of tradition that came here with my great-grandfather. There may still be nine dragons that rule the universe, but most of these newcomers don't know where to find them.

My ghosts are rapidly floating away. They are getting lost in a neighborhood where there is no longer the gleam of mother-of-pearl, and where karaoke has replaced centuries-old Cantonese opera. Canal

Street is full of Hong Kong jewelers, their windows draped with vulgar gold necklaces and bracelets which say nothing about artistry, but everything about the god of money, which is seemingly the only god worshipped these days. In Columbus Park, across from the funeral parlors, the smoke from burning paper effigies of Mercedes-Benzes, garish mansions, and obscene stacks of thousand-dollar bills rises to the clouds, giving Chinatown's new generation of Ancestors their own riches in heaven.

The village has grown into a sprawling city, where OTB has obliterated the need for bookies, and Big Shots don't need to swagger on Mott Street any longer. Instead, power lunches are given by business-suited lawyers and real estate dealers at a Chinese Holiday Inn. They then climb into their stretch limos so they can catch the Concorde to London before they go on to make deals in Singapore, and Kuala Lumpur, and Hong Kong.

There is none of our family left in Chinatown now. In a replay of 1973, Great-Uncle Sun and Great-Aunt Dor died on the same day in 1982, he of cancer, and she of a heart attack a few hours later, as her two daughters arrived at their Long Island home. Cousin Alison, two weeks away from graduating from medical school, was powerless to help either one of them.

Great-Uncle Fong lived until 1987. He had moved permanently out to Bradley Beach, where his easy and genial nature made him popular at the Italian restaurant where he tended bar and the track was just a short drive away. Great-Aunt Ruth didn't die on the same day that he did, but she might as well have. Totally helpless on her own, she stopped eating and within weeks was installed in a nursing home where she still sits, all alone ten years later. Now that Fong isn't there to watch her play solitaire anymore, she acknowledges no one and does nothing but sit in her chair and stare at the wall.

The family banquets barely fill one table now, and they are held in vast restaurants where uniformed hostesses brandishing walkie-talkies meet customers at the door and send them up escalators to a madhouse of noise and rush and confusion. Oh, the food is always delicious, and the service prompt, even though there is no one left who remembers how to make those magically deboned roast chickens that are filled with glutinous rice.

But sometimes I walk up to the second floor of the big grocery store that took over the Port Arthur and remember. It is now just another big over-bright room, filled with housewares and restaurant supplies. Still, I can see through them to the past. Over by the display of electrified household shrines was the table where my mother once proffered Chinese Cheerios. Next to the shelf with the electric rice cookers was where Great-Aunt Ek was standing when she shouted "Bruce is here! Everybody sit down!" before commanding a wonderful meal to appear, course after course, before my hungry young eyes. It seemed then as if there was all the time in the world.

But in restaurants nowadays the waiters hustle you out as soon as you are finished to make room for the next group—even if there isn't a next group waiting. I stand in the space that once was the Port Arthur, and wonder if anyone still has time to clear the table for gossip and cut-throat games of mah-jongg. I wonder if anyone still flies caterpillar kites twelve feet long from the roofs of buildings, just for fun. I wonder where to find the embroidered silks and brilliant colors that once marked the start of every New Year. Does anyone still hold poetry contests? Is there still a place in New York where Cantonese Opera is performed? And where is the restaurant where the owner will greet his favorite bookie with a big smile, a plate of dumplings, and a complementary pot of Tea that-Burns?

NOTES

.

CHAPTER 1

PAGE

8 *about three* lis *away*: One *li* equals half a mile.

9 *the Toi-shan district of Kuang Tung Province*: Or Toishan of Guangdong.

9 *in far-away Peking*: Or Beijing.

9 *Emperor Tao Kuang*: Or Daoguang, ruled 1821–1850.

10 *for four months out of twelve*: Betty Lee Sung, *Mountain of Gold*.

10 *away in Canton*: Or Guanghou.

10 *monarchs of the Ch'ing*: Or Qing.

10 *young Prince Hsien Fêng*: Or Xiangfeng.

11 *the previous century*: Lynn Pan, *Sons of the Yellow Emperor*, p. 43.

11 *in 1851, the Tai-ping*: Or Taiping.

11 *maniac named Hong Hsiu-ch'üan*: Or Hong Xiuquan.

11 *provinces of Kuang Tung and Fukien*: Or Fujian.

11 *ruin upon their enemies' lives*: Stanford M. Lyman, *Chinese Americans*, p. 12.

12 *successor was Tung Chih*: Or Dongzhi.

12 *more like sixty million*: Elmer Clarence Sandemeyer, *The Anti-Chinese Movement in California*, p. 14; Pan, *Sons of the Yellow Emperor*, p. 44.

13 *Emperor Tao Kuang, a.k.a. 1848*: See *New York Times*, November 3, 1852 and November 18, 1870; Jack Chen, *The Chinese of America*, p. 5.

13 *treasure beyond the sea*: Chen, *The Chinese of America*, p. 5; *New York Times*, November 3, 1852.

15 *death in their floating prison*: *Pall Mall Gazette*, as quoted in the *New York Times*, May 25, 1874.

15 *gave up and committed suicide:* Lynn Pan, *Sons of the Yellow Emperor,* pp. 49–50.

15 *"buried in the sea are the same":* Pyau Ling, *Annals,* XXXIX, p. 80, as quoted in Sandemeyer, p. 14.

16 *snakes for use as medicine:* San Francisco *Bulletin,* July 2, 1875.

17 *$30 per month in gold:* New York Times, June 29, 1869.

17 *killed in those five years:* Dorothy Hoobler and Thomas Hoobler, *The Chinese American Family Album,* pp. 58–61.

18 *countrymen who had preceded them:* Report to the U.S. Commissioner of Education, as reported in the *New York Times,* November 18, 1870.

18 *something vastly more rude:* See Hoobler and Hoobler, *The Chinese American Family Album* p. 96, among many other sources.

18 *producing the same amount:* Sandemeyer, *The Anti-Chinese Movement in California.*

18 *eaten in California by 1872:* "Food Habits of Nineteenth-Century California Chinese," *California Historical Society Quarterly* 37, 1958.

19 *most prosperous region in China:* Betty Lee Sung, *Mountain of Gold.*

19 *great fan of the Chinese:* Jack Chen, *The Chinese of America,* p. 129.

19 *many pet dogs:* Contrary to popular belief, the Chinese did not eat all their dogs, and often kept them as pets—at least until times of famine. See Hoobler and Hoobler, *The Chinese American Family Album,* pp. 12–13.

20 *passage to San Francisco:* San Francisco *Bulletin,* July 2, 1875.

20 *now styled Dowager Empress:* Or Zoushi.

22 *"a few lucky words":* From interview testimony in Chinese Immigration Files, National Archives, Northeast Division.

24 *"in all respects a desirable population":* Milwaukie Sentinel, as quoted in the *New York Times,* September 27, 1852.

25 *filling the quayside air:* New York Times, September 9, 1874.

25 *in one 1887 raid:* Ibid., August 20, 1995.

25 *white thugs in 1877:* Ibid., March 19, 1877.

25 *burned by angry white mobs:* Ibid., September 18, 1877.

25 *"would think it unsafe":* San Francisco *Bulletin,* July 16, 1870.

25 *"some evils we now suffer . . .":* From a speech given by Fung Tang to a group of politicians and business leaders in San Francisco, June 25, 1869. *New York Times,* July 4, 1869.

25 *"health, decency, and morality . . .":* Marin [County] *Journal,* March 30, 1876.

CHAPTER 2

27 *expand on his story:* New York Times, March 9, 1880; see also *New York Tribune,* March 4, 1880.

27 *five Chinese servants:* Jack Chen, *The Chinese of America,* p. 4.

27 *in New York in 1808:* S. W. Kung, *Chinese in American Life,* p. 203.

27 *school in Cornwall, Connecticut:* Ibid., pp. 4–5.

28 *named after his father*: John Kuo Wei Tchen, "Quimbo Appo's Fear of Fenians," p. 7.

28 *rich in the opium trade*: Ethan A. Nadelman, "Should We Legalize Drugs?" *American Heritage,* March 1993.

28 *"has yet visited Christendom"*: From "Ten Thousand Things on China and the Chinese," the Brochure of the "Chinese Collection," 1850.

28 *"exhibited" as late as 1847*: Information comes from John Kuo Wei Tchen, "New York Before Chinatown," an unpublished dissertation at New York University, 1992.

29 *"cats and mice and pupies"*: Beekman Papers, Box 25, Folder 2, New-York Historical Society.

29 *"sink and common sewer"*: Kenneth T. Jackson, *The Encyclopedia of New York City,* p. 250.

30 *five crooked floors*: Helen Campbell, *Darkness and Daylight,* p. 400.

30 *one murder per week*: Rohit T. Aggarwala, "The Good Old Days Were Pretty Bad," *Columbia,* Summer 1993.

30 *"'price of blood'"*: Report of Board of Health, New York, 1869, p. 346.

30 *"sticky with constant moisture"*: Jacob A. Riis, *Battle with the Slums,* 1902, p. 22.

30 *"within a* foot and a half *of the seats"*: Campbell, *Darkness and Daylight,* p. 410.

30 *easy collection and disposal*: Otto L. Bettmann, *The Good Old Days . . . They Were Terrible!*

30 *room for 100 families*: Riis, *Battle with the Slums,* p. 25.

30 *cellars made "horribly foul"*: Ibid., pp. 24–25.

31 *for eight-hour stretches*: Campbell, *Darkness and Daylight,* p. 400.

31 *nicknamed "Death's Thoroughfare"*: Riis, *Battle with the Slums.*

31 *typhoid in a single year*: Ibid., p. 22.

31 *reckoned as one in five*: Ibid., p. 29.

31 *for lack of patronage*: Ibid., p. 282.

31 *near Chatham Square in 1645*: Herbert Asbury, *All Around Town,* p. 256.

31 *from "Russian Poland"*: U.S. Census, 1870, New York City, 4th and 6th Wards.

31 *outside of Dublin*: Jackson, *The Encyclopedia of New York City,* p. 415.

31 *a few small luxuries*: *New York Times,* January 21, 1996.

31 *"if necessary . . . starve together"*: Campbell, *Darkness and Daylight,* pp. 404–5.

33 *first Chinese-owned business in New York*: *New York Tribune,* June 21, 1885.

33 *"[and] a devoted Christian"*: *New York Herald,* September 4, 1847.

33 *their classic opera tragedies*: Tchen, "New York Before Chinatown." See also *New York Herald,* June 29, July 27, 1853.

34 *"our unfortunate fate"*: *New York Herald,* July 27, 1853.

35 *interpreter Leong Mun Gao, and two cooks*: Spelling is mine, based on contemporary newspaper versions.

35 *At 391 Pearl Street:* See *New York Times,* December 26, 1856, for a full description of the establishment.

36 *or even Mr. Akkbc:* Ibid.; see also *This Was New York!* p. 41. I base his age on the assumption that this is the same "Akomb" in the *Times,* August 11, 1878, having lived in the U.S. for "nearly 30 years."

36 *treaty ports like Amoy:* Now Xiamen.

36 *American factory worker:* Campbell, *Darkness and Daylight,* p. 734.

37 *first Chinese to do so:* Maxwell F. Marcuse, *This Was New York!* p. 41.

37 *"known as Chinese candy":* New York Times, December 27, 1873.

37 *sell for a penny apiece:* Campbell, *Darkness and Daylight,* p. 734.

37 *"wearing a shawl, and all that":* New York Times, December 26, 1856.

37 *on the road to prosperity:* New York Times, July 11, 1878.

37 *since 1855 of Ah Bao:* New York Times, June 20, 1859.

38 *vaguely Western first name of Quimbo:* Asbury, *All Around Town,* p. 254; *New York Times* of December 26, 1856 spells it "Crimpo."

38 *"the interior of China:* Beck, *New York's Chinatown,* p. 8.

38 *"a very intelligent Englishwoman":* New York Times, December 26, 1856. Some sources list Ah Bao as the first resident of Chinatown, but this article shows that he arrived at least five years after Ah Ken.

38 *almost exclusively the Irish:* U.S. Census, 1870, New York City, 4th and 6th Wards.

38 *actually Eurasian:* While the "politically correct" term is "Amerasian," neither of the groups involved were American citizens.

38 *their natural depravity:* See Riis, *Battle with the Slums,* p. 321.

38 *"suspected of liaisons with white women":* Tchen, "New York Before Chinatown."

39 *dint of his Chinese blood:* Beck, *New York's Chinatown,* p. 251.

39 *composition of her false leg:* Asbury, *All Around the Town,* p. 254; Beck, *New York's Chinatown,* p. 9

40 *Mother and child are d-owned:* See Tchen, "New York Before Chinatown."

40 *in his father's footsteps:* Beck, *New York's Chinatown,* p. 252.

40 *and his family name:* Tchen, "New York Before Chinatown." *The American Metropolis,* p. 403.

40 *undoubtedly low:* For this and the following description, see U.S. Census, 1870, New York City, 4th and 6th Wards. I have tried to reconstruct the proper spelling of Chinese names from the census-takers' guesses. Street addresses are not given.

41 *Irish woman named Kitty:* New York Times, August 18, 1878.

41 *the middle 1850s:* See New York State Census, 1855.

42 *to deny Chinese that right:* Tchen, "New York Before Chinatown."

42 *"negro girl with two heads":* New York World, June 16, 1870.

43 *"shown a second time":* New York Times, July 9, 1870.

43 *"no distinction of race or color . . .":* Ibid.

43 *"manifested no resentment":* Ibid.

43 *Chinese immigration in general: New York Times,* July 1, 1870.
43 *"compete with free white[s]": Ibid.,* July 1, 1870.
44 *New York and Brooklyn: New York Tribune,* June 21, 1885.
44 *the Chinese population: New York Times,* July 30, 1883.
44 *explode outward from California: New York Times,* June 26, 1873.
44 *retained $1,200 in "fees": New York Tribune,* June 21, 1885.
45 *"looked the visitors in the face":* Ibid.
45 *in the Eastern United States:* Beck, *New York's Chinatown,* p. 11; *New York Sun,* March 7, 1880, *New York Tribune,* June 21, 1885.
45 *grand total of 172:* New York State Census Enumeration, 1875.
46 *comes out as "Aslug": New York Times,* December 27, 1873.
46 *Greenville section of Jersey City:* Beck, *New York's Chinatown,* p. 225.
47 *to a curious visitor: New York Times,* December 27, 1873.
47 *The "Poolon Kun Cue":* Ibid. A white reporter's spelling of an unknown Chinese name.
47 *the inscrutable reply:* Ibid.
48 *"usages there instilled," they say: New York Times,* February 16, 1874.
48 *paid $80 to perform: New York Times,* December 13, 1872.
48 *"room full of insane women": New York Times,* December 20, 1872.
48 *scope out commercial opportunities: New York Times,* August 13, 1869.
49 *calendar is conspicuously empty: New York Times,* August 23, 1877.
49 *selling cigars without a license:* For this and the following, see *New York Times,* August 11, 1878.
50 *mystery surrounding her: New York Times,* March 21, 1879.
50 *with her family in 1869:* Arthur Bonner, "The Chinese in New York," 1991, Chapter 5, p. 11.
50 *to Cuba with her husband:* New York *Sun,* March 7, 1880.
50 *"Boston Beauty, No. 6":* New York *World,* April 29, 1877.
51 *"so he buy . . .":* New York *World,* March 9, 1880.
51 *depending on whom you ask:* New York *World,* March 6, 9, and 22, 1880.
51 *at 103 Park Street:* U.S. Census, 1880.
51 *new Chinese benevolent society: New York Times,* April 28, 1880.
51 *$22.50 per pound: New York Times,* June 13, 1880.
52 *known as "Wily Charly":* U.S. Census, 1880.
52 *brand new name—China Town: New York Times,* March 22, 1880.

CHAPTER 3
53 *"around Christmastime" in 1881:* Chinese Immigration Records, U.S. National Archives, Northeast Division, Ho Wong, Box 246.
53 *basement of Number 15:* U.S. Census, 1880. E.D. 47, p. 22.
54 *thundered Henry Ward Beecher: New York Times,* February 19, 1879.
54 *association of New York Merchants: New York Times,* February 21, 1879.
54 *Central Committee of New York: New York Times,* February 23, 1879.
54 *found in San Francisco:* 21,745 according to George F. Seward, *Chinese*

Immigration, in Its Social and Economical Aspects (Charles Scribner's Sons, New York, 1881), Appendix.

54 *laughed and did nothing*: New York Times, September 10, 1880.
54 *stabbing him to death*: New York Times, May 7, 1881; New York Tribune April 29, 1881.
55 *integrity of the entire nation*: New York World, March 3, 1879.
55 *"servile characteristics of his race"*: Bonner, "The Chinese in New York,' 1991, Chap. 16, pp. 5–6.
55 *"laborers, skilled or unskilled"*: New York Times, August 18 and September 29, 1882.
56 *to a virtual standstill*: New York Post, February 28, 1884.
57 *the New York Times recounts*: Ibid.
57 *agent of the circus*: New York Times, November 11, 1883.
57 *dropped to 1,560*: New York Times, May 18, 1883.
58 *store at Number 5*: New York Times, August 1, 1883.
59 *"Brotherhood of Masons"*: New York World, February 28, 1880. New York Times, Feb. 28, 1880.
59 *charges were dropped*: New York Herald, February 5, 1879; New York Sun, March 22, 1879; New York Times, September 15, 1881.
60 *"mutual succor in distress"*: New York Times, April 28, 1880.
60 *"Hall of United Patriotism"*: Stewart Culin, "The I Hing or 'Patriotic Rising,'" p. 3; Culin, "Chinese Secret Societies in the United States."
60 *emigration to California*: Bloodworth, The Chinese Looking Glass, pp. 151–155.
61 *one's ability to pay*: Culin, "The 'I Hing' or 'Patriotic Rising,' a Secret Society Among Chinese in America."
62 *"Chinamen or negroes"*: New York Post, May 10, 1880.
62 *spirits that they recognize*: New York Times, September 15, 1881.
62 *entire State of New York*: Seward, Chinese Immigration.
62 *"all that work for them"*: Chester Holcombe, The Real Chinaman (New York: Dodd, Mead & Co., 1895), p. 104.
64 *demi-emperor of the neighborhood*: New York Times, September 16, 1881.
64 *entire New York Chinese community*: New York Tribune, June 23, 1885.
64 *"tobacco and opium' shop*: New York Times, January 30, 1881.
64 *by raising rents*: New York Times, April 7 and April 12, 1883.
64 *staggering $1 million*: New York Tribune, June 2, 1885.
66 *Seventh Street Methodist Church*: Bonner, The Chinese in New York, 1991, Chap. 9, pp. 12–19.
66 *fruits of his endeavor*: New York Times, July 24, 1888.
66 *doing so by 1883*: New York Times, July 39, 1883.
67 *"cannot be overstated"*: New York Times, June 12, 1883.
67 *depart in high dudgeon*: New York Times, September 4, 1888; September 20, 1891.
67 *"white Christians to the blush"*: New York Times, July 30, 1883.
68 *"neighborhood a perfect hell"*: New York Post, May 8, 1883.

68 *"education which you would give them"*: New York Evening Post, December 9, 1875.

69 *snapped* Harper's Weekly *in reply:* "Wong Ching Fuo," by the editors of Harper's Weekly, "Wong Ching [sic] Foo," May 26, 1877, p. 405.

69 *"after Jesus came"*: The ninth year of Kuang Hsü would start in three days, after the coming of the Chinese New Year.

71 *A slave?*: Chinese American, February 3, 1883.

71 *consisting of some 700*: New York Times, June 18, 1888.

71 *righteous Wong Chin Foo himself*: Chinese American, June 14, 1883, as translated in the New York Tribune, March 4, 1885.

71 *at Tong headquarters*: New York Tribune, March 4, 1885, July 24, 1888; New York Times, March 4, 1885; Puck, January 1, 1888.

72 *for the coming year*: Bonner, The Chinese in New York, Chap. 6, pp. 22–25; New York Times, February 19, 1882.

73 *as many as four of them*: New York Times, November 25, 1886.

73 *"Look at their pants!"*: New York Tribune, January 28, 1884.

74 *his illustrious presence*: New York Times, January 28, 1884; New York Tribune, January 28, 1884, Newark (N.J.) Star-Ledger, February 14, 1996.

75 *knows whereof he speaks*: New York Times, February 1, 1885; New York Tribune, February 15, 1885.

76 *to exposure or accident*: Ellen Scheinberg, "Evidence of 'Past Injustices,'" The Archivist, (Vol. 20, No. 2, 1994), p. 26.

77 *a name like Hor Sek*: New York Times, August 31, September 28, November 30, 1884; San Francisco Chronicle, November 1, 1884.

77 *"won't take negroes!"*: New York Times, April 15, 1880; New York Post, January 31, 1884.

77 *an absolutely enormous sum*: New York Times, September 17, 1880; New York Tribune, June 21, 1885, and October 7, 1893.

77 *for those who live in*: New York Times, December 8, 1884.

78 *estimated 1,000 by 1885*: New York Sun, June 29, 1879; New York Tribune, June 21, 1885.

78 *who work there as well*: Frank Leslie's Illustrated Weekly, Sun, June 29, 1879 May 5, 1875.

78 *Chinese always pay*: Yearbook of St. Bartholomew's Church, 1896, p. 83; Baldwin, Letter to Christian Advocate, May 26, 1887.

79 *soap, 95 cents*: Chinese American, February 3, 1883.

79 *until you do*: Wong Chin Foo, "The Chinese in New York," Cosmopolitan Magazine, June, 1888.

80 *at every imaginable opportunity*: New York Post, May 8, 1883.

80 *"bestial practices" of its own*: Bruce Edward Hall, Diamond Street, p. 17.

80 *"blood in their veins ran pure"*: George W. Walling, Recollections of a New York Chief of Police, pp. 427–429.

81 *"conveniences are taken away"*: Wong Chin Foo, "The Chinese in New York," Cosmopolitan Magazine, June, 1888.

81 *$5 per table per week*: "Report and Proceedings of the Senate Committee

Appointed to Investigate the Police Department of New York," testimony of Ching Hing Tong

81 *at a manageable level:* Lyman, *Chinese Americans*, p. 97.

83 *guaranteed ways to dream: New York Herald*, February 5, 1879; *New York Times*, January 21, 1884; December 8, 1884, *Cosmopolitan Magazine*, June, 1888.

84 *reserves for his pagan neighbors: New York Tribune*, May 11, 1883.

88 *where opium is openly sold: New York Times*, August 11, 1878; *New York Tribune*, July 21, 1875; Beck, *New York's Chinatown*, pp. 146–149.

88 *posthumous terrestrial journey: New York Times*, June 25, July 10, and July 14, 1888.

90 *manage to enter the country:* Chen, *The Chinese of America*, p. 157.

CHAPTER 4

90 *four are women:* Ira Rosenwaike, *Population History of New York City*, p. 78; Wong Chin Foo, "The Chinese in New York," p. 308. While the census figure is undoubtedly low, Wong Chin Foo guesses that there are 10,000 Chinese in New York, which is far too high, and at any rate includes the number of Chinese living in Brooklyn, which was then still a separate city, New Jersey, and the rest of the Greater New York area. See also *The New York Times*, November 25 and 26, 1886.

91 *single Chinese to be found:* See the New York City Police Census of 1890.

91 *no Christians allowed: New York Times*, July 23 and 24, 1888.

92 *stomach, health, and the hereafter: New York Times*, April 17, 1887 and June 18, 1888.

92 *"raindrop ever thought of": New York Times*, June 18, 1888.

92 *calls himself "Guy Maine":* Huie Kin, *Reminiscences*, p. 50.

93 *to defend his brethren: New York Times*, March 18, 21, 23, and 1890.

94 *from being overwhelmed: Yearbook of St. Bartholomew's Church*, 1889–1892.

94 *or the Brooklyn Bridegrooms:* The Giants won the first World Series in 1888. The Bridegrooms played to a draw in the series of 1890.

94 *"why should we abstain":* Wong Chin Foo, "The Chinese in New York."

95 *puppies and stray cats: New York Times*, August 1, 1883.

96 *out into the street: New York Times*, July 17, 1884; *Cosmopolitan Magazine*, June 1888, pp. 306–308.

96 *just with his fingers: Evening Post*, March 23, 1901.

96 *exaggerating about the drunkard:* Wong Chin Foo, "The Chinese in New York," p. 308.

96 *breaks into applause New York Times*, November 19, 1887 and May 18, 1888.

96 *give up their studies: Yearbook of St. Bartholomew's*, 1893, p. 54.

96 *try to kill himself: New York Tribune*, May 27, 1893.

97 *"by force of arms:* Some Reasons for Chinese Exclusion," as quoted in Chen, *The Chinese of America*, p. 132.

97 *"facial hirsute adornment"*: New York Times, August 10, 1892; see also *New York Times*, August 26, 1885.

97 *"residence in the United States"*: New York Times, August 10, 1892

98 *doesn't have the proper forms*: New York Times, June 3, July 22, and September 23, 1892; *New York Tribune*, September 23, 1892 and March 3, 1893.

98 *(Quong Yuen Shing has seventy-four)*: According to an internal document in Chinese, dated February 18, 1914, which also firmly states the date of Quong Yuen Shing's founding as August 1891.

99 *8Opera house at 5 Doyers*: The first performance was on March 25, 1893.

99 *"business as such merchant"*: New York Times, November 26, 1893.

99 *(as he is wont to call Chinese)*: J. Thomas Scharf, "The Force of the Chinese Exclusion Laws," p. 96.

100 *deck of an arriving ship*: New York Tribune, October 7, 1893.

100 *Tong bullies in Chinatown*: New York Tribune, October 29, 1893; Frank Moss, *The American Metropolis*, pp. 415–417.

100 *interpreter Joseph Singleton*: Also known as Jee Man Sing.

101 *Cleveland's term, and beyond*: New York Times, August 2, 1894; November 30, 1896; August 21, 27, and October 14, 1897.

101 *From 1891, onward*: In 1891 St. Albans, Vermont and several other Canadian border towns were declared official U.S. Ports of Entry.

CHAPTER 5

106 *was a prostitute*: Beck, New York's Chinatown, p. 117.

106 *south Asia and California*: New York Times, July 30, 1869, and August 29, 1875.

107 *two hundred to one*: Lyman, Chinese Americans, p. 88. The average Chinese male-to-female ratio in the U.S. between 1860 and 1900 was 196.4 to 1.

107 *bride-price of $900*: Moss, The American Metropolis, p. 424.

108 *asked her opinion*: New York Times, July 31, 1873.

108 *husband was fined $2,500*: New York Times, June 17, 1890.

108 *"slaves and prostitutes"*: Beck, New York's Chinatown, p. 29.

108 *their duty was done*: Ibid., p. 108.

108 *pimps—like Tom Lee*: George W. Walling, *Recollections of a New York Chief of Police*, 1887, p. 428.

108 *"Chinese woman looked like"*: Committee of Fifteen report, 1901.

109 *"reconcile these statements?"*: From documents from the New York Chinese Bureau, dated May 8, 1905–June 4, 1908, in immigration file of Hor Yin, U.S. National Archives, Northeast Division.

109 *Are you sure of this?*: Ibid.

110 *"defined by the regulations"*: Ibid.

110 *"relationship does not exist"*: Ibid.

110 *"They don't bring daughters!"*: Helen Wong, as quoted in Hoobler and Hoobler, *The Chinese American Family Album*, p. 45.

110 *at 19A Mott Street*: Files of Hom Mon Why, June 30, 1896; Hor Gon [sic]

She, June 14, 1912, Chinese Immigration Records, U.S. National Archives, Northeast Division.

110 *if they were married:* New York City Police Census of 1890, Book 44.

112 *prestigious place to live:* According to the Federal Census, 1900.

112 *bathing is grossly unhealthy:* Harry M. Shulman, *Slums of New York,* p. 174–200.

112 *"in all its appointments":* Beck, *New York's Chinatown,* p. 263; *Seeing Chinatown: The Official Guide,* N.Y., 1906.

115 *142 women were also counted:* While the population of New York City's Chinese had been listed at only around 2,000 in 1890, in 1898 the boroughs of Brooklyn, Queens, the Bronx, and Staten Island were incorporated into the City, vastly increasing its size. One could estimate that perhaps one-half to two-thirds of New York's Chinese lived in Manhattan's Chinatown proper. See Stuart H. Cattell, "Health, Welfare and Social Organization in Chinatown, N.Y.," p. 12.

116 *"too awful to print":* New York Times, December 28, 1902.

119 *determined was by weight:* Chester Holcombe, *The Real Chinaman,* p. 331.

120 *Best Restaurant that Ever Was.*

120 *in 1897 or thereabouts:* Joan Feldman *New York on $5 & $10 a Day,* 1968–69, p. 87.

121 *"roast beef of Old England":* Lucien Adkins, in Appendix to Beck, *New York's Chinatown,* pp. 295–296.

121 *asked the Prince:* New York Times, June 15, 1904.

121 *a five-dollar bill:* The Pittsburgh Dispatch, as quoted in the Malone (N.Y.) *Palladium,* August , 1895.

122 *"remember anything about it":* New York Tribune, July 12, 1895.

122 *his ravings forever:* See also New York Tribune, October 14, 1894; Tchen, "New York Before Chinatown."

123 *"humanity to be found":* Committee of Fourteen, Investigative Reports, 1912.

123 *next group was due:* New York Sun, February 26, 1912.

123 *"from the Chinese quarter":* New York Times, December 19, 1903; Herbert Asbury, *The Gangs of New York,* pp. 315–324.

124 *"help yerself to a twist":* New York Times, December 19, 1903.

124 *on East 42nd Street:* Yearbook of St. Bartholomew's, 1897, p. 81.

125 *"gathered about the door":* Moss, *The American Metropolis,* p. 405.

125 *"incarnation of the Christian spirit":* Ibid.

125 *Doyers Street quarters:* New York Times, April 30, 1905.

125 *patched up bodies upstairs:* Beck, *New York's Chinatown,* p. 240.

125 *"Christian way of living":* Ibid., pp. 242–243.

126 *"ordinary-sized radish":* New York Times, May 19, 1895.

127 *reformers such as Jacob Riis:* Although Jacob Riis, himself a Danish immigrant, was a tireless champion of the poor slum-dweller, he had absolutely nothing good to say about the Chinese. At the beginning of the "Chinatown"

chapter in his famous 1890 *How the Other Half Lives*, he writes, "I state it in advance as my opinion, based on the steady observation of years, that all attempts to make an effective Christian of John Chinaman will remain abortive in this generation; of the next I have, if anything, less hope" [p. 77]. Even the natural cleanliness of Chinese he uses against them: "He is by nature as clean as the cat, which he resembles in his traits of cruel cunning and savage fury when aroused" [p. 80]. In his 1902 *Battle with the Slums* his sole reference to Chinatown describes how a "Chink husband" brought about the downfall of an otherwise virtuous Italian girl [p. 321].

129 *their exalted guests:* Moss, *The American Metropolis*, pp. 412–413.

130 *Thy spectral ship,* Beck, p.301.

CHAPTER 6

132 *"all vice in Chinatown":* New York Times, September 6, 1892.

133 *jail for ten years:* Beck, *New York's Chinatown*, p. 285.

133 *off his back:* New York Tribune, June 28, 1894; New York Times, April 27, 1905; Herbert Asbury, *The Gangs of New York*, p. 302.

133 *other Hip Sing crusaders:* Moss, *The American Metropolis*, pp. 404–429.

134 *ideas to be "amusing":* Ibid., pp. 420–421.

134 *Lee and the Sixth Precinct:* New York Tribune, June 28, 1894.

134 *"language may be pursued":* New York Times, November 8, 1896.

135 *uproar for nearly an hour:* Brooklyn Eagle, September 26, 1897.

136 *as if nothing had happened:* Bloodworth, *The Chinese Looking Glass*, pp. 152, 179.

136 *venture outside of Chinatown:* New York Times, July 10, 31, 1900; New York Tribune, September 27, 1901; Yearbook of St. Bartholomew's, 1900, 1901, 1902.

137 *stray bullet and dies:* A 1906 newspaper account says that it was the mother who died "a few days later." Perhaps they both did. Or perhaps it was just an invention of the press. See *New York Times*, February 19, 1902, and February 13, 1906.

138 *some limited consolation:* See Moss, *American Metropolis*, p. 424; *New York Times*, February 3, 1906; New York World, February 3, 1906.

139 *"a good time together":* Chinese Immigration files, National Archives, Northeast Division, Hor Mei Wong file, dated May 21, 1907.

140 *died in Singapore:* Chinese Immigration Documents for "Hor You" and Hor Mei Fun, dated 1902–1918, National Archives, Northeast Division.

141 *brothel at Number 8:* New York Times, February 16, 1902.

141 *"hoochy-coochy" music:* Committee of Fourteen, Special Grand Jury Report, 1910.

142 *empty for a long, long time:* Leong Gor Yung, *Chinatown Inside Out*, pp. 40–43.

143 *seeds in an orange:* New York Times, March 20, 1907; Asbury, *The Gangs of New York*, p. 304.

143 *chain mail under his shirt: New York Times*, March 19, November 3, 4, 1904; Asbury, *The Gangs of New York*.

143 *vice in Chinatown at the time: New York Times*, February 25 and May 16, 1905.

143 *chests of mah-jong tiles: New York Times*, April 16, 1905.

144 *"worst farce he ever saw": New York Times*, April 25 and 27, 1905.

144 *"when they are in trouble": New York Times*, April 27, 1905.

145 *"plant flowers on graves": New York Times*, May 31, 1905; *New York Tribune*, May 31, 1905.

146 *jails him on $1,000 bond: New York Times, New York Post*, and *New York Tribune*, August 7 and 8, 1905.

146 *building at 18 Pell: New York Times*, and *New York Tribune*, August 13 and 21, 1905.

146 *handing out to children: New York Times*, January 25, 1906.

147 *another thirty-five years: New York Herald-Tribune*, September 7, 1939.

147 *forbidden to vote:* Tom Lee and the small handful of other Chinese who had managed to become naturalized citizens before 1882 were arrested when they tried to vote in the 1904 local elections. Their citizenship was stripped at that time. See the *New York Tribune*, August 17, 1904.

147 *collect the correct tariffs:* Chinese Chamber of Commerce, 50th Anniversary, pp. 28–34.

147 *reform in the homeland:* Legend has it that while in Chinatown, Dr. Sun hid in the loft of the *Chinese Reform News* office on Canal Street, in order to elude secret agents of the Dowager Empress. See also Huie Kin, *Reminiscences*, pp. 68–71.

147 *their own pogrom in 1903: New York Tribune*, May 24, 1903.

147 *nearly forty years ago: New York Times*, July 4, 1869.

148 *gravity of the occasion: New York World*, February 3, 1906.

148 *Port Arthur is bigger:* Wong Get had returned to New York from China some time in 1905. See *New York Times*, February 12, 13, and 21, 1906.

148 *in an opium haze:* The relationship of this girl (Ha Oi) to Mock was complicated. She was half Caucasian, having been born to one Lizzie Smith and her Chinese husband in San Francisco. After the mother's death soon after her daughter's birth in 1901, the father married a Chinese lady, Tai Yu, and after he died, Tai Yu married Mock Duck, bringing the child with her. To his credit, Mock reportedly doted on his adopted daughter. See *New York Times*, March 20, 1907; *New York Sun*, March 20 and 23, and April 1, 1907; *New York Evening Post*, March 19, 1907; Asbury, *The Gangs of New York*, pp. 306–307.149

149 *Hor Ting Sun:* The adopted sons in China, Hor Mei Wong and Hor Mei Fun, would technically be considered First and Second Great-Uncles, respectively.

149 *actually on their persons:* see *Yearbook of St. Bartholomew's*, 1903, p. 94.

149 *baffled by this reaction:* John W. Foster, "The Chinese Boycott," pp. 122–124.

150 *at its own expense:* Huie Kin, *Reminiscences,* pp. 106–107.

150 *attics for years afterwards:* See Richford (Vt.) *Gazette,* April, 1904; *St. Albans* (Vt.) *Daily Messenger,* July 1, 1903; *Malone* (N.Y.) *Palladium,* January 2, 1902, March 14, 1903, and July 2, 1903; Malone *Farmer,* July 1 and 8, 1903; *New York Times,* June 21, 1904. The kite story is from the memories of Mr. W. Burns Garvin in a letter to the *Richford Journal-Gazette,* some time in 1950.

150 *my dreams are not sweet; ever return from battle; and small gains, return home early:* From *Carved in Silence,* a 1987 film by Felicia Lowe.

151 *return home early:* Hoobler and Hoobler, *The Chinese American Family Album,* pp. 42–43.

151 *next Canadian-Pacific steamer:* From Hor Mei Wong's immigration file, National Archives, Northeast Division. According to later interviews with other family members, Hor Mei Wong apparently eventually made it into the U.S., sneaking over the border and living in Washington, D.C., for a few years, before moving to New York. The U.S./Canada border is long and sparsely populated, providing many a Chinese with the opportunity to simply walk into New York State through the woods and then get on a train for Boston or New York City.

151 *discovered to be missing:* New York Times, July 15, 1907.

152 *Four die:* New York Times, August 3, 1907, and March 8, 1908.

152 *two years old:* New York Times, November 17, 1908.

153 *"six months or a year":* New York Tribune, July 12, 1909. See also *New York Times,* June 22 and 24; July 4 and 6; and August 1, 1909.

154 *horror when he came home:* New York Times, August 16, 1909 and January 5, 6, 7, 8, and 11, 1910; Asbury, *The Gangs of New York,* p. 313.

155 *some women acrobats:* New York Evening Post, February 9, 1901.

155 *first time in its history:* Asbury, *The Gangs of New York,* pp. 310–311; *New York Times,* December 30 and 31, 1909.

156 *the wonders of electricity:* John S. Burgess, "A Study of the Characteristics of the Cantonese Merchants in Chinatown, N.Y." Master's Thesis, Columbia, 1909.

156 *when the Tong paid a call:* Asbury, *The Gangs of New York,* Chapter 14; *The Chinese Annual,* 1911, p. 13; *New York Times,* January 5–8 & 11, April 11–15, 17, 23, June 27, July 16, October 9, 24–27, 30, and December 5, 1910; January 3, 1911; *New York Post,* June 27, 1910; *New York Tribune,* January 24, April 22, 23, 25, July 28, and December 30, 1910.

158 *exactly what has happened:* New York Times, April 4, October 14, and October 23, 1911; New York *World,* January 28, 1912.

158 *"for Mrs. Morin and myself:* New York Times, January 26, 1911 and Committee of Fifteen Reports.

158 *(. . . barrels of flour):* New York Tribune, June 22, 1888.

159 *"small change in bad coins"*: New York Times, February 10, 1911.

159 *it reads*: New York Times, October 8, 1911.

159 *placidly surveys the carnage*: New York Times, January 6, 1912. The *Times* actually quotes him as saying, "Velly bad business." I have tried to remove the racism from the reportage.

161 *was promptly deported*: Titanic Insurance Claim Nos. B-176–180. Archibald Gracie *The Truth About the Titanic*, part of *The Story of the Titanic as Told by Its Survivors*, pp. 186, 253, 195, 258–264. The author classifies all Asian passengers as "Japanese," but my identification of them is based on passenger and survivor lists and survivor letters. See also *A Night to Remember*, pp. 191–199 and *The Night Lives On*, p. 93, and Logan Marshall, *The Sinking of the Titanic* and *Great Sea Disasters*, and *Titanic, Untold Stories* , a film by David Elisco, 1997.

CHAPTER 7

164 *well-formed Chinese characters*: From a document dated June 14, 1912, from the Chinese Immigration files for Hor Ting Sun, National Archives, Northeast Division.

166 *a wide berth*: Committee of Fourteen, Investigative Reports of 1907 and 1910 and Special Grand Jury Testimony, 1910.

169 *marriageable age in Chinatown*: Ibid.

169 *Exclusion Law has done its work*: U.S. Census, 1900 and 1910; Ira Rosenwaike, "Population History of New York City," p. 141.

169 *two at teachers' college*: The Chinese Annual, 1911, p. 23.

170 *Ph.D.'s in Philosophy*: Ibid.

170 *"hands of shyster lawyers"*: Not to be confused with the young man admitted to the State Bar in 1888. See the *New York Times*, July 2, 1915.

170 *the police sergeant takes*: New York Times, August 23, 1915.

174 *still wearing queues*: New York Times, January 2, 1913.

174 *Forty people attend*: Asbury, *The Gangs of New York*, pp. 320–321.

175 *covered by Columbus Park*: Mulberry Bend Park was renamed Columbus Park in 1911.

175 *not have to suffer alone*: Albert W. Palmer, *Orientals in American Life*, p. 169.

175 *"I'm an American, see?"* New York Herald-Tribune, June 9, 1929.

176 *called pai gao poker*: New York Times, June 18, 1913.

177 *trade annually by 1910*: Chinese Immigration files for Hor Mei Fun, 1910–1918.

179 *absolutely identical language*: In the Chinese Immigration testimony at the National Archives are page after page of virtually identical statements from different, apparently "paper" fathers.

181 *many thought he was older*: New York Times, January 11, 1918; "The Passing of Tom Lee, Mayor of Chinatown, by the editors of Literary Digest, February 9, 1918.

Notes

182 *"food of white customers*: New York Times, February 16, 1925.
182 *funeral four years before*: New York Times, April 24 and 25, 1915.

CHAPTER 8

184 *as does the Chinese*: Dr. Leighton Parks in the Preface to the *Yearbook of St. Bartholomew's Church*, 1916.
185 *"Me no savee Inglis"*: New York Times, April 26, May 4, 1919.
185 *meant to be chewed*: New York Post, July 15, 1955.
185 *eggs and rotten vegetables*: New York Herald, December 19, 1923.
186 *("a man of minimal ability")*: Jackson, *Encyclopedia of New York City*, pp. 577–578.
192 *by the name of Ng Ah*: Clement Wood, *The Truth About New York's Chinatown*, p. 32.
192 *if the* New York Times *is to be believed*: New York Times, October 12, 1924.
193 *vast majority are eventually released*: New York Times, April 12, 1926.
193 *collapses from a stroke*: "Death didn't stop Lee To." Found in the files of the Museum of the Chinese in the Americas.
193 *"He was a real Jew"*: Palmer, *Orientals in American Life*, p. 169.
198 *Court thinks is poetic justice*: New York Times, January 5, 1929.
200 *not a bad deal*: See Chinese Immigration Documents, "Harry Haw," 1917–1932.
200 *eight to one*: American Journal of Sociology, May, 1951; Stuart H. Cattell, "Health, Welfare, and Social Organization in Chinatown, New York," August 1962.
205 *"a lover of man"*: "Yearbook of St. Bartholomew's, 1890," pp. 75–76; "1930," p. 8.
206 *elected president of her class*: Florence Burger, "The Chinese American Girl," pp. 165–180.
207 *"would be desirable"*: Letter dated March 19, 1931, in Chinese Immigration File for George Pun Hor, National Archives, Northeast Division.
211 *treasury after his departure*: Leong Gor Yun, *Chinatown Inside Out*, pp. 29–50.
211 *for better overall conditions*: Ibid., pp. 85–101.
212 *"this city has ever seen"*: New York Times, February 29, 1932.
212 *one-to-one basis*: Burger, "The Chinese American Girl," pp. 25–26.
214 *"from the time they met"*: Daily News, August 24, 1934. See also New York Times, August 24, 1934; World-Telegram, August 28, 1934; Daily Mirror, August 24, 1934.
214 *"weeping to weep"*: Daily News, August 24, 1934.
215 *looking death in the face*: Paul Gallico, "The Weekly Aviation Column," Daily News, August 25, 1934.
215 *Chinese motherland of her enemies*: The Chinese Nationalist Daily (New York), August 30, 1934.

216 *to stop his Japanese foe:* See: Iris Chang, *The Rape of Nanking: The Forgotten Holocaust of World War II.*

220 *around World War I:* New York Herald Tribune, June 7, 1959.

225 *shouts to her brother, "Pretty!":* New York Times, March 2, 1943.

225 *"Chinese Air Force . . .":* Ibid.

225 *"until the very end . . .":* Ibid.

225 *78,000 Chinese in the country:* Down from nearly 104,500 in 1890.

226 *sixty-year-old Exclusion Law:* Chen, *The Chinese of America,* pp. 202–207.

CHAPTER 9

230 *it costs them $60,000:* New York Herald-Tribune, January 7, 1949.

230 *for this monument: $500,000:* New York Times, November 7 and 9, 1950.

233 *with 10,560 Chinese men:* Stuart H. Cattell, "Health, Welfare and Social Organization in Chinatown," New York, p. 12.

236 *two boys during the War:* See the *New York Herald-Tribune,* March 11, 1945; *New York Times,* April 29, 1946.

236 *in five months:* Keith Buchanan et al., *China, the Land and the People,* p. 379.

238 *"commerce in human misery":* New York Times, April 29, 1952.

239 *arrested by Immigration authorities:* New York Times, February 15, March 17, April 20, and May 4 and 5, 1956; February 20, March 6, 1957; *New York Herald-Tribune,* May 4, 1956.

241 *unusual red hair:* New York Herald-Tribune, October 8, 1956.

241 *printed on nontoxic paper:* New York Herald-Tribune, June 7, 1959.

244 *"American as the Negro":* New York Herald-Tribune, January 31, 1965.

251 *the Immigration Service:* New York Times, January 15, 1964.

252 *nonwhite population in New York:* New York Times, September 9, 1963.

252 *Chinese-American Times:* New York Times, January 15, 1964.

253 *"I thank you":* New York Post, July 13, 1955.

253 *"family will suffer disgrace":* New York Post, July 12, 1955.

253 *"nothing to do here":* New York Post, July 13, 1955.

254 *"I cannot speak English":* New York Herald-Tribune, January 31, 1965.

254 *"a 100 percent increase":* Ibid.

EPILOGUE

261 *live in Chinatown in 1985:* Jackson, *The Encyclopedia of New York City,* p. 215.

263 *"which is questionable":* New York Times, September 7, 1997.

REFERENCES
AND
BIBLIOGRAPHY

·

BOOKS

Asbury, Herbert. *All Around Town*. Alfred A. Knopf, New York, 1934; *The Gangs of New York: an Informal History of the Underworld*. Alfred A. Knopf, New York, 1928.

Auchincloss, Louis. *The Hone & Strong Diaries of Old Manhattan*. Abbeville Press, New York, 1989.

Backhouse, Sir Edmund T. and J. O. P. Bland. *Annals and Memoirs of the Court of Peking (from the 16th to the 20th Century)*. Houghton Miffin, Boston, 1914.

Beck, Louis J. *New York's Chinatown*. Bohemia Publishing Co. New York, 1898.

Bettmann, Otto L. *The Good Old Days—They Were Terrible!* Random House, New York, 1974.

Bercovici, Konrad. *Around the World in New York*. The Century Company, New York, 1924.

Bloodworth, Dennis. *The Chinese Looking Glass*. Farrar, Straus and Giroux, New York, 1966.

Bonner, Arthur. *Alas! What Brought Thee Hither? The Chinese in New York, 1800–1950*. Fairleigh Dickinson University Press, Madison, New Jersey, 1997.

Browne, G. Waldo. *China, the Country and Its People*. Dana Estes & Company, Boston, 1901.

Buchanan, Keith; Charles P. FitzGerald and Colin A. Ronan. *China: The Land and the People*. Crown Publishers, Inc., New York, 1980.

Campbell, Helen. *Darkness and Daylight, or Lights and Shadows of New York Life*. A. D. Worthington & Co. Hartford, 1891.

Chang, Iris. *The Rape of Nanking: The Forgotten Holocaust of World War II.* Basic Books, New York City, 1997.

Chen, Jack. *The Chinese of America: From the Beginning to the Present.* Harper & Row Publishers, San Francisco, 1980.

The Chinese Annual. Published by the Members of the New York Chinese Students Club, New York City, 1911.

Clayre, Alasdair. *The Heart of the Dragon.* Houghton Mifflin Company, Boston, 1984.

Clemens, Samuel Langhorne; William Dean Howells, and Charles Hopkins Clark. *Mark Twain's Library of Humor.* Charles L. Webster & Co. New York, 1888.

Colman, Elizabeth. *Chinatown, U.S.A.* The John Day Co., New York, 1946.

Connors, Chuck. *Bowery Life.* Richard K. Fox, Publisher, New York, 1904.

Crossley, Pamela Kyle. *The Manchus.* Blackwell Publishers, Cambridge, 1997.

Dun J. Li. *The Ageless Chinese: A History.* Charles Scribner's Sons, New York, 1965.

Ellis, David Maldwyn *New York State and City.* Cornell University Press, Ithaca, 1979.

Ellis, David M.; James A. Frost, Harold C. Syrett, and Harry J. Carman. *A History of New York State.* Cornell University Press, Ithaca, 1957.

Fairbank, John King. *The Great Chinese Revolution, 1800–1985.* Harper & Row, New York, 1987.

Feldman, Joan and Norma Ketay. *New York on $5 & $10 a Day, 1968–69 Edition.* An Arthur Frommer Publication for KLM, 1968.

Gilfoyle, Timothy J. *City of Eros: New York City, Prostitution, and the Commercialization of Sex 1790-1920.* W. W. Norton & Company, New York, 1992.

Gracie, Archibald. *The Truth About the Titanic.* Mitchell Kennerly, New York, 1913.

Hall, Bruce Edward. *Diamond Street: The Story of the Little Town with the Big Red Light District.* Black Dome Press, Hensonville, New York, 1994.

Hahn, Emily. *China to Me: A Partial Autobiography.* The Blakiston Company, Philadelphia, 1944.

Hanly, Rev. Denis. *The Catalogue of A Pictorial History of Early Chinatown, New York City, a Permanent Exhibition in Celebration of the American Bicentennial by the Chinese Community of New York.* Published by The Arts, New York, 1980.

Headland, Isaac Taylor. *Court Life in China: The Capital, Its Officials, and People.* Fleming H. Revell Company, New York, 1909.

Holcombe, Chester. *The Real Chinaman.* Dodd, Mead & Company, New York, 1895.

Hoobler, Dorothy and Thomas Hoobler. *The Chinese American Family Album.* Oxford University Press, New York, 1994.

Huie Kin. *Reminiscences.* San Yu Press, Peking, 1932.

Jackson, Kenneth T. *The Encyclopedia of New York City.* Yale University Press, New Haven, 1995.

Kinkead, Gwen. *Chinatown, A Portrait of a Closed Society.* HarperCollins, New York, 1992.

Kohler, Max J. *Immigration and Aliens in the United States.* Block Publishing Co., New York, 1936.

Kung, S. W. *Chinese in American Life: Some Aspects of their History, Status, Problems, and Contributions.* University of Washington Press, Seattle, 1962.

Leong Gor Yun. *Chinatown Inside Out.* Barrows Mussey, New York, 1936.

Lewis, Elizabeth Foreman. *Young Fu of the Upper Yangtze.* Holt, Rinehart, and Winston, New York, 1932.

Lin Yutang. *The Vigil of a Nation.* The John Day Company, New York, 1945.

Lo, Karl and H.M. Lui. *Chinese Newspapers Published in North America, 1854–1975.* Center for Chinese Research Materials, Association of Research Libraries, Washington, D.C., 1977.

Lockwood, Sarah M. *New York: Not So Little and Not So Old.* Doubleday, Page, & Co., New York, 1926.

Lord, Walter. *The Night Lives On.* William Morrow and Company, New York, 1986; *A Night to Remember,* Henry Holt and Company, New York, 1955.

Lyman, Stanford M. *Chinese Americans.* Random House, New York, 1974.

McCabe, James D.. *New York by Gaslight.* Greenwich House, New York, 1984. (orig. published as *New York by Sunlight and Gaslight,* Hubbard Brothers, Philadelphia, 1882.)

Marcuse, Maxwell F. *This Was New York!* LIM Press, New York, 1969.

Marshall, Logan. *Sinking of the Titanic and Great Sea Disasters.* L. T. Meyers, New York, 1912.

Money vs. Muscle, or Chinese Emigration. "Season" Press, New York, n.d. (1870s?)

Moscow, Henry. *The Street Book: An Encyclopedia of Manhattan's Street Names and Their Origins.* Fordham University Press, New York, 1978.

Moss, Frank. *The American Metropolis from the Knickerbocker Days to the Present Time.* Peter Fenelon Collier, New York, 1897.

Moule, Ven. Arthur E. *New China and Old, Personal Recollections of Thirty Years.* Seeley and Co. Limited, London, 1891.

New York; A Collection from Harper's Magazine. Gallery Books, New York, 1991.

Official Chinatown Guide, 1939. N.P. Printed for the 1939 New York World's Fair.

Palmer, Albert W. *Orientals in American Life.* Friendship Press, New York, 1931.

Pan, Lynn. *Sons of the Yellow Emperor: A History of the Chinese Diaspora.* Kodansha International, New York, 1994.

"Pilgrim." *Chinatown as I Saw It.* A. W. Knox, New York, 1895.

Riis, Jacob A. *Battle with the Slums.* The Macmillan Co., New York, 1902. *How The Other Half Lives: Studies Among the Tenements of New York.* Dover

Publications, Inc; New York, 1971. (Reprint of 1901 Charles Scribner's Sons edition. Originally published in 1890.)

Roosevelt, Theodore. *New York*. Longmans, Green and Co., New York, 1903.

Rosenwaike, Ira. *Population History of New York City*. Syracuse University Press, Syracuse, N.Y., 1972.

Rudy, Stella M. *Children of China*. Rand McNally & Co., Chicago, 1937.

Sandemeyer, Elmer Clarence. *The Anti-Chinese Movement in California*. University of Illinois Press, 1939.

Sante, Luc. *Low Life*. Vintage Books, New York, 1992.

Scidmore, Eliza Ruhamah. *China the Long-Lived Empire*. The Century Company, New York, 1900.

Seaver, Frederick J. *Historical Sketches of Franklin County* [New York] *and Its Several Towns*. J. B. Lyon Company, Albany, 1918.

Seeing Chinatown: The Official Guide. Rigner Publishing Company, New York, 1906.

Seward, George F. *Chinese Immigration, in Its Social and Economical Aspects*. Charles Scribner's Sons, New York, 1881.

Sharman, Lyon. *Sun Yat-Sen, His Life and its Meaning*. Archon Books, Hamden, Conn., 1965.

Shulman, Harry Manuel. *Slums of New York*. Albert and Charles Boni, New York, 1938.

Spence, Jonathan D. *God's Chinese Son; The Taiping Heavenly Kingdom of Hong Xiuquan*. W. W. Norton & Company, New York, 1996.

Sui Sin Far. *Mrs. Spring Fragrance and Other Writings*. Edited by Amy Ling and Annette White-Parks. University of Illinois Press, Chicago, 1995.

Sung, Dr. Betty Lee. *Mountain of Gold*. Macmillan, New York, 1967.

Swinton, John. *The Chinese American Question*. American News Co., New York, 1870.

Ten Thousand Things on China and the Chinese, being a picture of the Genius, Government, Agriculture, Arts, Trade, Manners, Customs, and Social Life of the People of the Celestial Empire, as illustrated by the Chinese Collection. J.S. Redfield, Printer, New York, 1850.

The Truth About Chinatown. N. P. 1926.

Van Loon, Hendrik. *The Story of Mankind*. Garden City Publishing Company, Inc., Garden City, New York, 1939.

Van Norden, Warner M. *Who's Who of the Chinese in New York*. Privately published, New York, 1918.

Walling, George W., *Reflections of a New York Chief of Police*, Caxton Book Concern, Limited, New York, 1887.

Wood, Clement. *The Truth About New York's Chinatown*. Haldeman-Julius Company, Girard, Kansas, 1926.

WPA New York City Guide, 1939. The Guilds' Committee for Federal Writers' Publications, Inc., New York, 1926.

Yan Phou Lee. *When I was a Boy in China*. D. Lothrop Company, Boston, 1887.

Yearbook of St. Bartholomew's Church, New York. E. P. Dutton & Company, 1889–1930.

ARTICLES, DISSERTATIONS, AND PAPERS

"A Daughter is Just Passing Through: Women and the Chinese Family." By the editors of *Stagebill, Public Access,* the Program for "The Golden Child," by David Henry Hwang at the Public Theater, New York, 1996. Vol. 3, #2.

The American Journal of Sociology. May, 1951, summarized in the Bonner Papers, New York Public Library, Manuscript Division.

"A Trip to Chinatown," *23rd Annual Report of the Rescue Society,* The Rescue Society, Inc., New York, 1915.

Baldwin, (Mrs.) S. L. A Letter to *The Christian Advocate.* May 26, 1887.

Becket, Henry. "Why Chinese Kids Don't Go Bad." *The Post,* July 11, 1955; "How Parents Help Chinese Kids Stay Out of Trouble." *The Post,* July 12, 1955; "Spare the Rod, Love the Child." *The Post,* July 13, 1955; "The Chinese in New York." *The Post,* July 14, 1955; "How Chinatown Has Changed." *The Post,* July 15, 1955.

Berger, Mike. "Dingy Chinatown Shop is Counterpart Here of Old General Store in New England." *The New York Times,* November 6, 1953; "Facts for Story of Chinatown Being Sought." *The New York Times,* May 6, 1957; "New York Chinatown." A report prepared for the Chinese Chamber of Commerce, 50th Anniversary, 1957.

Bonner, Arthur. "The Chinese in New York and American Reactions to Them." 1991. Unpublished. On file at the Museum of the Chinese in the Americas.

Bordages, Asa. "Dead Chinese Flier to Get 'Iron Coffin' He So Desired." *World-Telegram* (New York), August 28, 1934.

Boyer, Richard O. "Chinese Thought Dead by Police Heads Hip Sings." *New York Herald Tribune,* July 29, 1931.

Bruen, Edward J. "New Territory is Taken Over by Chinatown." *New York Herald Tribune,* June 9, 1929.

Burger, Florence. "The Chinese American Girl, A Study in Cultural Conflicts." Master's Thesis, New York University, 1935.

Burgess, John Stewart. "A Study of the Characteristics of the Cantonese Merchants in Chinatown, New York as Shown by their Use of Leisure Time." Master's Thesis, Columbia University, 1909.

Callahan, John P. "Changeless' Chinatown Bows, But Only Slightly, to Progress." Newspaper article with no further attribution. In the collection of the Museum of the City of New York.

Carrs, Nancy. "The Early Historical Evolution of Chinatown, New York City." Spring 1980. On file at the Museum of the Chinese in the Americas.

Catell, Stuart H. "Health, Welfare, and Social Organization in Chinatown, New York. A Report Prepared for the Chinatown Public Health Nursing Demonstration." Dept. of Public Affairs, Community Service Society, 105 E 22nd St. New York, N.Y., Aug. 1962.

"Chinatown." *Our Town,* Vol. 1, No. 3. No further attribution. In the collection of the Museum of the City of New York.

Ching, Frank. "Street Crime Casts a Pall of Fear Over Chinatown." *The New York Times.* January 19, 1974.

Culin, Stewart. "The I' Hing or 'Patriotic Rising'." A report read before the Numismatic and Antiquarian Society of Philadelphia, November 3, 1887; "Chinese Secret Societies in the United States." A paper read at the Annual Meeting of the American Folk-Lore Society, Nov. 28, 1889; "Customs of the Chinese in America," *The Journal of American Folk-Lore.* July–Sept. 1890; "America, the Cradle of Asia." *Harper's Monthly Magazine,* March, 1903.

"Death Didn't Stop Lee To." By the editors of *The Literary Digest,* undated, in the files of the Museum of the Chinese in the Americas.

Emery, Stewart M. "Chinatown is Chinatown Still." *The New York Times Magazine,* September 7, 1924.

Faison, Seth. "'Godfather' of Chinatown is Laid to Rest." *The New York Times,* August 20, 1994.

Ferretti, Fred. "New York's Chinatown." *Gourmet,* Feb. 1979.

Foster, John W. "The Chinese Boycott." *The Atlantic Monthly,* Jan. 1906.

Fried, Joseph P. "Man Accused in Smuggling of Chinese is Extradited." *The New York Times,* October 4, 1997.

Fuchs, Lawrence H. "New York's Forbidden City." *The New York Times Book Review,* July 5, 1992.

Fulton, Gordon. "19th Century Housing Conditions: An Overview." Spring 1980; "The Pattern and Image of Chinatown—The Built Environment: Ownership and Construction." 1980. Both on file at the Museum of the Chinese in the Americas.

Gallico, Paul. "Weekly Aviation Column." *Daily News,* Aug. 25, 1934.

Harding, Gardner L. "Chinese Tongs Thrive on Protected Gambling." *The New York Times,* December 14, 1924.

Heyer, Virginia. "Patterns of Social Organization in New York's Chinatown." Ph.D. Dissertation, Columbia University, 1954.

Holder, Charles Frederick. "The Chinaman in American Politics." *The North American Review,* Feb. 1898.

Irwin, Will. "The Drama That Was in Chinatown." *The New York Times Book Review and Magazine,* April 10, 1921.

Jean, Helen Wong. "Playing the Palace Theatre: A Chinese American's Recollections of Vaudeville." On file at the Museum of the Chinese in the Americas.

Jerrold, Julian. "A Chinese Dinner in New York." *The Illustrated American,* September 4, 1897.

Kifner, John. "On Sunday; Benny Ong: A Farewell to All That." *The New York Times,* August 21, 1994.

Lieber, Leslie. "The Inside Story of the Chinese Fortune Cookie." *This Week* (the Sunday Magazine of the *Herald Tribune*), June 7, 1959.

Lii, Jane H. "Neighborhood Report: Chinatown; on Pell Street, only Memories of a Violent Past." *The New York Times,* June 12, 1994; "Neighborhood Report: Chinatown; Tongs and Gangs: Shifting the Links." *The New York Times,* August 21, 1994.

Louie, Elaine. "A Little Museum That Could." *The New York Times,* January 25, 1996.

Martin, Douglas. "After Benny Ong, Silence in Chinatown." *The New York Times,* August 8, 1994.

McCombe, Leonard. "America's Chinese." *Life Magazine,*. January. 8, 1951.

McFadden, Robert D. "Benny Ong, 87, the Reputed Godfather of Chinatown Crime." *The New York Times,* August 7, 1994.

Meade, Hon. Edwin R. "The Chinese Question." A paper written for the Social Science Association of America, Saratoga, New York, September. 7, 1877.

Millstein, Gilbert. "On a Sunday in Chinatown." *The New York Times Magazine,* February 27, 1955.

Morehouse, Ward. "Positively the Last Queue in Chinatown." *New York Tribune,* April 24, 1921.

Nadelmann, Ethan A; David T. Courtwright. "Should We Legalize Drugs? History Answers." *American Heritage,* March, 1993.

"New York City Mission and Tract Society, Annual Reports [1859–1866]."

"New York Foreigner's Mission, Report 1901–1905."

Page, Patricia. "Chinatown: Not East, Not West." *The New York Times,* December 15, 1946.

Peck, Robert B. "Charley Boston, Long a Power in Chinatown, Dies." *New York Herald Tribune,* January 5, 1930.

Ranzal, Edward. "Red Extortion is Laid to Chinese Daily Here." *The New York Times,* April 29, 1952; "Chinese Leader is Indicted Here." *The New York Times,* May 4, 1956.

"Report and Proceedings of the Senate Committee Appointed to Investigate the Police Department of the City of New York," January. 18, 1895.

Rice, Diana. "Left Their Pigtails Behind Them." *The New York Times Magazine,* March 30, 1924.

Rosenquist, Doris. "A Flushing Old-Timer Welcomes Asians No More." A letter to the City Section, *The New York Times,* Sept. 7, 1997.

Scharf, J. Thomas. "The Farce of the Chinese Exclusion Laws." *The North American Review,* Jan. 1898.

Scheinberg, Ellen. "Evidence of 'Past Injustices'." *Archivist Magazine.* Nov. 2, 1994.

"Sixth Annual Report of the Chinatown and Bowery Settlement for Girls," 1910.

"Sixty Second Annual Report of the Missionary Society of the Methodist Episcopal Church for the period 1880–1906."

Speed, John Gilmer. "Food and Foreigners in New York." *Harper's Weekly,* September 8, 1900.

Spier, Robert F. G. "Food Habits of Nineteenth-Century Californian Chinese." *California Historical Society Quarterly,* No. 57, 1958.

Strauss, Theodore. "Theatre in Chinatown." *The New York Times,* February 15, 1942.

Tchen, John Kuo Wei. "New York Before Chinatown," a Dissertation, New York University, 1992; "Quimbo Appo's Fear of Fenians: Chinese-Irish-Anglo Relations in New York City." Asian/American Center and Urban Studies, Queens College, City University of New York, 1993.

Telemaque, Eleanor Middleton. "Chinatown in the Year of the Serpent." *Herald Tribune,* January 31, 1965.

The Woman Citizen. December, 1927, summarized in the Bonner Papers at the New York Public Library, Manuscript Division.

Weisberger, Bernard A. "The Chinese Must Go." *American Heritage,* March, 1993.

Wong Chin Foo. "The Wail of Wong Chin Foo; Experience of a Chinese Journalist." *Puck,* January 1, 1888; "The Chinese in New York." *Cosmopolitan, A Monthly Illustrated Magazine,* June, 1888.

"Wong Ching [sic] Foo." by the editors of *Harper's Weekly.* May 26, 1877, p. 405.

NEWSPAPERS
Ballou's Pictorial
The Boston Globe
Brooklyn Eagle
The Bulletin (San Francisco)
The Chinese American (New York)
The Chinese Nationalist Daily (New York)
The Daily Graphic (New York)
The Daily Mirror (New York)
The Daily Sun (Vancouver)
Daily World (Vancouver)
Leslie's Illustrated
Malone (N.Y.) *Farmer*
Malone (N.Y.) *Palladium*
Manitoba Free Press
Marin (County) *Journal*
New York Herald
New York Herald Tribune
New York Post
New York Evening Post
New York Times
New York Tribune
New York World
Ottawa Free Press
Plattsburgh (N.Y.) *Press-Republican*
Richford (Vt.) *Gazette* (later *Journal-Gazette*)
St. Alban's (Vt.) *Daily Messenger*

References and Bibliography

San Francisco Call & Post
Star-Ledger (Newark, N.J.)
Sun (New York)
Toronto World
World-Telegram (New York)

COLLECTIONS
Beekman Papers, New-York Historical Society
Bonner Papers, New York Public Library
Emile Bocian Collection, Museum of the Chinese in the Americas
Jip F. Chun Collection, Museum of the Chinese in the Americas
George Hall Collection, New-York Historical Society
Jacob Riis Collection, Museum of the City of New York
Landauer Collection, New-York Historical Society
Richard Hoe Lawrence Collection, New-York Historical Society

MISCELLANEOUS
"The Lt. B. R. Kimlau Chinese Memorial Post, 1291, American Legion, 50th Anniversary Special Issue." Commemorative program for the ceremonies marking the 50th anniversary of American Legion Post 1291. June 3, 1995.
"Carved in Silence," a film by Felicia Lowe. Felicia Lowe Productions, 1987.
Chinese Immigration Records, Canadian National Archives, Ottawa.
Chinese Immigration Records, U.S. National Archives, Northeast Division.
"Committee of Fifteen." Report on an investigation into vice in New York City, 1901. Manuscript Division, New York Public Library.
"Committee of Fourteen." Report on an investigation into vice in New York City, 1910–1912. Manuscript Division, New York Public Library.
Funeral Records for Edmund On Wong, Benjamin Kimlau Funeral Home. Handwritten, Aug. 30, 1934. Private collection.
"The Haircut," a video by Paul de Silva and Ann O'Brian for *Inside Stories* television series.
"Handbook of the City of New York, Prepared Especially for the Eighth International Congress of Applied Chemistry," Sept. 4–13, 1912.
Letters from the Wong family to Betty Wolff Wong, 1923–1955, Private collection.
"New York Chinese Save Our Country Fundraising Committee's Contributors List." Handwritten, 1938. Private collection.
New York City Death Records, Municipal Archives.
New York City Directories, 1880–1920.
New York City Police Census, 1890. Books 44, 45, & 48.
New York State Census and/or Enumerations; 1855, 1875, 1895.
Passenger List; *Empress of Russia.* November, 1913. On file with the Canadian National Archives, Ottawa.

Records from the Ancestors' Shrine, Hor Lup Chui village, Toi-shan District. Canton Province, People's Republic of China.

Titanic Insurance Claims. National Archives, Northeast Division.

Titanic; Untold Stories. A film for the Discovery Channel, written and produced by David Elisco, 1997.

"Trust in God Baptist Church, Sanctuary Dedication. The Lord's Day, June 12, 1983, New York City." Program for commemorative service.

U.S. Census and/or Enumerations; 1850, 1860, 1870, 1880, 1890, 1900, 1910, 1920.

Vaudeville, An American Masters Special. A film by Greg Palmer produced by Thirteen WNET-TV; KCTS/9 Television; and Palmer/Fenster Inc., 1997.

Voice of the City. A radio play by Barron Collier, Jr. Broadcast on WHN, New York, Feb. 16, 1938. Sponsored by the Street Railways Advertising Company. Museum of the City of New York.

ACKNOWLEDGMENTS

·

This part is always tricky, because there are always so many people who contribute so much to a project like this, and invariably someone who gets overlooked when the thank-you notes go out. But here goes anyway.

I guess the easiest place to start is with my family, who have been so generous and supportive throughout, both morally and physically. I have particularly to hold up for praise the Richard Hoe family. Cousin Marika Hoe took up a substantial portion of her summer vacation from college in the tedious job of tracking down and copying an endless list of newspaper articles that I wanted, all with nary a complaint or a mistake. And then, after she went back to school her mother, Susan, took over for her. My second uncle Richard himself was very generous with his time, driving me all over the Northeast in pursuit of old ladies to interview and new sources of roast-pork buns to ply them with. Even the taciturn cousin Jonathan provided a couple of good stories with which to lace my pages.

My Uncle Roy Eng gave wonderful insights into traditional Chinese family relationships, as well as some exquisite translations of old letters and newspapers written in an archaic but beautiful Chinese that my younger friends from Canton and Hong Kong could barely decipher.

And of course all of my other relatives have patiently fielded sometimes bizarre-sounding questions about the minutiae of their personal lives. My favorite time was when I called my Uncle Everett out of the blue and asked him to tell me what he had for dinner on a certain night in 1926. "I don't remember *everything* I've ever eaten!" he protested—but then he told me anyway. My cousins Carl and Sookie Hom shared invaluable memories, and Cousins Karen Fung and Alison Ho have been generous with their photographs and their time. My sister Amy was always there with constructive, logical advice. And then of course there are my parents, who had the idea for me to do this book in the first place, and who have staunchly supported me throughout this long process.

And now we get to the people "on the street" who kindly shared so much about their lives in Chinatown. Especially I wish to thank Mrs. Grace Mok, Mr. Kaimon Chin, Mr. Norman Kee, Mr. Bruce Ho, Miss Jadin Wong, Mr. Jip F. Chun, Pee Wee Wong, Paul Lee, Patty Typond Maba, and the Liu family for spending so much time reminiscing and laughing over old times. Mrs. Anne M. Chan sent me stacks of pictures and tracked down other people to find out information for me. Mr. and Mrs. Lee Hen Shung and their son Jan and I spent many pleasant hours in the back of their exquisite shop on Mott Street—in a space where one of my Ancestors had worked over a hundred years ago—and where I learned about the moon festival, the eighteen saints of the Taoist religion, and the proper way to drink tea. And of course I can't forget a certain retired doctor, ninety-one years old at the time of our interview. He loves a good story, but is a little deaf, requiring one to speak loudly to get the goods.

So as we sat on the porch of his house on a sleepy, quiet street in a little seaside town, and he told me about one particularly vexing problem he had to face early in his practice, I found I had to raise my voice so he could hear my next question.

"How did you cure the VD?" I shouted in a voice that rattled windows and caused heads to pop out of doors up and down the block. As the good doctor chuckled and told me, I realized that the neighbors were wondering what to do with this tasty new bit of gossip. It was a moment of sublime surreality that I wouldn't have dared dream for.

Acknowledgments

And then there are all those people who helped me in a professional or semiprofessional way, such as Sushan Chin and the staff of the Museum of Chinese in the Americas (which everyone ought to visit, by the way), John Celardo and the staff of the National Archives, Northeast Division, Ellen Scheinberg at the Canadian National Archives in Ottawa, as well as the folks at the New York Municipal Archives, the New York Public Library, the Museum of the City of New York, and Dale Neighbors of the New-York Historical Society, who has actually read my other work and so deserves special mention for feeding my vanity.

Christopher Gray, architectural historian and columnist for the *New York Times,* was very accommodating in sharing his research, as was Percy Preston, Jr., in making available the archives of St. Bartholomew's Episcopal Church, even to the point of getting pictures copied for me on his own time. Then, of course, there were my friends Ron Drummond and Geraldine Fitzgerald, who offered hours of help in research through piles of microfilm and musty documents.

On my trip up to the Canadian border towns of Malone, New York, and St. Albans and Richford, Vermont, I was met with nothing but kindness and helpfulness at every turn. Sue Hogan at the Kilburn Manor B&B enthusiastically introduced me to people like Marj Mahler, Director of the Franklin County Historical Society, and Kitty Murtagh down at the County Courthouse, who graciously gave up her lunch hour as she got on the phone to track down leads in my quest for the history of Chinese immigration through that town.

This happy experience was only repeated in St. Albans, Vermont, when Anna Neville and her daughter Jennifer Bright at the Old Mill River Place B&B eliminated days of tedious groundwork for me with a few judicious phone calls to people like Clare Sheppard at the St. Albans Historical Museum, who dug out old articles (and old people) to supply the information I needed. But no one could hold a candle to Rhoda Berger in nearby Richford, who not only knew where to find all sorts of valuable source material, but carefully transcribed years' worth of antique newspaper articles (in longhand), provided invaluable photographs, and polished it off with a meticulously detailed driving tour of tiny Richford, Vermont, complete with a full dossier on all of its inhabitants past and present—enough for very juicy book indeed, if one were so inclined.

I also must not overlook my agents, Neeti Madan and Charlotte Sheedy, who knocked on every door in town; my editor, Norah Vincent, who convinced The Free Press to take a chance on me; and Ms. Deborah Harkins, a former editor with *New York* magazine, who in 1993 published my article called "Ghosts" and showered me with encouragement. It is upon that article that this book is based.

Last, but not least, I must thank Andy Padre for putting up with my moods, photocopying old articles, and faithfully reminding me to remember to keep doing the frivolous things in life—like sleeping and eating.

If all of these people hadn't been so unselfish with their assistance, this book would have taken twice as long to write. That is, if it had ever got written at all.

INDEX

•

Index

Index